A Guidebook for Teaching
WRITING
IN CONTENT AREAS

A Guidebook for Teaching
WRITING
IN CONTENT AREAS

SHERRY HILL HOWIE
University of Michigan—Flint

Allyn and Bacon, Inc.   **Boston • London • Sydney • Toronto**

This book is part of A GUIDEBOOK FOR TEACHING Series

Library of Congress Cataloging in Publication Data

Howie, Sherry Hill, 1941—
   A guidebook for teaching writing in content areas.

   1. Language arts. 2. English language—Study and
teaching. 3. English language—Composition and
exercises. I. Title.
LB1576.H68 1984   808′.042′07   83-13379
ISBN 0-205-08070-7

Printed in the United States of America

10 9 8 7 6 5 4 3 2 1   88 87 86 85 84 83

Contents

Preface

This is a pioneer attempt to provide a guide for teachers in all classrooms who are interested in teaching their students to communicate content fields in writing. James Moffett in *Teaching the Universe of Discourse* said, "To compose is to comprehend," and so to have a student write out an idea in a subject field is to have a student understand the idea. This book is not meant to put an extra burden on content area teachers who feel their responsibility is to teach the subject. Rather, it is meant as a guide and resource to aid them in getting student feedback in written form regarding their teaching and student learning. To teach a subject is to teach communication in that subject.

This guidebook is intended to be practical and immediately usable in the classroom by the busy teacher, who may duplicate the reproducible pages of student exercises and teach writing from them. Teachers at the upper elementary, secondary, and college levels will find student exercises, teacher presentations, and teaching suggestions applicable or adaptable to their classroom needs. This book is meant to be not only a resource book, but a methods book for use in teacher training. It may be used effectively in inservice training for teachers and in college education courses for preservice teachers. Because it is divided into ten chapters, the book may be used as a textbook over the course of a semester with in-depth study of each of the ten major topics. The Resources provided at the end of each chapter may stimulate rich research into major areas of concern that teachers have in teaching communication in each field.

The major thrust of the book is to identify what the elements of written language in each content area are, how to teach those elements, and how to evaluate student expression of those elements. All of the current research obtainable as well as information available to me has been collated, synthesized, and distilled into one comprehensive volume. The underlying philosophy is guided by a combination of theory, teacher experience, and classroom testing of exercises and beliefs. All of the student exercises and worksheets have been field-tested in the classroom, if not by me (a teacher for twenty years), then by experienced teachers who have reported success with the recommended approaches.

Although the activities, teacher presentations, and sequencing of learning is suggested, the teacher clearly has the option to choose which strategies and exercises to use. The choice would be based on suitability and applicability to the teaching situation and the students involved. Perhaps adaptation of the materials would be more workable at times, and teachers should feel free to use the suggestions and ideas in ways that work for them.

In general, each topic is presented in the *Guidebook for Teaching Writing in Content Areas* in this manner:

1. An introduction to the concepts in the chapter.

2. A list of objectives that the methods and activities help the students achieve.

3. Teaching strategies that include teacher presentations and student activities with worksheets, notebook resources, and whole-group and small-group exercises.

4. A wealth of learning experiences that give students personal experience in learning concepts.

5. Sample evaluation devices for determining student progress in achieving the objectives of each unit.

6. An annotated list of resources for use in further research on that topic.

In order to know if the *Guidebook for Teaching Writing in Content Areas* has been helpful to those who use it, the Feedback Form in Appendix D has been provided. It can be easily torn out and mailed. Your response will be replied to personally and will be most sincerely appreciated. Your suggestions, questions, and concerns are most welcome and will be used to guide future revisions of this book.

Although most of the material in this book is derived from my teaching experience, acknowledgment and thanks are certainly due to others who have made contributions. I am grateful to Nancy Marshall for her ideas on modes of composition. Although she developed her ideas for teaching reading comprehension of the different types of text, the ideas are directly applicable to the teaching of writing. Contributions were made by Richard Sinatra, with whom I have collaborated on projects involving visual compositions and the teaching of writing. Numerous other colleagues and friends, especially at the Universities of Colorado and Michigan–Flint, have been encouraging and supportive, and to them I am thankful. My mentor, Philip DiStefano, provided much of the inspiration and direction for this book in his guidance of my studies and research. Donna Quigley helped with typing and preparation of the manuscript. The many students who tested the materials and made invaluable comments are greatly appreciated, especially those at Saint Edwards School in Vero Beach, Florida. Above all, however, I wish to thank William Howie for his constant encouragement, his belief in me and in the project, and his never-failing support. This book could not have been written without him.

1

Assumptions for Teaching Writing in Content Areas

Teaching writing has long been the domain of the English teacher, and it is assumed that the skills learned by students in English class will automatically transfer to other content areas. Since other content area teachers are not "English majors," they often feel that teaching writing is not their concern or their problem. When students do not write well in the content area classes, it is believed that it is probably the fault of the English department or the elementary school teachers who "did not teach those kids to write." Non-English teachers often have not faced the task of teaching communication skills in their subject area, feeling that their concern is the content, not the expression of it.

There are reasons why most non-English, content area teachers feel this way. First, they have not been taught the usage of language in their subject field and do not feel comfortable dealing with it. Clear differentiations were not established in their training between creative or narrative uses of language in the English textbooks and the expository, procedural, and technical uses of language in many other content area texts. What the English teacher teaches about usage of language many times does not pertain to other modes in other subject fields. Therefore, neither students nor their teachers are well prepared to deal with language as it is used in different subject areas. It should be the responsibility of all teachers to be knowledgeable about language as it is used specifically in their field if they want their students to be able to read and write about the subject matter.

A second reason content area teachers are reluctant to teach writing is that they have to grade it, which takes knowledge and time. Most content area teachers feel they are not "expert enough" to grade a composition, not realizing that the process can be greatly simplified and diversified by using numerous methods of evaluation.

The following are certain assumptions about writing that the content area teachers should consider in learning to teach language and writing skills to students.

EVERY TEACHER IS RESPONSIBLE FOR TEACHING WRITING

Every teacher in every subject area is a communications expert. The art of teaching involves communication of the subject matter sufficient to impart knowledge of it to learners. Communication involves use of language both oral and written. Every teacher should be trained in the ways language is used in the subject field.

Usage of language varies depending on its purpose, its mode, its audience, and its vocabulary. For example, social studies texts using narration of an event in history will differ in language use from a mechanics manual in an industrial arts class, which uses the procedural mode. The mechanics manual will use different sentence structure, more graphics, and very technical vocabulary. The purposes in the two texts will differ in that the social studies text is designed to tell about an abstract event in history, whereas the mechanics manual serves to instruct in a concrete procedure. Each teacher of each course should be aware of the way language is used in the subject matter in order to teach students to communicate in the field.

Teachers should teach students that writing is a process involving *prewriting* activities, which include gathering information, becoming interested, and making decisions on what to write and how to write it. The initial draft is just that and should never be considered a finished product. The major part of the writing process is revision and editing of the initial and subsequent drafts until a final result is produced. Realizing that writing involves a process and a procedure, a teacher can foster growth and development of language skills within the subject area by teaching the process—the behavior—of writing.

WRITING IS DISCOVERY

Henry Miller, well-known American author, said, "Writing, like life itself, is a voyage of discovery." Writing is discovery of what one wants to say because oftentimes a writer knows what he or she wants to say only when it is down on paper. Writing is thinking, a mental process that seems to unleash ideas as the pen moves across the page. Every thinking person should be given the training and the opportunity to experience these revelations of what he or she knows, understands, and remembers. This can be experienced in every subject field when the teacher provides opportunities for it.

Because writing is discovery of what one knows, it is a personal, meaningful experience that can result in greater memory retention of the subject matter. What persons experience firsthand is always most likely to remain with them. The writing experience results in better learning and longer memory retention, yet in many content area classes objective tests are solely used. Surely students are being robbed of rich cognitive adventures when they are not asked to write about their learning in every subject field.

Writing is not only a cognitive exercise, but a tactile experience as well that allows students another modality of learning. Too, most of our society are visual learners who need the reinforcement of seeing their ideas graphically. Writing is a reinforcement of learning and leads to learning through discovery and personal involvement. Every subject area can benefit its students by allowing learning through writing.

WRITING CAN HELP DEVELOP MATURITY

Writing is the highest animal evolvement in learning to communicate. To write effectively is to reach the heights of communication. There is no wonder why learning to write is not easily achieved or why teaching writing is so complex. Certainly a maturity is reached in young persons when they learn to express themselves effectively in written form.

Writing is not simply spoken language written down; it has a jargon, an organization, and a structure all its own. Consider how communication is aided by the use of gestures, bodily movements, and intonation in oral expression. In writing, punctuation is used in place of oral pauses and gestures; proper spelling and usage of words give sentences their meaning and distinguish word groups as *to, too, two,* which are not differentiated in spoken language by sound. A greater maturity level in communication is achieved when students understand such differences between spoken and written language.

Learning to write to different audiences will help a student to mature. The differences are vast between writing in a diary to oneself, writing a letter to a friend, and writing an article for publication in a school newspaper, for example. The differences range from egocentric to sociocentric stages of maturity in communication. As writers mature, they grow from seeing only the self in the universe to recognizing others in ever-increasing distances. Writing for publication is communicating to an unknown, distant audience that gives no immediate feedback. Consideration of this kind of audience can result in a greater maturity of communication.

When students are taught options in using language, they can begin to appreciate the variety and flexibility of their language, which they will use throughout life. Among such options are sentence arrangements, modes of composition, text factors, and vocabulary usage. Appreciation of language and its use will indicate an increase in maturity in communication by young learners. Experience in written communication should be given students in every content field to assure their growth and maturity in communicating.

EDITING MUST BE TAUGHT AS A SKILL

Because students have been graded on their initial drafts throughout most of their schooling, they will tend to believe that being required to rewrite a composition is a punishment "for not getting it right the first time." The teacher who teaches quality writing will have to overcome this misunderstanding by assuring students that editing and revising are skills every writer must develop, whether professional or amateur, experienced or beginning.

Explain to students what one professional American author, John Updike, has said: "Writing and rewriting are a constant search for what one is saying," Updike means that rewriting helps a writer to refine, rethink, and rework language so that ideas take clear shape. Language can be manipulated and experimented with until it becomes a precision instrument for what one wants to express. In rearranging language elements through rewriting, one becomes aware of options for expression of what may at first have been a dim idea. Language gives shape and substance to the idea, and its expression may be a surprise. Students who are allowed the opportunity to rework their initial drafts may discover what it is they really want to say. Perhaps they can be taught to appreciate the skills involved in rewriting.

Rewriting skills concern understanding the purpose and audience one initially had in mind, then deciding if the initial draft is effective in achieving the original intentions. It may be that the writer changes the original purpose and audience during the course of writing, and that is all right. The writer then has to reformulate the decisions regarding the changed purpose and audience; but those factors must be clear to the writer, and subsequently to the reader. The rewriting would be directed toward effective achievement of the decisions about purpose and audience that the writer has made. Decisions would involve language usage, sentence structures, level of vocabulary, and the mode and genre of composition most effective for purpose and audience.

EVERY TEACHER CAN DEVELOP A WELL-PLANNED WRITING CURRICULUM

No matter what the subject area, every teacher can allow students the opportunity to discover their own ideas through writing them out. The opportunity should be well planned so that the writing exercise is meaningful to students and fits into the time schedule of the course work. The design of the writing opportunity may take into consideration factors of age level of students, time allotted to the experience, justification for the exercise, and procedures and evaluation. Such a design would give purpose, meaning, and structure to the writing experience for students in every subject area. When a writing experience is well planned, students will tend to value it and gain more from it. Best of all, the content area teacher will feel more confident about the justification for its inclusion in the learning of the subject matter and in the allotment of time for the writing experience. In creating the design for a writing experience, the following structure is suggested:

Design for Writing in Content Areas

Grade level

Time estimated

Rationale (justification)

Objectives (from students' point of view)

Procedures

    Motivation

    Process (behaviors)

Evaluation

    Rationale

    Objectives

    Procedures

Such a design may be written out by the teacher in order to facilitate thinking about what is to be achieved by this experience. The procedures to follow include developing some form of motivation for the experience to build background, stimulate interest, and develop involvement on the part of the students. Chapter 9 offers some ideas on how to motivate students to write and how to stimulate their participation. The process or behaviors for students to follow should involve some prewriting, initial draft, and revision experiences. Chapter 2 can help in establishing writing behavior. Teacher decisions will have to be made in the type of evaluation to use for the writing, but the teacher should not feel restricted to using only one type, as there are several methods to choose from. The decision on which method to use should be based on its meaningfulness to the entire writing experience, the time constraints of the teacher, and the stage of development of students toward their ability for self-evaluation, the highest goal in evaluation. Chapter 10 can offer ideas for methods of evaluation.

Writing is thinking, and giving students a well-planned writing experience will help them think through their ideas and understanding in every content field. Such an experience should be given to students in every subject they are taught.

The chapters in this book are designed to meet the foregoing assumptions for teaching writing with relevant philosophy, activities for students, and meaningful evaluation of learning. With use of this guidebook, teachers in every content field should be able to give students opportunities to express ideas in the subject matter through written expression.

2

Teaching Students the Behaviors of Writing

CONTENT OVERVIEW

To teach students to write is to teach them to perform certain actions, to operate in a systemized manner, to undergo a prescribed process. In other words, to teach students to write is to instruct them in how to behave like a writer. Not only are these behaviors meant for the classroom, but they should carry over into lifelong writing endeavors. Once the behavioral process is learned and practiced, it should become natural and nonthreatening as the way to communicate anything in written form. The results of the students' products will be well worth the efforts of teaching them the process.

Most writing assignments given in the classroom are actually unnatural to the process that writers undergo in real life. The topic is posted on the board and students are asked to give an immediate written reaction within the classroom period of time. For example, in social studies an assignment may be to compare the legislative branch of government to the judicial branch. The compositions, designed for the teacher, are turned in and read only by the teacher. The papers, which are actually initial drafts, are returned by the teacher with a grade and some remarks in red ink scribbled in the margins. Students look at their grades, see the red ink, and toss their papers into the trash can. Why?

The teacher's investment of time and energy into each student's paper in this typical writing assignment was probably greater than the students'. An initial draft requires little involvement and investment of one's self; therefore, the writing exercise had little interest to or meaning for the students. It is no wonder the papers were tossed. Involvement and commitment to the point of actually caring about the writing exercise is the crux of teaching writing. Writing is discovery that takes time in thinking and planning, writing and rewriting, and sharing and caring. The teacher of writing must allow time for students to experience the great joy and satisfaction of hard work done well. Writing is difficult, which is why students resist doing it, but teaching writing is teaching discipline and pride in accomplishment.

Teaching discipline in writing is also teaching behavior, and there are five steps to the performance. Step 1 involves **prewriting** activities designed to stimulate, involve, and adequately prepare the students for the writing experience. Step 2 is the **initial draft,** the actual writing in its preliminary stages. Before editing the draft, step 3 (**preparing to revise the draft**) allows preparation time and enrichment through deeper interaction with the written communication. **Editing the draft,** step 4, is a critical step toward student growth in critiquing, judging, and revising so that personal commitment to the paper is inevitable. Then step 5, **finalizing the composition,** provides for the lacquering on the finished product. Although these five steps appear to be time-consuming for the content area teacher, once they are taught to students, they should require no more time than otherwise since evaluation time will be cut drastically. The objective is to ensure that student revision will result in superior papers that greatly reduce teacher time in grading the papers.

OBJECTIVES

As a result of the learning experiences in this chapter, students should be able to:

1. Make a transition from thinking to writing by forming their impressions and associations of a topic into sentences, using an outline, and developing paragraphs.

2. Understand how to narrow down a broad topic for their purpose in writing.

3. Address a specific audience other than the teacher.

4. Write an initial draft with the recognition that it is a preliminary effort.

5. Develop some editing skills.

6. Recognize the importance and value of rewriting the initial draft.

7. Rewrite the initial draft with better understanding of language, form, and content.

8. Write a final draft that is more polished and of higher quality than the initial draft.

9. Better understand the behaviors of a writer.

10. Appreciate the hard work and efforts that produce a well-written composition.

LEARNING EXPERIENCES

Topic I: Understanding and Using Step 1, Prewriting

1. *Teacher Presentation.* Present Reproduction Page 2–1 to students and tell them that the writing process that they are to learn is in five steps. The five steps will enable them to produce a polished composition that they will be proud of because they will have explored the topic, thought about it, and shaped and reshaped what they have to say about it. Tell them that the steps will be taught to them sequentially and slowly enough so that they will be able to grasp and practice the concepts. Explain

that step 1 will require the most time because embodied in it are the elements of motivation, self-direction, free choice, thinking, discrimination, involvement, and commitment. This step is also partly social in contrast to step 2, which is a solitary activity by necessity.

2. *Activity.* Teacher experience seems to indicate that student writing is more effective when it is directed than when students are allowed total freedom in choosing a topic. The following is a suggested exercise in guiding students to compose a group composition based on a directed topic. The group composition exercise is excellent as an icebreaker for stimulating human interaction and cooperation in a group endeavor. It is nonthreatening and may help poor writers realize that language manipulation and creation of ideas in written form can be fun and satisfying. As well, the exercise teaches the concepts of sentence combining, outlining, organization, transition and connectors, summarization, logical thinking processes, and paragraph structure. Finally, the exercise provides a method for teaching students to progress from thinking to writing, and thus communicating their feelings, impressions, and associations.

   Write a topic of interest to the class on the board from the content area. In science, for example, a topic may be "The sun is 93 million miles from the Earth." Ask the class for their reaction to this statement. Ask students what their impressions are of the statement. List one-word and phrasal associations on the blackboard as students give their impressions and reactions.

   Then have students combine the ideas they've given into three sentences. Have them choose the ideas that are most closely related to each other and group them into three groups. Three major groups for the given science topic may relate to the solar system, heat, and weather, for example. Mark numbers 1, 2, and 3 by the related ideas. Write the three sentences students create on the blackboard. Have students condense these ideas into a fourth sentence that summarizes the three sentences and write the fourth sentence on the blackboard.

   From the fourth sentence, create an outline so that students may organize their ideas in logical order. As they outline, have them think of connectors such as *for example, first, however* that they can later use in their writing to show the logical order they're following. Choose one idea to be the topic statement. Write the topic statement as number I in the outline and add the details as students enumerate them for the outline.

   Ask students to identify the major ideas in the outline (A, B, C, and so forth). Combine the columns into logical sentences using the connectors discussed when the outline was formed. (Write the sentences on the board in paragraph form as students dictate.) Summarize them in a concluding sentence. Write the concluding sentence students create. Call on a student to read the group composition aloud to the class. Ask for changes, additions, or deletions.

3. *Activity.* Discuss with the class a general topic of concern that emanates from the subject matter under consideration. Have students identify specific aspects of the general topic. As an example in math, the discussion could center around the general topic of *infinity.* Specific aspects would be concepts of *time, space,* and *quantities.* Further narrowing of the topic could focus on questions such as: What is the largest number? Where does space end? What is the value of measurement? Where do I fit in in the time frame of the history of the earth?

4. *Activity.* Using Reproduction Page 2-2, the Student Worksheet, ask students to choose an aspect of the topic in Activity 3 above. Tell them to narrow the topic to what interests them personally and to state it in one sentence on the Student Worksheet. In writing about this topic, what is their purpose? Tell students to make a decision about whether they want to argue a point, explore a question, create a fictional possibility, and so on, and to write this decision under *Purpose* on the Worksheet.

5. *Activity.* Ask students to decide on the kind of audience they want to create to read their paper. Who in their lives (living or dead) do they want to communicate this topic to? Write out the specific characteristics of the audience to be addressed on Reproduction Page 2-2. (See Chapter 4 for suggestions.)

6. *Activity.* Present the list of feelings on Reproduction Page 2-3 to students. Have them identify the specific feelings they have toward their topic from Activity 4. How will these feelings influence the way they will write about the subject, the tone they will generate? Have the students fill in the *Attitude* section of Reproduction Page 2-2.

7. *Teacher Presentation.* In the content field, teachers will know the reference materials available and the authorities and resources where students may gain further information on their topic. Enlist the aid of the librarian and the curriculum coordinator of the school and school district in order to compile a list of references for your students. Students should be aware of their own existing knowledge of the topic and where to go to learn further. Have them fill in this information under *Experience* on Reproduction Page 2-2.

8. *Activity.* Tell students that in writing they are playing a role as they approach their audience. Awareness of audience will help focus their writing and provide a persona or approach that will determine the level of language, style, and mode of writing. Students should decide whether their role is to be that of an equal writing to a peer, an authority writing to provide information to the unknowledgeable, or a character they have created to portray the topic. (See Chapter 4 for audience and purpose considerations.) Ask students to write this information for their topic under *Persona* on Reproduction Page 2-2.

9. *Activity.* Providing students with flexibility in their writing is preparing them for lifelong writing options. Choice of mode or form of composition will be determined by their purpose and their audience. Present the following choices to students to guide them to their decision, then have them write their decision for their topic under *Mode* on Reproduction Page 2-2:

Narration/Description

● Tell a story using description, characters, a plot; compare and contrast using coordinating conjunctions such as *but, or, yet.*

Story Components
goal

characters

time

place

incidents

resolution

theme

Procedural

- A direction or step-by-step relating of a process using words of transition.

Components

sequence

imperative sentences (commands)

unstated steps

abbreviations and symbols

referents

product or final outcome

Time-Order Exposition

- Events are in a time sequence with characters often mentioned; there is a problem to be solved, and the sequencing is often cause and effect.

Components

cause and effect

causality/motivation

final events most important

Topic Exposition

- An argument or clear topic is presented; a statement is made with supporting details and logical connections.

Components

no event sequence

main idea or topic

supporting details or examples

relationships connected logically

specialized vocabulary

often abstract information

If students select a different mode other than these alternatives, have them define it and list its characteristics as has been done here.

10. *Activity.* For developing note-taking abilities, an excellent, teacher-tested technique is a **listening guide** that is constructed by the teacher for student use. It is a pictograph in which students write what they hear or read sequentially. It trains students to focus on main ideas and quickly jot down details about each. Figures 2–1 and 2–2 are examples of useful listening guides. Construct a listening guide for use with a lecture. As you lecture, have the students fill in the spaces with details from the lecture that may be used later in their writing.

11. *Activity.* A junior high teacher, Bonnie Dowler, suggested the use of "Jogging Notes" to train students in outlining and notetaking. Tell students to fold their paper into thirds. Write the heading "Main Ideas" on one third and "Details" on the other two-thirds of the page. Have students record their discriminations between the main ideas and the details of the new information. Then review the notes to determine the logical order of the details as to time sequence, cause and effect, comparison and contrast, and so forth. This knowledge will help the student to organize the composition and to select appropriate connectors and transition words to convey the logical order of the ideas. Present the following partial list of connectors and transition words to students as a guide to organizing their details in their writing (see Chapter 7).

Connectives as Pattern Signals

Compare and Contrast		*Cause and Effect*	*Time*	*Listing*
likewise	otherwise	thus	finally	first
similarly	in spite of	therefore	while	second
many	although	consequently	when	third
	conversely	accordingly	soon	next
	however	hence	at the same time	in addition
	less	as a result	next	also
	though	because	first	
	yet	since	second	
	on the contrary	so that		
	nevertheless			
	notwithstanding			
	on the other hand			

12. *Activity.* Another method for teaching outlining skills is a class outline. Have all the students fill in an outline together with the teacher, holding discussions on their choices and procedures. Also, distribute a teacher-constructed, skeletal outline to students for individual exercise; then discuss it and evaluate it as a group.

Topic II: Understanding and Using Step 2, the Initial Draft

1. *Teacher Presentation.* Tell students that they now are prepared to write their initial draft after the prewriting activities because they have had experiences of a social

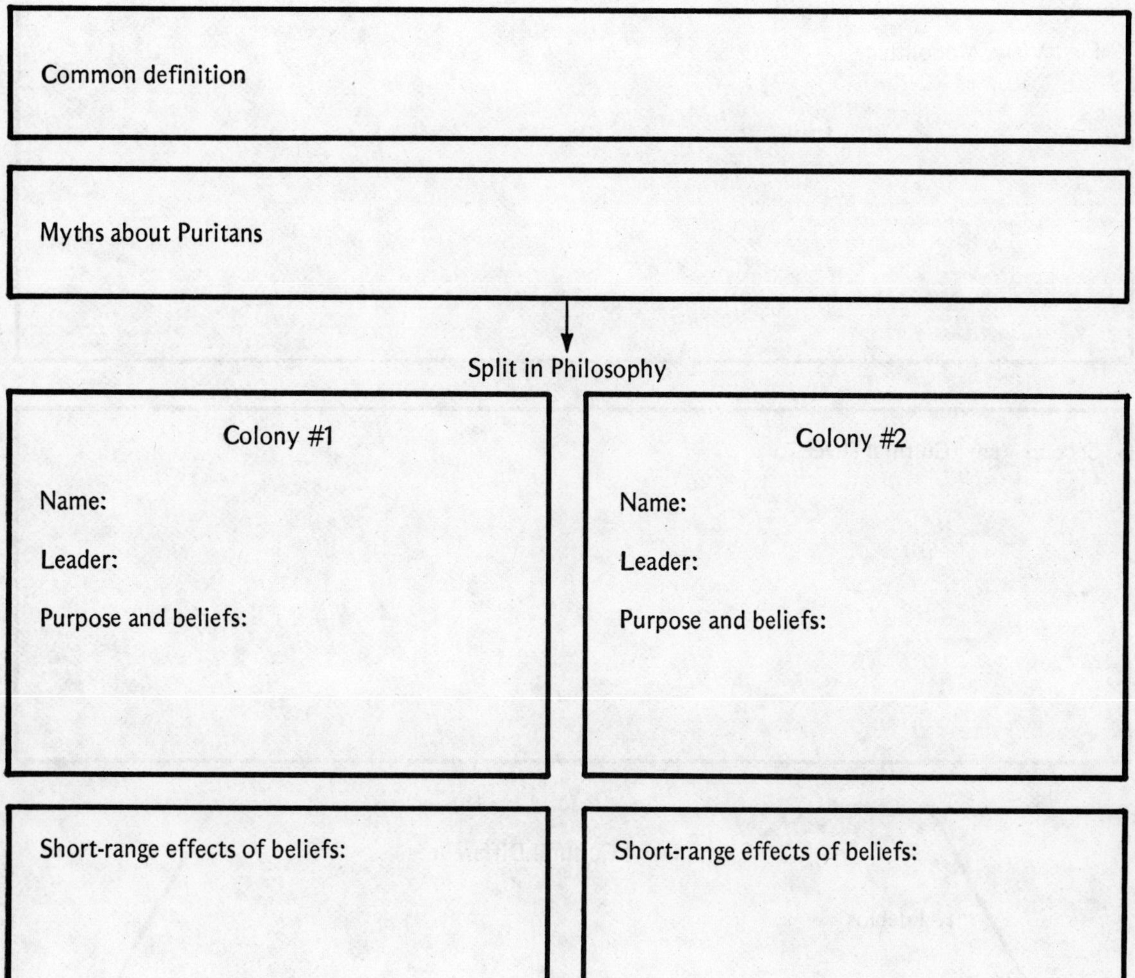

Common definition

Myths about Puritans

Split in Philosophy

Colony #1	Colony #2
Name:	Name:
Leader:	Leader:
Purpose and beliefs:	Purpose and beliefs:

Short-range effects of beliefs:

Short-range effects of beliefs:

Long-Range Effects

Government:

Work ethic:

Spiritual:

Educational:

Social:

Figure 2–1. Listening Guide: American Puritanism. (Prepared by secondary school teacher Linda Crowe.)

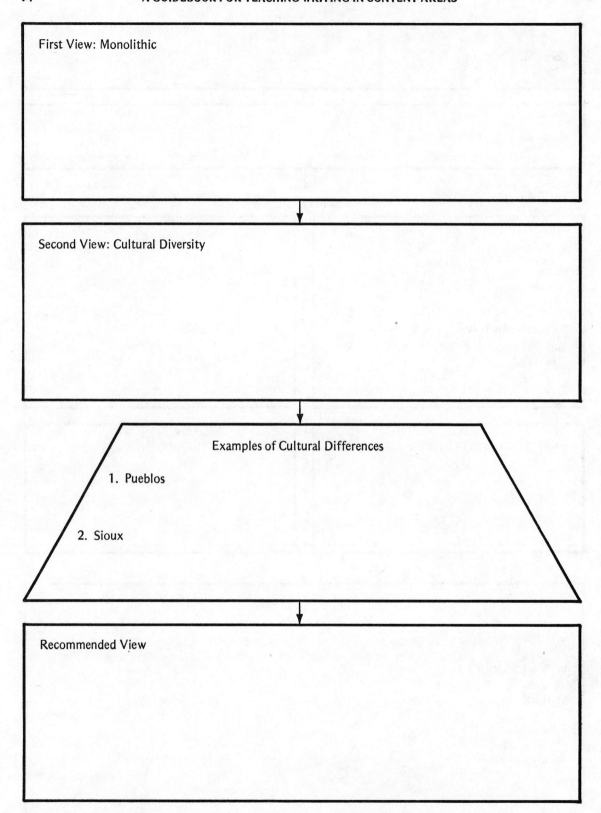

First View: Monolithic

Second View: Cultural Diversity

Examples of Cultural Differences

1. Pueblos

2. Sioux

Recommended View

Figure 2-2. Listening Guide: Two Views of Native American History. (Prepared by secondary school teacher John Pickett.)

nature—exchanging ideas with other people about the topic—and of a solitary nature—incubating and organizing what they will write. The actual writing experience should be less threatening at this point because students have lived with their topic and it has become part of them and personally meaningful.

2. *Activity*. Assign the initial draft, either as a class activity with teacher guidance readily available, or as a home activity where students have more time to think about and write out their ideas based on their previously constructed outlines and worksheets. If particular groups require more structure in learning writing behaviors, the class activity for writing the initial draft is highly recommended.

3. *Activity*. Collect the drafts but *do not grade* them at this stage. Have the class work on them further before they are assigned a grade. Students will know what kind of preliminary efforts go into writing an initial draft, so they know as well as does the teacher that the writing is only partly completed.

Topic III: Understanding and Using Step 3, Preparing to Revise the Draft

1. *Teacher Presentation*. Tell students that their Initial Draft is just that, a preliminary sketch through which they discover just what it is they want to express. It is a trial run, an experiment in which students practice and gain experience and confidence in proceeding to the next step of mastery. If the initial draft is red-penciled by the teacher at this step, the self-confidence and learning students should experience may be lost. Good teaching always has as its end result the independence of the student, and teaching writing is no exception when it comes to revision and editing. Have the students criticize and red-pencil their own papers before the teacher does. Tell students that the revision step is a natural, essential part of writing, not a punishment for doing it incorrectly the first time. Read aloud this statement on the necessity for revising their writing by James Michener, a well-known writer:

> I have never thought of myself as a good writer. Anyone who wants reassurance of that should read one of my first drafts. But I'm one of the world's greatest rewriters. I find three or four readings are required to comb out the cliches, line up pronouns with their antecedents, and insure agreement in number between subjects and verbs. It is, however, this hard work that produces a style. You write the first draft really to see how it's going to come out. My connectives, my clauses, my subsidiary phrases don't come naturally to me and I'm very prone to repetition of words; so I never write anything important in the first draft. I can never recall anything of mine that's ever been printed in less than three drafts.[1]

Revision, so essential, is neglected in the classroom writing assignments children most often undertake. Teacher judgments in red pencil and grades are frequently made on initial drafts and impromptu exercises, which do not allow time and practice in rewriting. Allow class time for this revision process, with guidance and reinforcement from you, and emphasize the importance of this step as part of the composing process.

---

1. Donald M. Murray, *A Writer Teaches Writing: A Practical Method of Teaching Composition* (Boston: Houghton Mifflin, 1968), pp. 241–242.

2. *Activity.* Instruct students to read aloud to themselves their own writing. Tell them to *listen* to their sentences to hear if each expresses a complete thought, sounds as if it flows smoothly, and is related to the other sentences. Tell students to focus first on the way their sentences sound and then on what the sentences mean individually and in relationship to each other. Students will be surprised at how much they already do know about language and their abilities to find errors in their own writing.

3. *Activity.* Using an opaque projector or distributing copies of student papers, display examples of good student writing. Be careful to use no names or else obtain permission of students beforehand to use their papers as examples. Point out effective use of language, excellent development of ideas, many aspects considered executed well that you want students to emulate. This positive approach will be encouraging and exemplary to students, who will begin to believe they can write that well too, now that they know what is considered good writing.

4. *Activity.* Using examples from unidentified student papers, present a lesson on one specific weakness such as comma usage, capitalization, lack of detail, paragraphing, and so on. Have students rewrite their papers focusing on this one specific problem.

5. *Activity.* Have students compile a list of commonly found errors in students' papers with examples for students' clear understanding. Have students do it themselves from their own papers. Students will be surprised at how much they already know about their language, and their sense of responsibility will increase as well as their confidence.

6. *Activity.* Read aloud to students in order to model use of language and to illustrate effective written language. Ask them to listen to the rhythm, flow, and music in the language; then discuss with students why it sounds so good. The effective use of language sounds good because of variety of sentences, construction of sentences, and balance between sentences. (See Chapter 8 for details.)

7. *Activity.* Using Reproduction Page 2–4, have students edit their own papers by checking the *Yes* and *No* columns for each category given. For all *No* checks, students should reconsider and change aspects that trouble them, with teacher assistance.

8. *Activity.* Conduct teacher-student conferences on student writing. Emphasize positive aspects of the writing in order to build confidence and determination to improve strengths. All students have language abilities, but most do not have practice in writing language. Emphasize their language strengths so that they will want to attempt writing.

9. *Activity.* Once a class has developed some proofreading skills, groups can be formed that have specific editing responsibilities. Have each group develop its own guide for editing a skill. Have students volunteer to be in a group of "capital-letter lookers," a group of "comma checkers," or a group of "sentence-fragment searchers," for example. Build editing confidence with this type of peer evaluation. Tell these editing groups that they can be the experts in the class on their particular problem area and can serve as counselor-instructors to the class, perhaps presenting a lesson on their expertise. Each group should have a handbook available as a reference for marking papers and for developing expertise. *The Writing Book* by Joan Roloff and Robert Wylder is an excellent reference for this activity (see resources at end of the chapter).

10. *Activity.* Break students into groups of five or less. The members of each group will read and discuss only the papers of their own group. Have the group members make suggestions for correcting errors and for developing ideas more clearly. Use Reproduction Page 2-4, which concerns editing the first draft, as a guide for the groups to follow in their evaluations, discussions, and recommendations. Use this activity later in the semester after students have gained confidence and knowledge in writing and editing and a cooperative working arrangement with peers. (See Chapter 9 on motivating students.)

11. *Activity.* Have each student mark the initial draft and turn it in to you; then make comments or have a student-teacher conference on the student's own editorial marks. This kind of guidance toward writing independence will be motivational and instructive for students, who will have numerous questions about their editing and writing that the teacher can deal with. Deal not only with errors but with concerns of the students as well.

Topic IV: Understanding and Using Step 4, Editing the Draft

1. *Teacher Presentation.* Tell students that there are two editorial acts in the revising process (see the two Donald Murray references in the *Resources* at the end of this chapter). Internal revision is the first act, which includes "everything writers do to discover and develop what they have to say." Have students read their writing to discover where their content, form, language, and voice have led them. Tell students that in internal revision their audience is one person, themselves.

   Tell students that the second act "is what writers do to communicate what they have found they have written to another audience." This act of externalizing the communication is where writers "pay attention to conventions of form and language, mechanics, and style." Internal revision is a necessary part of step 3 in our writing behaviors, and preparing to revise the initial draft, step 4, concentrates on externally revising the writing so that an audience beyond the writer is reached. This is the actual rewriting step now that the preparation has been done to make it effective.

2. *Activity.* Have students rewrite their initial drafts in the classroom, where the teacher may serve as a counselor and reference. Refer questions students have to a writer's handbook or discuss them on the spot to give immediate feedback and reinforcement on decisions they are making while rewriting.

3. *Activity.* Have students exchange their completed papers with a partner for proof-reading and for further editing.

4. *Activity.* If rewriting a second time is justified, have students complete this activity at home. Students will have to be reminded of what John Updike has said: "Writing and rewriting are a constant search for what one is saying."[2] This step is where the joy and excitement of using language and making discoveries about it may develop for some students.

---

2. Charles R. Cooper and Odell, Lee. *Research in Composing.* Urbana, Ill.: NCTE, 1978, p. 103.

5. *Activity.* Have students rewrite awkward, run-on, and choppy sentences by combining ideas using coordination and subordination as suggested in Chapter 8. Ask students to read their sentences aloud to themselves, listening for awkward sentences, the ones that should be rewritten. (See Chapter 8 for further details.)

Topic V: Understanding and Using Step 5, Finalizing the Composition

1. *Teacher Presentation.* Explain to students that once the editing and revising activities have been completed, they may rewrite the composition in its final draft. Discuss with student writers that if they feel knowledgeable and confident, then they are ready for this final step.

2. *Activity.* Have students write their final paper during class time. Be on hand as resource and as advisor and have reference materials and writing handbooks available to students in order to check out last-minute uncertainties.

3. *Activity.* Using Reproduction Page 2–5, the Proofreading Guide, have students check *Yes* or *No* to each of the pertinent points of composition listed. If students have a question regarding a point, tell them to use a reference book or teacher resource.

4. *Activity.* When students have completed the final copy and have proofread it, ask for discussion of problems, feedback on the writing process, and suggestions from students about future writing activities. Ask students to evaluate their own papers with specific comments. This may provide valuable information about student feelings of production, confidence, reality, and so forth. Self-evaluation will be diagnostic.

5. *Activity.* Compare teacher's evaluations of final papers to those of students'. Use the comparisons as the basis for student conferences so that comparative evaluations may be understood by students in their efforts to improve.

6. *Activity.* Without revealing names on papers, differently ranked writing may be displayed on an opaque projector to students. Thus A-graded writing can be discussed in class for its superior attributes so that students may learn and see comparisons to their own writing development. Be sure to obtain permission beforehand to display student work.

ASSESSING ACHIEVEMENT OF OBJECTIVES

Ongoing Evaluations

The extent to which students master each step of the writing behaviors can be measured by having them submit for evaluation the products of the Activities.

Final Evaluation

For an overall evaluation of students' ability to recognize and apply the concepts of the writing behaviors, assign an essay. Some of the following questions could be used to assess whether students have met objectives:

1. Did students list all their impressions and associations of the topic before they started writing?

2. Were these prewriting impressions formed into sentences and outlined?

3. Was the topic sufficiently narrowed and a specific audience chosen?

4. Did students select a particular mode or form of composition suitable to the topic?

5. Was the second, revised draft an improvement over the initial draft in language, form, and content?

6. Did the final draft evidence overall improvement over the other drafts?

7. In discussion, do students express their understanding of the writing behaviors that produce a well-written composition?

RESOURCES FOR TEACHING THE BEHAVIORS OF WRITING

Below is a selected and annotated list of resources useful for teaching the subject matter in this chapter. Resources are from journal articles and books.

Britton, James. "The Composing Processes and the Functions of Writing." *Research on Composing* (editors Cooper and Odell). Urbana, Ill.: NCTE (1978). This article explores the relationship between the writer and the reader and how that relationship affects the composition process. Sense of audience determines the role the writer plays in his or her interaction with the reader and the purpose for writing. The points presented are theoretical and of interest to researchers of the writing process.

Cooper, Charles R., and Odell, Lee (editors). *Research on Composing*. Urbana, Ill.: NCTE (1978). The book presents recent research on the composing process, discourse theory, and revision procedures. The editors present ten essays by prominent researchers in the field of composition that focus on these problems and suggest implications for further research. The essays raise questions concerning our understanding of the term *composition* and how to teach it most effectively.

Draper, Virginia. *Formative Writing: Writing to Assist Learning in All Subject Areas*. Berkeley, Calif.: Bay Area Writing Project, University of California, Curriculum Publication No. 3, 1979. The pamphlet proposes that writing assists learning in all content areas and suggests some activities for integrating writing and learning of subject matter. Such integration requires formative activities such as exploration, development, and discovery, which constitute the process common to both writing and learning. The writing activities suggested address this process.

Moffett, James, and Wagner, Betty Jane. *A Student Centered Language Arts Curriculum, Grades K-13*. Boston: Houghton Mifflin, 1968. The book is a wealth of ideas, activities, and approaches to integrating all the language arts, defined here as communication, in a school-wide program. Background theory for teaching writing is given practical application for the classroom. Particularly, Chapter 22 is valuable for its discussion of ways to assess student growth in communication skills based on brain hemisphere theory.

Murray, Donald. "Internal Revision: A Process of Discovery." *Research on Composing* (editors Cooper and Odell). Urbana, Ill.: NCTE, 1978. This article explains writing as a discovery process in its three stages: prevision, vision, and revision. Prevision is everything preceding the first draft, which is a "discovery draft." Revision is what the writer does to the first draft, the vision, in order to understand and communicate his or her initial discovery. Revision is writing and writing to find out what one wants to say because one has to allow language to lead into meaning. Included are pages of quotations from professional writers on the discovery process in their writing.

Murray, Donald M. *A Writer Teaches Writing.* Boston: Houghton Mifflin, 1968. The book is written by a professional writer who tested his ideas for teaching writing with secondary teachers. His approach is to explain the processes a writer undergoes and the skills a teacher must possess in order to guide the growth process. There are plenty of examples, suggestions, and illustrations to use as guidelines for teaching secondary students to write. Even daily and weekly lesson plans are included. Most valuable of all is his philosophy that writing is discovery and that students can be led into the joy and excitement that this discovery brings.

Roloff, Joan, and Wylder, Robert. *The Writing Book.* Encino, Calif.: Glencoe Publishing, 1978. This paperback book links reading and writing practice by providing short reading selections followed by writing exercises. Included also are photographs that serve as visual stimuli for the progressively more abstract writing exercises presented. The last section is a valuable reference for the writer on usage, punctuation, and spelling.

Wagner, Eileen N. "How to Avoid Grading Compositions." *English Journal.* 64:3 (March, 1975), 76–78. The article suggests that the reason most teachers do not assign compositions is that they do not want the drudgery of grading them. It recommends alternatives to grading each one separately, such as random grading, blanket grading, peer grading, and no grading. The point is to provide students with practice in writing, but not everything has to be given a grade.

Weigl, Bruce. "Revision as a Creative Process." *English Journal.* 65:6 (September, 1976), 67–68. This article approaches revision as a "revisiting" time and again. The original conception of the writer is not that important, for that will probably change as she or he discovers what is to be written about. Revision is a creative endeavor that must be faithful to language that communicates clearly to the reader. A revision checklist for the writer and teacher is included.

West, William W. *Developing Writing Skills.* Third Edition. Englewood Cliffs, N.J.: Prentice-Hall, 1980. The book provides processes, activities, and examples for students to follow in learning to write in various modes such as exposition, argument and persuasion, and narration. Designed for senior high, it also instructs in developing a library resource paper and in criticism of prose and poetry. It is comprehensive in its approach to teaching writing through the many styles and modes of composition.

3

Teaching Kinds of Writing in Content Area Texts

CONTENT OVERVIEW

Each content area has its own specific mode or modes of composition that best suit its subject matter and purpose. There are four such modes of composition that generally pertain to content area types of writing: narration and description, procedure, time-order exposition, and topic exposition. Each mode has its own components, structure, and requirements of expression. Learning how to compose in the mode demanded by the subject matter should also aid comprehension in reading of the content. Certain modes require more explicit text than others, which may be more implicit. Reader or audience considerations will help to determine how explicit or implicit a writer may be with his information. Students may develop writing fluency in the different modes through practice in building cumulative sentences and exercise in creating sentence parts. Such fluency is built on modification and elaboration of the main point, which results in more sophisticated sentence structure and development of the idea. The cumulative sentence may also affect style and student realization that language can be manipulated. This chapter teaches students to write in the mode or modes that best suit each content area and to increase fluency in each mode.

OBJECTIVES

As a result of the learning experiences in this chapter, students should be able to:

1. Recognize the four different modes of composition found in their textbooks.

2. Locate different modes of writing used in their different school subjects.

3. Understand the components and the structure of the different modes of writing and realize they are used for different purposes of communication.

---

4. Recognize which mode to use for essay test questions in their different school subjects.

5. Judge the language used by the author in their textbooks in regard to organization and structure, purpose, logical development, sentence variety, and concept presentation.

6. Comprehend their reading of the different modes found in textbooks much better because of their knowledge of the components and structure of each mode.

7. Be more aware of reader requirements in making written text explicit and in assuming certain reader background and experience for implicit text.

8. Realize that the different modes of writing have different text factors and reader factors that determine explicitness and implicitness of the writing.

9. Develop a greater sense of style of language use through sensitivity to and practice with the cumulative sentence.

10. Use different kinds of modifiers to develop images in readers' minds in narrative and descriptive modes of writing.

11. Use different transition and connector words to link modifiers to the subject in the expository mode of writing.

12. Understand and develop fluency in their own writing.

13. Construct more sophisticated sentences with use of different kinds of modifiers.

14. Develop a sense of rhythm and style in language use.

LEARNING EXPERIENCES

Topic I: Understanding and Using Different Modes of Composition

1. *Teacher Presentation.* Duplicate and distribute the Modes of Composition presented in Reproduction Page 3-1. Explain the components of each mode and that each one may be accounted for in the composition for each mode. Explain that the **narration/ description mode** tells a story and describes characters, times, places, and so forth. Examples of such writing can be found in social studies, English, and science textbooks. The **procedural mode** gives directions and relates step by step a process to be followed. Math problems, recipes, and scientific experiments are examples of procedural writing. **Topic exposition** develops one major argument or point that is developed with details. See Reproduction Page 7-9 for transition "ties" such as *in fact, as an illustration, such as,* and so on, to connect details. This type of writing is commonly found in social studies, English, and science textbooks. Lastly, **time-order exposition** deals with solving a problem or explaining cause and effect, that a certain effect was achieved in later time due to a causation prior. For this mode also see Reproduction Page 7-9 for transition ties such as *then, after, once,* and so forth. This mode suits writing in social studies, physical education, home economics, and industrial arts, among others.

Tell students that understanding the mode of their composition and its components should help them to express the type better and to fulfill its requirements for communication.

2. *Activity.* Using Reproduction Page 3-1, ask students to locate examples of the modes of writing they find in their own textbooks. Have them write out the passages they find so that by copying they may experience the language use and style of a professional writer of their text. Ask students to identify in the writing the components of the mode and to justify their choices according to the definitions provided them on Reproduction Page 3-1.

3. *Activity.* When students have copied the passages that substantiate their choice of mode of writing, ask them to read the passages aloud to the class so that students may *hear* the language and style of the writer. To hear the written language is a training that students can benefit from, as it exposes them to the rhythm and fluency of the language they want to emulate in their own writing.

4. *Teacher Presentation.* Explain to students that each of their subject areas has certain modes each employs that are suited to the purposes and communication of the subject. If students understand the mode use of their textbooks, then greater reading comprehension may result because identification of the components of the mode can help in locating the main points of the communication. Knowledge and recognition of textual mode can help the students in their own written expression in the different content fields. The students can better understand how to structure their composition and what components of it to include. Ask students to guess which of their classes use certain modes of writing in the textbooks and in the essay test questions asked. Have the students substantiate their guesses with reference to Reproduction Page 3-1.

5. *Activity.* After students have made their guesses on the modes of composition used in different content fields, present the following list on the blackboard. Ask students if they agree with the list and to substantiate their agreement or disagreement. Ask students to explain how knowledge of mode of composition may help them in taking essay tests in their different classes.

Mode of Composition	Content Area
Procedural	physical education
	math
	industrial arts
	art
	home economics
	music
	science
Narration/description	English
	social studies
	science

	math
	foreign languages
Topic exposition	social studies
	English
	science
	home economics
Time-order exposition	physical education
	home economics
	science
	math
	English
	social studies

6. *Activity.* Reproduce and distribute Reproduction Page 3-2, Probable Essay Questions in Subjects. Ask students to identify the probable content field of each essay question. Then have students identify which mode of composition would best suit the different essay questions. Have students give reasons for their choices by referring to the components and structure of each mode presented on Reproduction Page 3-1. Ask students to explain in detail the differences between each mode and what each one attempts to accomplish. What are the purposes for writing in each mode?

7. *Activity.* Make up several essay questions for students in your own content field. Present them to students for their analysis of what mode is suggested for each question, what the components and structure are for each question, and what the purpose is in each question according to the mode indicated. Ask students if knowing the mode indicated for each essay question helps them in knowing how to write it and to communicate the subject better. Have students explain why or why not.

8. *Activity.* Ask students to list the components and the structure for one of the essay questions you present to them. Have students refer to Reproduction Page 3-1 for the components and structure of the mode they have chosen for use for the essay question. For example, students could select an essay question that uses a time-order exposition mode. They would list the cause and the effect the essay elicits, the sequence of events to be detailed and the final events. They would list probable motivations and causes of such final outcomes. Have students write their purpose for writing the composition with reference to the definition of the mode.

9. *Activity.* When students have listed the components and structure of the essay question in specific detail, ask them to write out an initial draft of the composition, including all of the components and structure they have listed. Have them underline the transition ties they used in the composition, so that they are aware that they are using them and need to provide transitions between ideas. Collect the initial drafts for later work.

10. *Activity*. Reproduce and distribute Reproduction Page 3-3 that gives textbook examples of modes in different content fields. Divide students into small groups and have each group choose a passage to analyze. Ask students to determine the different modes asked for in each passage. Have students identify the components and structure of each passage according to its mode. Ask each group to determine which subject area textbook the passage probably came from.

Passage 1 came from the social studies textbook *Many Americans—One Nation* (Noble and Noble, 1974) and it can be considered to be in the time-order expository mode.

Passage 2 came from *Macmillan Mathematics* (Macmillan, 1977) and illustrates the procedural mode of composition.

Passage 3 is from the same math textbook as passage 2 and is in the topic exposition mode.

Passage 4 is from Jack London's short story "All Gold Canyon" found in *Types of Literature* (Ginn & Company, 1970) and demonstrates the narration/ description mode.

Passage 5 is from *Rise of the American Nation* (Harcourt Brace Jovanovich, 1977), a social studies textbook and is in the time-order exposition mode with cause-and-effect sequencing.

Passage 6, from *General Science* (Holt, Rinehart & Winston, 1979), displays the topic exposition mode and uses transition ties such as *since, also,* and *for example*.

Passage 7 is from *Chemistry* (Silver Burdett, 1978) and demonstrates the narration/ description mode with its use of comparison and contrast. Notice the use of the coordinating conjunction *but*.

Passage 8 illustrates the procedural mode and is from *Modern Biology* (Holt, Rinehart & Winston, 1981). It relates a process in a step-by-step sequence and ends with the product of the process.

Passage 9 is the narration/description mode in poetic form, which uses metaphorical language. The poem is by Robert Browning from "Pippa Passes" and was found in *Types of Literature* (Ginn & Company, 1970).

11. *Activity*. Ask each group of students to read aloud the passage they have chosen to analyze to the rest of the class. Then each group can present its views on choice of mode for the passage with reference to the components and structure of the passage. Solicit agreement or challenge from the other students, so that the choice each group makes has to be defended.

12. *Teacher Presentation*. Explain to students that in writing the different modes, the information given has certain text factors the writer should be aware of to make the communication as clear as possible to the reader. These text factors involve how explicit information should be, how much the writer may assume the reader already knows, and the amount of implicit or inferential ambiguity the writer may permit. In other words, there are three factors in text that influence comprehension of readers which writers must address: explicit, implicit and reader factors. Discuss

with students the concept of writing to a reader so that information and communication is best given. Present the following text and reader factors involved in writing to a reader.

Explicit factors: literal statements, direct information, and denotative (dictionary) word meanings.

Implicit factors: inferential aspects of language that require a reader to draw conclusions and make logical connections, connotative word meanings, ambiguity in meaning, symbols, and abbreviations.

Reader factors: background and experience in the subject, knowledge of the mode and type of writing, ability to tie in known ideas with new ideas in the writing, ability to follow the logic in the writing, and knowledge of symbols and abbreviations.

Discuss with students the complexities of writing clearly to a reader.

13. *Activity.* Reproduce and distribute Reproduction Page 3–4, on the recipe, the equation, and the poem, which are representative of different content fields such as home economics, mathematics, and English. Ask students to identify the explicit words and the implicit factors in each of the three forms of writing. What would a reader have to know in order to understand each form of writing? What do writers have to consider when they write in order to make meaning clear? What kinds of readers are there to write to: possibly inexperienced ones (who have never baked a pie before or worked an equation problem), very experienced ones (teachers and adults), and peers (who may have the skills to understand)? Recognizing these text factors should help students be aware of difficulties readers may have and how they as writers may have to be more explicit at times in their writing depending on their readers.

14. *Activity.* Present to the students the following modes of writing and the text factor considerations for each mode. The text and reader factors are what writers have to consider in making their communication clear to the reader.

Mode	Text Factors	Reader Factors
Procedural	explicit: direct information, precise word meanings, literal statements implicit: abbreviations and symbols, hidden steps, connotative words, conclusions to be drawn	knowledge of text mode and technical words ability to visualize the end-product, apply information, fill in unstated steps
Topic exposition	explicit: literal statements, direct information, details	knowledge of mode ability to find main idea ability to follow the logic

	implicit: ambiguity in referents and transitions, connotations, implications that require inferencing	understand new concepts deal with abstract information build relationships from old to new concepts background knowledge of subject ability to synthesize information
Time-order exposition	explicit: literal statements, direct information, denotative words implicit: causal inferences, connotative words, ambiguous associations and connections, synthesis of events, conclusions implied	knowledge of mode ability to follow sequence of events inferencing and synthesizing skills summarizing and visualizing abilities
Narration/ description	explicit: literal statements, denotative words implicit: connotative word meanings, metaphors, symbolism, levels of meanings (literal and figurative), ambiguity in motivations, events, clues (foreshadowing), theme implied	knowledge of mode and form (poetry, short story, etc.) imagination visualization intuition ability to infer, synthesize, and use background knowledge fill in unstated information apply old knowledge to new concepts

15. *Activity.* Discuss with students the considerations of factors in their own writing. Ask students to apply the reader factors to themselves as readers of textbooks in their subject areas. How could their knowledge of such reader factors help them to become better readers of the different modes of text in each content area?

16. *Activity.* From Activity 9, return students' initial drafts on the essay questions using a specific mode. The initial drafts should be unmarked and ungraded at this time because they are only preliminary. Ask students to rewrite their compoisitions in light of the different text and reader factors they have learned. Tell students to identify at the top of the page who their reader is to be, whether a peer, a younger person (not experienced), or a more experienced person (teacher, editor, or parent). Who the student names as the reader will help determine how explicit and implicit the writing may be. Collect the students' rewritten compositions.

17. *Activity.* Using students' compositions, but blacking out the students' names on the papers, project on the opaque projector some of the especially well-written ones. Discuss with students the mode used and the components and structure of the mode (see Reproduction Page 3–1) that can be identified in each one. Discuss with students the text factors found in the compositions. How much explicit information appears to be given and what are the implicit factors that can be identified? In view of the reader each student selected (as given at the top of the page), is the meaning intended communicated well with appropriate vocabulary, full-enough development of concepts, and explicit-enough information? Have students point out the strengths seen in these compositions. Also, can any improvements be made and what should they be?

18. *Activity.* Return students' compositions to them, still ungraded and unmarked at this time. Ask them to critique their own papers in light of the foregoing display and discussion of some effective student compositions. Tell students that editing and revising are learned and developed skills that take practice, but that they should learn to edit their own writing for lifelong value. They will not always have a teacher to "correct" their writing; they must learn to do it themselves. When students have decided on changes they want to make, a brief teacher-student conference would be helpful to discuss changes and problems students have. After the conferences, ask students to write a final draft, which will be collected, graded and marked at this time. Then collect the papers. The time you spend editing and correcting should be minimal on this final rewrite.

19. *Activity.* Reproduce and distribute Reproduction Page 3–5, the Language in Your Textbook form. Using the content area textbook, discuss with students one representative passage in the book. Have students fill in the information requested on the instrument as students discuss the answers. At the end on the last page, ask students to write their impressions and their judgment of the readability, its difficulty and its conceptual problems. What text factors and reader factors help or hinder their understanding of the passage? Why is it or isn't it written well?

20. *Activity.* Divide students into small groups. Using Reproduction Page 3–5, have students in groups select and analyze two other passages in their textbooks. Ask them to indicate the page numbers of the passages and to fill out the questions on the form for each passage. Discuss as a class the passages chosen and analyzed. Determine students' critical reactions to and judgment of their own textbook. Perhaps it is not well written and students have difficulty understanding it because of that. Student criticism can be valuable information for a teacher to use in selecting student reading material and textbooks. Help students to transfer their discoveries about their own textbook writing to their writing in the subject. Their analysis of effective and ineffective features of the writing should be applied to what they should or should not do in their own compositions. Tell students that they should try to use in their own writing the factors they liked in their analysis.

Topic II: Understanding and Developing Fluency in the Modes of Writing

1. *Teacher Presentation.* Explain to students that when they write they not only express a subject and a verb of some kind, but also add information; thus their

writing is a process of *addition*. This process of addition is how their ideas are developed, elaborated on, and communicated more fully to the reader. What is added to the subject and the verb is called a **modifier,** and the addition process itself is one of modification or expansion. Modification is achieved through adding single words to a subject, verb, or both, as in the following sentence:

> The young boy bought a pencil.

The adjective *young* is additional information for the subject.

> The young boy nervously bought a pencil.

The adjective *young* and the adverb *nervously* are single word modifiers for the subject and the verb. Consider the way modification is achieved in the next sentence, however.

> The boy on the bicycle bought a pencil from the blind man.

Notice that two phrases have been added to modify the subject and the verb. The phrase *on the bicycle* adds information to the concept of the boy, and *from the blind man* modifies *bought*, telling where he bought the pencil. There is one other way that modification can be developed in a sentence:

> The boy who was on the bicycle bought a pencil.

This time the modifier is a clause that adds information to the subject and serves to emphasize it. Modification, therefore, may be achieved in a sentence through single words, phrases, and clauses added to develop detail about and elaborate on the images the writer wants to create in the mind of the reader. In the previous sentence example it is not any boy who bought the pencil, but it is specifically one, the one on the bicycle (the emphasis is different if commas are placed before and after the clause because then the added information becomes more incidental to the subject).
Consider this final sentence:

> The young boy who was on the bicycle nervously bought a pencil from the blind man.

In this sentence all three kinds of modifiers are used to develop the main points. Single-word modifiers are *young, nervously,* and *blind*. Phrases are *on the bicycle* and *from the blind man*. The clause that develops the subject is *who was on the bicycle*. Further elaboration can be used for the sentence, of course, in developing the concept of the blind man. Also, the modifiers can be changed and moved around for emphasis. Students should be led to understand the flexibility and fun of our language, especially in the use of modification that involves the imaging and creativity of the writer.

2. *Activity*. Present the following subject to students: "boy." Ask students to list on their own papers what they can visualize about the subject. Tell students to write four things that describe the subject. Next, ask students to visualize what the subject

is doing and to write a verb for the subject. Tell students to write four describers of the action, the verb that they selected. Now ask students to form a sentence out of as many of their modifiers as they can that will describe in detail the subject and the verb. Have students write their sentences on the board to share with other students their use of modification. Point out and underline the kinds of modifiers and the single words, phrases, and the clauses that students used in their elaborations. Most importantly, point out how the image of the subject radically changes from sentence to sentence depending on the modifiers that each student used. The modifiers build understanding between writer and reader and are essential to communication.

3. *Activity*. Review with students the four different modes of composition as presented on Reproduction Page 3-1. Tell students that—with the use of the different kinds of modifiers, single words, phrases, and clauses—sentences can be built that will add detail to the images created in a reader's mind. Such sentences have been called "cumulative sentences" by Francis Christensen, and they can be used to develop sentences in most of the modes of composition in most content areas.

Reproduce and distribute Reproduction Page 3-6 to students. The narration mode of composition is found in their English, social studies, science, and other subject textbooks. These examples come from secondary school reading materials. Ask students to read the two examples aloud for sensory detail. Tell them to notice the punctuation of each sentence: the dashes, commas, and periods. Ask students to explain what is being modified or described in each sentence. In the first two examples the elaboration is of the verbs, *glimpsed* in the first sentence and *increased* in the second sentence. The modifiers heighten the effect of the verbs. Therefore, when students write out the practice sentences, they are to add descriptive modifiers to the verbs *crashed* and *posed* for each sentence. The following are examples:

1　The waves crashed to the shore,

　　2　smashing the sand castle

　　2　and scattering the strolling sandpipers.

1　The model posed for the artist,

　　2　shivering on the platform,

　　2　balancing on the stool.

The number 1 indicates the main clause, the main subject and verb of the sentence. The other numbers depict the modification; by counting and averaging the number per sentence, the depth of modification can be found (see Chapter 8 for sentence weights). Point out to students that the main clause can come after its modifiers, that clauses and modifiers can be moved around in a sentence. Be careful, though, to place a modifier next to what it describes so that it will make sense. Tell students that the narration mode, because it tells a story, is concerned with action primarily. So the modifiers they add in this mode will serve to heighten the effect of the verb. This is in contrast to the descriptive mode, which tends to elaborate on nouns—the persons, places or things to be described. All of the practice sentences for students in this exercise will emphasize description and elaboration of the verb. Tell students to check their modifiers in each practice sentence to make sure they have described the verb, the action word in the sentence. Have students read their sentences aloud to the class, or write them on the blackboard for students to discuss and share.

4. *Activity.* Ask students to find examples of modifiers in sentences in their own textbook writing. Tell them to copy out the sentences they find and to underline the single-word, phrase, and clause describers they locate in each sentence. Share the examples with the whole class. Have the students decide what the modes of writing are for the examples and which is being described—a verb or a noun—for each sentence. Ask students how understanding the modification in the sentences in their subject area writing can help them in both their writing and their reading in the subject.

5. *Activity.* From the class textbook, take five long sentences for examples. Write only the main clause on the board for students to see. Ask them to copy down the main clause and then to expand it with modifiers to build a longer, more detailed sentence from the main clause. Discuss the students' sentences for their expansion, elaboration, and logical development of the subject. Then have students read the original sentence as given in the textbook. Ask them to compare their sentence to the original and to discover what the textbook writer did in the sentence construction. Ask them to critique the writer's sentences for clarity, logic, and development of the subject.

6. *Activity.* Reproduce and distribute Reproduction Page 3-7. Tell students that the description mode of writing emphasizes the effect of the noun because it serves to describe a person, a place, or a thing. The modification, therefore, should be of the noun, not of the verb. Have students recognize the kind of detail—sensory, emotional, or metaphorical—that the practice sentences are emphasizing. **Sensory detail** has to do with the senses of sight, sound, feel, taste, and smell. The modifiers for those two practice sentences should therefore involve description of the senses. Ask students to decide which senses are being emphasized in each of the examples and practice sentences. For the **emotional detail,** have students explain the emotions that are described in each sentence. What emotions are being asked for in the practice sentences? **Metaphorical detail** involves using a comparison of the subject with an unlike thing. The first sentence compares the "man" to a "gorilla," and the second sentence compares the smell of the boy to that of a bird's nest. Metaphors can be fun and creative for students to think of and to use. They are very useful for creating images and humor in writing.

7. *Activity.* Ask students to find examples of descriptive modifiers in their textbook writing. Have them copy out the sentences and underline the describers they locate. Ask students to read their sentences aloud to the class to hear the rhythm and fluency of the sentences. Have students discuss the kind of detail—whether metaphorical, sensory, or any other they may discover—used to describe the noun in each sentence. How is the description developed in their subject area writing? Ask students if recognizing the development of descriptive detail helps them in their reading as well as their writing in their subjects.

8. *Activity.* From the classroom textbook take five sentences using descriptive detail. Write the main clauses of the sentences on the blackboard and ask students to copy them down. Have students develop the main clause of each sentence with descriptive detail that expands the noun of the clause. Tell them to use metaphorical comparison where it is appropriate and makes sense. Have them read aloud their

own sentences to the class. Analyze their sentences in regard to development of the noun, the kind of detail used, and the rhythm and fluency of the sentence. Ask students to compare their own descriptive sentences to the original ones in the textbook. How did the author develop the descriptive detail? Is it effective or not? Have students critique the textbook sentences for development of detail or lack of it, the kind of modifiers used, and the types of details used. Is the writing effective for the purpose of describing a person, place, or thing? Why or why not?

9. *Activity.* Reproduce and distribute Reproduction Page 3–8 to students. Tell students that the modification used in expository writing is more for the purpose of developing and expanding information than for creating images in a reader's mind. Expository writing is found in almost all subject area textbooks because it is the explanation and information kind of composition. This kind of composition is what students are probably asked most to write in their different classes. Exposition is explanation, and it can follow different arrangements. The two arrangements most commonly used in expository writing are the time-order and the topical developments. Transitions and connectors are very important in both arrangements because they indicate the kind of sequencing that is used. For instance, in the three time-order sentences given as examples, certain transition words are used such as *following, as,* and *soon* in the first sentence; *then* and *before* are the connector words in the second sentence; and *if* in the third sentence shows causation. All of these transition words provide cohesion (see Chapter 7) that link the ideas together and indicate sequencing. Not only are transition words used between sentences, but they must be used within sentences to show logical development. The transition words also introduce modifiers and help expand the main clause with informational clauses and phrases. With the use of the transition words (also see Reproduction Page 7–9 for a complete list), the cumulative sentence can be built in expository writing.

Notice in the topic exposition examples the transition and connector words used to build elaboration. Have students point out how the details are linked together in the expanded sentences. In the first sentence, *on the other hand* is a transitional phrase from the prior sentence, so it serves as a link from a previous idea to this contrasting idea. *Which* connects the modifying clause to the main clause and expands on *teachers* and *subjects,* giving more information. In the second example, *although, for,* and *as* connect the subordinate clauses, which modify the main clause and expand on the main idea. In the last example, *between* twice links modifying phrases to the idea of the swinging pendulum in the preceding phrase and to the alternating rhythm in the main clause. Have students discuss the uses of these linking connector words and how they serve expansion in the cumulative sentence.

Have students complete the practice sentences. Discuss their sentences and share with the class how they expanded each one with different transition words.

10. *Activity.* Have students locate sentences in their own textbooks that are examples of expository writing. Ask the students to copy down at least five of the sentences they find. Have students read aloud their sentences to the rest of the class in order to hear the fluency and rhythm of a professional writer's sentence. Have students identify the transition and connector words used in each sentence. What kind of sequencing do the transition words indicate: time-order, topical, or other? If students are in doubt, have them read the paragraph, the context from which the sentence came in order to discover the logical development used by the writer. Ask students to determine the *purpose* of the expository writing they examine. What

function does it serve: to explain what? To inform about what? This kind of questioning should help student understanding in reading expository writing as well as in learning to write it more effectively.

11. *Activity.* Take five sentences out of the classroom textbook that are examples of expository writing. Write only the modifiers on the blackboard for one sentence at a time. In class discussion ask students to provide a main clause to fit the modifiers logically. Compare the main clause the students provide to the original one given in the textbook. Discuss how the modifiers introduced by the transition and connector words provide clues to the main idea (the main clause) of the sentence. Explain to students that they provide contextual clues to meaning and comprehension for the reader. The writer must recognize the function of these clues in giving aid to the reader for effective communication.

12. *Activity.* Discuss with students the idea of fluency in their writing. Fluency means flowing smoothly with rhythm and ease. Ask students to examine the example sentences given on Reproduction Page 3–8 to see if they fit this definition. Ask the students in chorus to read aloud each sentence to discover if there is a smooth, flowing rhythm to the construction. How is it achieved? Discuss with students the use of modifiers that build the concepts in the sentences. Review with them what kinds of modifiers are single words, phrases, and clauses. The rhythm is achieved through a balance of these modifiers and the natural pauses (cadences) that they cause the reader to make. Sensitivity to the rhythms of language used well is valuable to writers in their discovery of style. With practice a writer develops a style in writing, a language use, that is the writer's own. Awareness of the music of spoken and written language should be part of the development of style and creative use of language.

13. *Activity.* Write a main clause, a statement, on the blackboard for students from the subject area. In class discussion have students build modifiers for the statement. Write suggestions on the board as students supply them, but have students determine *where* the modifiers should be placed. They should be written next to the word they describe in order to be logical. Help students to realize where modifiers should be placed to make sense. Language is flexible and sentence parts can be moved around for emphasis, but they should make sense. When the sentence is built, have students read it aloud in chorus. Discuss with students whether it has fluency or sounds choppy or cluttered. Do they like the sound of the sentence? Does it flow and have rhythm? If it sounds disagreeable, how can it be changed? When students are satisfied with the sentence they have built, ask them to copy it on their papers and to write other sentences related to it. Have students develop the statement into a paragraph for practice in writing longer forms beyond the sentence. Collect the paragraphs. In reading the students' compositions, assess whether their sentence structure has become more elaborate and detailed. Present some of the interesting sentences to the students to hear and discuss.

14. *Activity.* Discuss with students why the procedure mode of composition is not one that should be developed with modifiers in a cumulative sentence. Why should directions be simple statements (actually commands or requests) without much elaboration in each sentence? Ask students to look back at the recipe and the equation problem on Reproduction Page 3–4. What is the purpose of this mode of writing and why must it be explicit and brief? Its purpose is to provide directions for a final outcome, and the command sentences used must be short and to the point.

ASSESSING ACHIEVEMENT OF OBJECTIVES

Ongoing Evaluation

The extent to which students have understood and used the different modes of composition can be measured by having them submit for evaluation the final products of Activities.

Final Evaluation

For an overall evaluation of students' ability to understand and use different modes of composition and to increase their fluency in each mode, assign an in-class essay *before* they study this chapter and perform the learning activities. When students have studied this chapter, then assign an in-class essay on a similar topic and compare the two essays, one a prelearning experience and the other a postlearning experience. Compare the two essays according to the following criteria:

1. Has the student recognized the mode of composition by the components included and the structure used? Are they identifiable?

2. Are the sentences generally longer (more words per sentence) in the postexperience composition?

3. Is the sentence structure more complex because more modifiers are used in the postexperience composition?

4. Are the ideas more developed with greater elaboration in the second paper?

5. Is there evidence for growth of reader awareness from use of clear definitions, logical transition words, or specific images?

6. Does the postexperience paper warrant a higher grade than the preexperience paper in regard to greater detail, clarity of purpose, communication to the reader, and use of the appropriate mode?

Another method of evaluation is to display students' papers to the class (blocking out the names) on an opaque projector and solicit students' comments as to the effective and ineffective factors they find in the writing. Listen for the terminology students use in their critiquing. The extent to which they talk about mode components and structure and fluency, text, and reader factors will indicate their understanding and grasp of their learning experiences.

RESOURCES FOR TEACHING KINDS OF WRITING IN CONTENT AREA TEXTS

Below is a selected and annotated list of resources useful for teaching the subject matter in this chapter. The selections are from journal articles and from books.

Blaisdell, Thomas C. *Composition—Rhetoric*. New York: American Book Company, 1906. Chapter XXI is of interest in this book in that it presents the traditional "forms of discourse," which are narration, description, exposition, and argumentation. These differ from the modes of composition presented in this chapter, which cover most all content area composition in schools today. The value in reading Chapter XXI would be to gain a clearer definition and elaboration of the modes along with examples and exercises that may be used in the classroom. The book is rather quaint in its presentation of classic principles of rhetoric, but it is informational.

Christensen, Francis. "A Generative Rhetoric of the Sentence." *College Composition and Communication.* 14:3 (October, 1963), 155–161. The article develops the concept of the cumulative sentence that does more than just combine ideas; it also "generates ideas." The process of composition is a "process of addition," and the cumulative sentence is dynamic in generating addition in the form of modifiers. Several principles are discussed regarding the composing process, such as direction of modification, levels of abstraction, and texture of composition. This article would be of interest to teachers wishing to read the source of some ideas used in this chapter.

Lapp, Diane, and Flood, James. *Teaching Reading to Every Child.* New York: Macmillan, 1978. Chapter 9 presents several current theories of how readers comprehend text. Comprehension is information processing, analysis of connected logical discourse, analysis of propositions, or a "top-down, bottom-up" process. These theories of how a reader comprehends would be of interest to a teacher of writing because with them one may understand better how written communication should be presented to the reader. Of special interest is Bloom's Taxonomy, which helps clarify facets of text-explicit and implicit information. Explicit information is literal comprehension, and implicit information concerns inferential comprehension. Knowledge of reader functions should be part of teaching writing, for the focus is communication to the reader. This chapter provides many interesting theories of reader functions.

Pearson, P. David, and Johnson, Dale D. *Teaching Reading Comprehension.* New York: Holt, Rinehart & Winston, 1972. Chapter 2, "Factors Influencing Reading Comprehension," presents in detail the explicit and implicit factors to be considered in text that pertain to comprehension. Applied to writing, though, they should be understood by a writer in order to communicate to the reader. Here they are termed "factors inside the head" and "outside the head" and both kinds must be considered. Those "inside the head" pertain to the reader's linguistic development, interest, and motivation for reading. The authors do not delve into audience considerations that the writer would have to address in order to assess interest, motivation, and reading ability. Factors "outside the head" are ones of text, specifically its readability in structure and theme. This chapter is of interest to teachers desiring to pursue further the concepts of text and reader factors for teaching writing.

4

Teaching Choices of Purpose and Audience in Writing

CONTENT OVERVIEW

Two major assumptions in recent theories of writing refer to choices writers have that will influence their levels of language usage, style, mode, and vocabulary in writing. The first assumption is that the *purpose* for writing determines everything else in the process of writing. Four purposes are identified: expressive (expressing a viewpoint), creative (using the imagination), persuasive (persuading), and factual (informing). The aim of expressive writing is to express the writer's point of view on a topic, while the purpose of creative writing is to experiment with and manipulate the language to create images in the mind of the reader. Persuasive writing aims to evoke an action in the reader, and factual writing is concerned with data and logic. It would appear that in teaching writing, the purpose for writing would have to be communicated to the students and clearly perceived by them *before* they actually write.

The second assumption in recent theory is that the relationships between writer, subject, and audience (or reader) guide a writer's choices of style, mode, diction, and so forth. Communication relationships between writer and audience are described in terms of the "distance" between them. One kind of distance ranges from intimate to formal, for which the writer creates a "voice" or persona (mask) from which he or she speaks. Another kind of distance ranges from "reflection" within the writer, with its use of I-you (egocentric) relations, to "publication" for a large, impersonal, and anonymous group, which uses I-it (sociocentric) communication. The ability of a writer to use this range is dependent on maturity and intellectual development.

In teaching writing, teachers should make students aware of their choices in purpose for writing and audience to whom they are writing. Writers should be aware of how their language, style, and delivery differ according to their purpose for writing and to their readers. With this knowledge the writer may be able to realize choices available for varying language, style, and delivery and thus communicate more effectively.

OBJECTIVES

As a result of the learning experiences in this chapter, students should be able to:

1. Understand that writing is undertaken to achieve a purpose.

2. Identify their reasons for writing.

3. Realize that their purpose for writing will influence the audience to whom they write, the style, the language, the form of composition, as well as what they write.

4. Make clear their reasons for writing so that these are communicated effectively to the reader.

5. Understand the importance of the audience/reader in their writing.

6. Experience growth from writing for a very personal audience to writing for a larger, more impersonal audience.

7. Experience growth from writing on an informal level to writing on a more formal level, recognizing changes in language use, form of composition, and distance from audience.

8. Appreciate the differences in style and how these are created with consideration of varying audiences.

9. Identify their audience in the prewriting stage in order to appeal to the audience with appropriate language and relationship.

10. Write for a particular audience so that the communication is more effectively achieved.

LEARNING EXPERIENCES

Topic I: Understanding and Establishing Purposes for Writing

1. *Teacher Presentation.* Explain to students that when they write, they do so for a particular purpose. When they are clear about their purpose for writing, then they achieve communication much more effectively. *Before* they write, in the step 1, prewriting stage, students should be very clear about their purpose for writing. Tell students that there are generally four different reasons or purposes for writing in school essays. The first is to express their views or opinions on a topic they know about in a subject field. The second may be to use their imagination to create images in the reader's mind, as in a story. The third may be to persuade the reader to do something. And a fourth could be to present facts and data, probably the most prevalent writing assignment in school. Ask students to demonstrate verbally each one of the four possible purposes for the rest of the class. For example, one student can express an opinion about the military draft, whether or not boys and girls should be drafted. To illustrate the second kind of purpose, a second student could tell the story of Little Red Riding Hood with very descriptive words or make up another story. A third student could persuade the class to vote for a friend for class

president or whatever. Lastly, to demonstrate the fourth purpose, students could cite information they have read in the encyclopedia, such as the uses and sources of the element zinc. As a verbal exercise this should be fun for students and practice for them in understanding and using purpose. Have the class reiterate the specific purpose each student speaker has demonstrated.

2. *Activity.* Have students collaborate in groups to discuss other examples for each of the four reasons for writing. Each group can do all four, or each group can be responsible for just one reason to present to the rest of the class as an oral example of what they would write.

3. *Activity.* Duplicate and distribute Reproduction Page 4-1 to each student. Explain the four possible reasons for writing given on the worksheet and ask students to write several sentences illustrating each reason. They may write on the hint given for each reason, or they may write on another topic of their own choosing. Have students read aloud what they have written and have class discussion on the examples students provide. Have students identify other possible reasons for writing in their subject areas in school.

4. *Activity.* From the several sentences students wrote on Reproduction Page 4-1 in Activity 3, have them write a paragraph on one of the reasons. Ask students to expand on one of the topics they have chosen and to keep their purpose for writing clearly in mind as they write. Have students volunteer to read aloud their paragraphs when they finish. Discuss them in regard to purpose: is it clearly communicated to the reader? Is the development of the topic such that the purpose is carried out? Is the purpose achieved effectively? Why or why not? How can the paragraph in regard to its purpose be improved? After the class discussion, collect the paragraphs for later work. Do not grade them or red-pencil them at this time.

5. *Activity.* Duplicate and distribute Reproduction Page 4-2 to students. Ask students to identify in the reading selections from secondary textbooks what the purpose of each selection must be. Ask them to state the reason each writer had for writing each passage. Have students refer to the four reasons already presented to them on Reproduction Page 4-1 to understand possible purposes. Discuss students' reasoning. Ask them to explain why it is important in reading to understand the writer's purpose for the communication. As writers themselves, why should students clearly understand their purpose for writing to a reader?

6. *Activity.* Ask students to rewrite the passages given in Reproduction Page 4-2 into other *forms* of discourse. For example, selection 1, a biography, could be rewritten as a letter to a friend describing people students know personally. Selection 2, the poem, could be written as an essay. Selection 3, a tall tale, could be rewritten as a factual account or as a letter. Selection 4, a historical essay, could be rewritten as a letter, a diary or journal, or as a story. Selection 5, an essay, could be a biography or an autobiography. Finally, selection 6, the advertisement, could be rewritten as a description or a fictional story with the student as its owner. Have students decide when they change the form if the purpose of the communication is changed at all. Is one form better than another for communicating the writer's purpose?

7. *Activity.* Write on the blackboard and present the following different writing assignments to students that might be typical of essay tests they may have in school in

different content areas. Have students discuss the purpose for writing asked for in each essay assignment. Refer to the four purposes given in Reproduction Page 4-1. Discuss with the students how knowing their purpose for writing will help their writing and their grade on the writing test.

Possible Writing Assignments in Content Areas

a. Continue the plot of the short story where the author leaves off. Provide further action and end it the way you would have the story end.

b. Explain what you think were the reasons for the outbreak of the Korean War during the 1950s.

c. Write an advertisement for the Louisiana Territory that the French could have written in 1803 when they sold it to the United States as the Louisiana Purchase.

d. Compare the basic differences between a red blood cell and a white blood cell.

e. Give your opinion on whether a person in our society is influenced more by heredity or by environment.

The probable reasons for writing for these essay assignments are the following: topic *a* asks for creative writing; topic *b* calls for facts and a viewpoint; topic *c*'s purpose is to persuade; topic *d* asks for facts; and topic *e* demands a viewpoint. Ask students in identifying each purpose for writing to substantiate their choices.

8. *Activity.* Return students' paragraphs to them from Activity 4. Review what they have learned about purpose in writing. Discuss with students what they can do in their paragraphs to establish purpose and to develop it more fully. How can they revise and rewrite their paragraphs to fulfill their purpose more effectively? For instance, in expressing a viewpoint, perhaps more opinions should be presented and more detail added to develop the point of view. In persuasion, maybe the appeal to the reader should be made clearer, whether it is emotional, logical, ethical, or all three. In creative writing, perhaps students can use more descriptive words, more varied sentences, and some dialogue with characters. Lastly, in presenting facts, the student could provide more information and more detail to fulfill the purpose for writing. Ask students to rewrite their paragraphs with the aim of fulfilling their purpose in writing more effectively.

9. *Activity.* When students have rewritten their paragraphs, collect them. Do not grade them yet, but select a few of the best-developed paragraphs and a few of the weakest ones. Ask students' permission to use their papers as examples in class. Cover the names on the papers and display the paragraphs to the entire class on the opaque projector. Have students discuss the strengths and weaknesses of the better and poorer papers and how these may be improved. The discussion should center on what the purpose of the writing is, how well it is carried out, and how effective it is in communication to the reader.

10. *Activity.* Return the paragraphs of Activity 9 to students for a final revision and rewriting. Tell them that this final draft will be collected and graded on how well they established and fulfilled their purpose for writing. Circulate and confer with students as they rewrite so that they have a resource for their understanding.

Topic II: Understanding and Creating an Audience in Writing

1. *Teacher Presentation.* Explain to students that in daily life in and beyond school people have a need to write to others. Their purpose for writing is probably the most important determinant for how they write, but a major consideration must be their reader. An analysis of the traits of the readers and how to appeal to them can be made once the purpose for writing about a subject is decided on. The writer visualizes the reader as being a recipient of and an interactor with the communication, whether in the form of an argument, a persuasion, a factual presentation, or an imaginative work. The writer must focus on the methods to be used in order to appeal to the reader in light of the purpose for writing. The writer considers the relationship to the reader: what distance is to be created? What language and tone should be used? What is the reader's experience or lack of it? What should be detailed and emphasized? Which voice should be used to appeal to the reader?

   Explain to students that their reader or audience is approached in several ways (see Moffett in the Resources at end of this chapter). The most personal is **reflection**: talking or writing just to oneself as in a diary. The next is **conversation**: gossip, anecdotes and informal reports in the form of dialogue between persons known to each other where response is possible. **Correspondence** is informal written exchange at a distance between people known to each other. This is writing to a small, familiar audience, whether in letter form or not. Lastly, the least personal relationship between a writer and audience is **public narrative**, a formal writing intended for a general audience removed from the writer. The relationships between writer and audience progress from informal to formal and from personal to impersonal. There are ways a writer achieves this progression that will be explored here.

2. *Activity.* Reproduce and distribute to students Reproduction Page 4–3, which explains writer-audience relationships. Ask students to provide three or more sentences to illustrate each of the relationships.

3. *Activity.* Discuss with students their illustrations on Reproduction Page 4–3 of writer-audience relationships. Point out the differences in the pronouns used in each one. Reflection would use the *I* pronoun, as this is a personal writing intended to be read only by the writer about oneself. Conversation uses I-you pronouns because it is a dialogue between two persons known to each other and who are responding to each other. Correspondence uses I-you and you-she, you-he to communicate over a distance. Lastly, public narrative uses no I or you pronouns, but is formal; it is used when the subject is impersonal.

4. *Activity.* Ask students to write a short (one-page) autobiography of their early lives. Tell them to provide details of where they were born and what happened in their early years. Do not collect the autobiographies at this time.

5. *Activity.* Duplicate and distribute to students Reproduction Page 4–4, two beginning "autobiographies," the first one from *Catcher in the Rye* and the second from *David Copperfield*. The characters of Holden Caulfield and David Copperfield are both created by the authors of the stories, but both characters are presenting their lives through the first-person point of view; they are telling their own stories

in the style and personality the authors want to project. Ask students to compare the two in terms of the relationships of writer to audience. Refer to Reproduction Page 4-3 to help students describe the relationships. How does the language use of each character establish their character? Discuss how the tone, the emotional effect on the reader, is created by the voice or persona in the language use and the style of each character. Walker Gibson describes tone as a "tough, sweet, or stuffy" voice. Which of these voices is being portrayed in each passage?

6. *Activity.* Ask students to compare their own autobiographies to those of the two characters on Reproduction Page 4-4. Are theirs more or less formal, personal, distant? Ask students to rewrite their autobiographies in a more formal style meant for publication in a magazine. Tell them to visualize a large, unknown audience who will be reading their autobiographies. Tell students to eliminate the slang and contractions and to avoid use of the second person *you*. Ask them to avoid using simple, short sentences and to try using more complex structures.

7. *Activity.* Ask students to volunteer to read their autobiographies aloud to the class. Have the class comment on the vocabulary used and the suitability of the style for publication in a magazine. Why or why not would the writing be effective? Discuss relationships of writers to audience and the factors that create them.

8. *Activity.* Tell the story of the "Three Bears" to students in the class. Divide the class into five groups and present the following kinds of audience to the class, each group choosing the audience it wants to address:

- a six-year-old child
- a peer (using slang)
- a college professor
- the president of a company
- a close friend

Have students identify their purposes for writing to their audiences, whether to present an argument, persuade the reader, present the facts, or just tell a story. Ask each group to retell the story of the Three Bears according to the group's purpose and audience. Each group should collaborate on the retelling while one person writes down the story as it develops.

9. *Activity.* Reproduce and distribute Reproduction Page 4-5, the Audience/Purpose Prewriting Worksheet. Ask each group to complete the worksheet before actually beginning to write their story of the Three Bears. Confer with each group regarding its choices while it is completing the worksheet. Collect the worksheets from the groups and ask each group to begin writing its version of the story.

10. *Activity.* Ask each group to read aloud its retelling of the Three Bears story. Have the rest of the class identify the audience, the purpose, and the appeal made for each story. Compare the prewriting worksheet for each group to their written stories. It is not necessary that the written story match the prewriting worksheet because the actual writing may have led the students into other adventures than what they

originally planned. This should be accepted because "writing is discovery" and may lead to other than what was originally intended. Discuss the differences in the original intentions and the written draft.

11. *Activity.* Have students individually rewrite their Three Bears stories into final form. Even though this was a group composition, have each student in the group experience an individual rewriting in their own words and style but directing the composition to the same audience that his or her group wrote to. Collect each student's composition. Evaluate compositions in terms of audience awareness using the criteria on Reproduction Page 4–3.

ASSESSING ACHIEVEMENT OF OBJECTIVES

Ongoing Evaluation

The extent to which students have gained a knowledge of choices for purpose and audience in writing can be measured by having them submit for evaluation the products of Activities.

Final Evaluation

For an overall evaluation of students' ability to recognize choices of purpose and audience in writing and to apply their knowledge, assign an in-class essay, one topic to be selected by the student from several that are given from the content subject area. Present at least four topics and ask students to choose one to write into a composition for a particular audience. Try to vary each topic in its purpose so that the purpose of one topic is persuasion, another to present facts and data, another to express opinions, and another to write creatively. Evaluate the compositions according to the following criteria:

1. Is the purpose for writing clearly stated by the student or perceived by the reader in the composition, preferably at the beginning?

2. Do the details that follow develop the purpose and fulfill it?

3. Is the purpose for writing restated or reinforced in the conclusion?

4. Has the writer attempted to create or identify an audience other than the teacher?

5. Is there awareness of the audience the student is addressing?

6. Is the language use (vocabulary, sentence difficulty, and so on) consistent with and appropriate for the audience the student has chosen to address?

7. Is the writer-reader relationship established in the tone, the formality or informality of the language, and the pronoun usage?

8. Is the writing effective in its establishment of purpose and appeal to a particular audience?

RESOURCES FOR TEACHING PURPOSE AND AUDIENCE

Below is a selected and annotated list of resources useful for teaching the subject matter in this chapter. Resources are from journal articles and from books.

Britton, James. "The Composing Processes and the Functions of Writing." *Research on Composing.* Urbana, Ill.: NCTE, 1978. This chapter discusses categories of audience found in secondary students' papers. Purposes for writing are also categorized and their functions analyzed. The author considers the writing process to have three stages—preparation, incubation, and articulation—and defines these stages in detail. This elaboration on audience, purpose, and the composing process should interest the teacher of writing because of its clarification of these concepts.

Cohn, Jill Wilson. *Writing, the Personal Voice.* New York: Harcourt Brace Jovanovich, 1975. This paperback book proceeds with its concept of using language as a medium through which we shape our relationships to people and things by regarding the process of maturation of students. From the very personal writing experience to interacting with others, to exploring impersonal issues, the growth in writing is presented developmentally to give students opportunities to extend their relationships to the world through language. Many examples of student writing are given to illustrate the points the writer makes, and exercises a teacher may use in the classroom are suggested to implement the ideas presented. This would be of interest to teachers in developing the concepts of audience and purpose in student composition.

Gibson, Walker. *Persona.* New York: Random House, 1969. A style book, the *persona* ("mask" in Latin) is presented as the voice the writer creates to perform the communicating. The voice affects the communication and its tone, attitude, and style. The first part of the book deals with understanding persona in our reading—in prose, newspapers, and the novel. The last part pertains to using persona in our writing so that we understand stylistic options.

Gibson, Walker. *Tough, Sweet & Stuffy: An Essay on Modern American Styles.* Bloomington: Indiana University Press, 1966. This book analyzes three styles or voices that a writer may choose to present to a reader. The tough talker is found in the narrative-hero and is characterized by the I-talker. The sweet talker is found in advertising and is depicted as the you-talker. The stuffy personality is the It-talker of authority and officialdom. These styles determine a writer's choice of words and his or her relationship to the reader. These are extremes in definition, but they are interesting categorically as descriptions of prose styles we recognize in modern writing. Teachers will find elaboration on these voices to be interesting and of value to suggest to students for their reading comprehension and their own writing.

Kroll, Barry M. "Cognitive Egocentrism and the Problem of Audience Awareness in Written Discourse." *Research in the Teaching of English.* 12 (October, 1978). This article traces classical theories of audience awareness to the present psychological theory of Piaget and finds that cognitive development from egocentric to sociocentric stages influences audience awareness. The research study conducted tested fourth-grade children's speaking and writing "decentration," or audience awareness, to determine if it was greater in oral rather than in written discourse. The result was that the children gave more information orally than in written discourse, so the conclusion was that audience awareness is greater in oral discourse than in writing, which lags behind. This article is of interest to teachers of writing in that it presents problems of teaching concepts of audience to children.

Long, Russell C. "Writer-Audience Relationships: Analysis or Invention?" *College Composition and Communication.* 31 (May, 1980). The article offers generalizations about the concepts of writer-audience relationships, classical and current, and argues the validity of the views. This is important for a teacher of writing to read since it is a critique of various philosophies that leads the author to suggest some instructional implications for the teaching of audience awareness. Specifically, the author contends that a writer must create an audience rather than search to identify one.

McCrimmon, James M. *Writing with a Purpose.* New York: Houghton Mifflin, 1963. This book encourages students to develop a purpose in their writing that will determine its unity and theme. The purpose becomes the dominant theme and suggests the direction of the composition. From the theme and the direction, then, a structure can be built to organize the writing. Purpose not only determines theme and structure; it dictates style as well. All of these factors of composition are developed in the book with many examples to illustrate. For teaching purpose in writing, exercises to give to students are included at the end of each chapter. The traditional concept of the paragraph is used, and there is a valuable section on coherence included in Chapter 4. This book would be of interest to teachers in teaching purpose for writing.

Moffett, James. *Teaching the Universe of Discourse*. Boston: Houghton Mifflin, 1968. The discussion in Chapter Two on "Kinds and Orders of Discourse" elaborates on the whole spectrum of mode, voice, writer-audience relationships, and genres of discourse. The kinds of discourse from reflection to publication are discussed in great detail as increasing distance between speaker and audience. Important to the teacher of writing is the theoretical base for teaching concepts of writer-reader relationships, development in use of abstraction from explicit to implicit communication and growth in wider language experiences beyond self for the student.

Odell, Lee; Cooper, Charles R.; and Courts, Cynthia. "Discourse Theory: Implications for Research in Composing." *Research on Composing*. Urbana, Ill.: NCTE, 1978. This chapter presents theories for teaching purpose and for teaching audience in composition. Current assumptions are presented for teaching both; then those assumptions are questioned in order to probe for understanding of the complexities of the concepts. This would be of interest to the teacher of writing for gaining new understanding for teaching audience and purpose.

Pfister, Fred, and Joanne F. Petrick, "A Heuristic Model for Creating a Writer's Audience." *College Composition and Communication*. Urbana, Ill.: NCTE, 1980. This article contends that sense of audience is difficult to develop in writers because the audience is unknown and unseen. Students have to fictionalize their audience, but it has to be close to reality. Proposed is a graduated model for teaching audience based on a series of questions the writer should ask regarding relationships of the audience to their environment, to the subject, to the writer, and to the form of composition. The authors' test of this model with students revealed that it did help audience identification in the detail provided, organization of the writing, and development of style. Audience awareness was greatly increased with use of the model.

5

Teaching Specialized Areas of Composition

CONTENT OVERVIEW

In the different content fields there are specialized kinds of writing that are more practical than creative. In contrast to imaginative writing, functional writing focuses on its use by the reader in its attempt to convey a clear, explicit meaning. In this kind of writing there must be no allowance for interpretation other than what the writer intends; if the language used is not concise, its purpose is defeated. Such writing includes career writing, media writing, and technical writing. These can be characterized as "doing the world's work" (MacIntosh in Cunningham and Estrin, 1975) because they are functional. They present factual information, explain concepts and laws, analyze data, and adapt materials for different audiences and circumstances. The problems in this kind of writing involve precision in semantics, effective syntax and organizational patterns including graphics, and sensitivity to audience and purpose. Utilitarian writing usually makes sense to students learning to write because they see it to be purposeful and useful for life beyond school walls. Training in these areas of writing is necessary for lifelong writing needs.

OBJECTIVES

As a result of the learning experiences in this chapter, students should be able to:

1. Recognize the different formats for writing business correspondence.

2. Write in the different formats depending on their purpose and their audience.

3. Compose effective business correspondence in order to convey the impression, the message, and the influence they need to accomplish a purpose.

4. Recognize the different forms of media writing.

---

5. Write in the different forms for the media according to the purpose and the audience for whom they are writing.

6. Develop an awareness of the differences between opinion and fact in reporting.

7. Use in their own writing the major patterns of news story writing.

8. Understand the great variety of written communication for the media.

9. Appreciate the precision of statement achieved through word choice, development of factual information, and principles involved in writing technically.

10. Compose effective compositions for conveying technical information.

11. Realize that technical writing is assigned in almost all content fields in school.

12. Apply principles of technical writing to everyday life needs for communication.

LEARNING EXPERIENCES

Topic I: Understanding and Practicing Career Writing

1. *Teacher Presentation.* Explain to students that people need a basic format for organizing their personal writing and business correspondence. Depending on the purpose of their writing and the audience to whom they are writing, the formats will vary in appropriateness. Letters must be coherent and concise because they are a "one-shot" representation of what one wants to say. Tell students that success in business and in higher learning is frequently dependent on one's ability to state ideas in clear, concise terms. The influence of the individual in social, community, and service areas of life is related to the ability to communicate in written form. As well, successful operation of private business is dependent on the ability to conduct advertising and sales promotions that involve written communication to customers. For economic reasons, most of this is carried out by the small business itself rather than a professional company or consultant. The necessary writing skills for these purposes must be learned for lifetime use. The following exercises can be used to develop some of these understandings and skills.

2. *Activity.* Tell students the following story while they take notes on the events that occur. Ask students to list the kinds of correspondence that they hear about in the story.

> You have read (a) a newsletter that was mailed to you describing and advertising a free-standing, wood-burning stove that saves energy and lowers the cost of heating your home. You go out to purchase the stove and notice that the newsletter solicits you to send for a free copy of a booklet of energy-saving hints in the use of your stove.
>   You send (b) a letter of request to this address:
>
> > Ms. Susan Gottheat, President
> > Energy Resources Association
> > 1382 Park Lane
> > Waschow, Pennsylvania 10832

Meanwhile, Ms. Gottheat has run out of the booklets because she did not anticipate such a huge response to the newsletter and she had underordered the booklets. She then sends you (c) a letter of response to your request explaining the situation and that a booklet will be forwarded as soon as available.

Ms. Gottheat's secretary receives the 1,000 booklets they had ordered and discovers that several pages are badly ink-smeared, an error by the printing company. She and Ms. Gottheat are angry at this inconvenience and delay and send (d) a letter of complaint to the printing company:

> Mr. Thomas Wordless
> Wordless Printing Company
> 831 Action Highway
> Canton, New Jersey 63002

Mr. Wordless is upset at the letter of complaint from this valuable customer, so he checks to find out where the error was made. He discovers that this printing job had been subcontracted to a smaller printing company because of the great backlog of orders at Wordless Printing Company. Mr. Wordless then sends (e) a letter of adjustment to Ms. Gottheat, explaining the situation and requesting that she return the defective booklets. He tells her that her order will be filled as a priority job. Mr. Wordless then sends (f) a memo to his boss requesting that the printing company they had used to subcontract jobs not be used again.[1]

Discuss the story with students. Divide the class into six groups and have each group be responsible for writing one of the six kinds of business correspondence.

3. *Activity.* Ask each group to read aloud their assigned type of business letter to the rest of the class. Have the class comment on the tone (feeling and attitude displayed), the development of the idea, and the appropriateness of the language used in each correspondence.

4. *Activity.* Explain to students the kinds of correspondence they have just written. The following identifies, from the sequence of the story in Activity 2, the types of business letters the students wrote and what should be considered when writing each type:

a. *Sales letter.* This promotes a service or a product and must be written with accurate and valid information. It must attract a reader's attention and arouse interest. Reader response should be made easy with a street map, an enclosed coupon, or clear instructions on how to make contact by telephone, letter, or both. Ways to use the product or service should be included.

b. *Letter of request or inquiry.* The writer asks for information or for a publication being offered. Keep the request simple with a minimum of direct, clearly stated questions. Number the questions if there are several and if it is clearer to do so. Express thanks for the trouble and consideration of the reader to respond. Include a return address within the letter to which the response should be sent. Sometimes it is appropriate to include a self-addressed, stamped envelope, especially if a particular favor from someone is being requested.

c. *Letter of response to an inquiry.* The writer determines if he or she is the proper person to respond to an inquiry. If not, the letter is forwarded on to the right

---

1. Adapted from *Writing That Works* by Walter E. Oliu, Charles T. Brusaw, and Gerald J. Alred. Copyright © 1980 by St. Martin's Press and used by permission of the publisher.

person. The response should be done promptly, answering every concern and question the writer indicated. The business response should be polite and courteous, with an offer to answer any further questions the inquirer may have.

d. *Letter of complaint.* The writer does not complain or show anger. The writer writes a direct and clear statement of the problem, including parts numbers, dates, and so forth. The problem must be explained rationally and specifically and what the reader (or company) should do to solve it. Past, positive associations with the reader (or company) should be pointed out if there have been any.

e. *Letter of adjustment.* In responding to a letter of complaint, the writer takes it very seriously because the reputation of the company, service, or person is at stake. This letter explains how a complaint is going to be handled and how the problems are going to be resolved. An apology should be offered for the problem at the beginning, with an explanation why the error occurred and what the company policy is regarding the problem. What will be done to solve the problem should then be specifically stated.

f. *Memorandum.* This correspondence takes place within an organization and ranges from short notes to reports of several pages. Memos follow a certain format, usually the following:

> *To:*   *Date:*
>
> *From:*
>
> *Re:* (regarding)
>
> *Subject:*

The tone can be informal or formal. Usually the body of the note is organized in paragraph form.

5. *Activity.* After students have discussed and studied the requirements of the types of business correspondence, have them rewrite the letter their group composed. Have students rewrite their letter individually this time so that each has personal experience with the type of written correspondence.

6. *Activity.* Ask students to share their papers with the other members of their original group. Have each student read aloud the paper to the group and have the group make comments on its effectiveness. Then have students in each group exchange their papers with another member, who will read it for spelling and other mechanical errors. Ask students to return the papers to their owners for a rewrite and final revision. Collect the final drafts and write comments on them for their effectiveness in communication according to the intent and purpose of the correspondence. Do not return the papers at this time.

7. *Activity.* Reproduce and distribute to students Reproduction Page 5-1. Discuss with them the format of the business letter, which is essential to learn for lifelong needs. Return students' business letters to them (see Activity 6). Ask students to write their correspondence in the format presented on Reproduction Page 5-1. Students with the memorandum correspondence will have to make up an address, but they can adapt their letter to the business letter format. Tell students to use either the block style or the indented style, whichever they prefer. Ask students to proofread

their own letters for errors and to check them against the model given. Collect the letters.

8. *Activity.* Select the best-written business letters and display them on the bulletin board in the room. Call students' attention to the format, content development, and effective features of the displayed letters.

9. *Activity.* Teach students to write a professional-looking resume with the following suggestions. Explain to students that there are many times when they will be requested to submit resumes of their work experience, education, and activities when they write applications for schools, jobs, and awards. Tell them that a resume is not an autobiography, but a carefully written summary of their experiences, education, and activities intended to be read by a personnel manager or selection committee who will evaluate it. Personal characteristics are optional and students should be told that they may include this information or not. The following information should be provided in a well-developed resume:

a. Name and address.

b. Personal characteristics (age, weight, height, marital status, social security number, and so forth).

c. Education (all schools attended with addresses, dates, diplomas, and degrees)

d. Work experience (starting with most recent, list dates, promotions, and positions held)

e. Professional, club, community, and service activities (include offices held and awards)

f. An ending paragraph stating your goals, aspirations, and employment desires.

Discuss this list and ask students to write down their own biographical information on a sheet of paper.

10. *Activity.* Reproduce and distribute Reproduction Page 5–2 as an example of the format students may follow for writing their own resume. Have students organize their biographical information in the outline format suggested. Discuss.

11. *Activity.* Teach students to write a letter of application with the following suggestions. Explain to students that throughout their lives they may have to respond to a job opening or prize opportunity or apply to a school by writing a letter of application. The letter is their first contact with an agency, and it should be a good representation of the writer and his or her qualifications. The letter of application will serve as a screening device for an agency to determine who will be called in for further consideration. The letter should follow this format:

a. It should be in the form of a good business letter and should be typewritten.

b. It may have three to four paragraphs. The first paragraph should state what is being applied for and give the source of information about it. The second should give the applicant's qualifications. The third may list references. And the fourth should express thanks for consideration of the application and suggest a possible conference or further communication.

12. *Activity.* Reproduce and distribute Reproduction Page 5–3 to students. Discuss the example of the format and content of the letter of application. Decide if the major points given in Activity 11 are included in the letter. Is the letter effective? Is it likely the applicant will get the job he or she is applying for? Why or why not? How would students change the letter?

13. *Activity.* Ask students to bring in a classified ad from the newspaper for a job opening. Using the model suggested in Reproduction Page 5–3, have students write a letter of application for the advertised job. Have students read aloud the ad and then their letter of application. Discuss the letters for their effectiveness and for their inclusion of the major points of writing this kind of letter.

14. *Activity.* Teach students to write a letter of persuasion with the following suggestions. A citizen in today's society frequently finds it necessary to react to situations in the community by making feelings and opinions known to other citizens in an effort to enlist enough support and enthusiasm to produce some action. Persuasion goes further than an argument. In an argument, the writer wants to convince the audience that his or her belief or opinion is right. The persuasive letter attempts to gain support to accomplish some action. A common letter of persuasion is the letter to the editor of a newspaper or magazine. The statement of opinions has to be exact, and the solutions proposed should be logical and supported by the opinions. A well-written letter to the editor should follow these guidelines:

a. Introduce the subject immediately.

b. Give information and data to make your opinion believable.

c. Take credit for the opinion by signing your name and thus standing behind what you believe.

15. *Activity.* Ask students to bring in letters to the editor from local newspapers and national magazines. Analyze the letters according to how effective they are and how the persuasion is achieved. What makes a letter effective, and how does the writer persuade the reader? How should some letters be changed in order to be more effective?

16. *Activity.* Present students with a hypothetical change in the school rules that only seniors may drive cars to school. Ask students to write letters to the school newspaper to persuade readers to agree or disagree with this rule. Read the letters aloud and discuss each for its effectiveness in convincing a reader to act—either to support or to change the rule.

Topic II: Understanding and Practicing Media Writing

1. *Teacher Presentation.* Explain to students that in writing for the media the emphasis is on the reader rather than the writer. The effectiveness of the writing depends on how much information it contains for the reader because the readers read it for knowledge. The information written must be concise, precise, and clear. It must be stimulating and presented interestingly to capture and to keep the reader's attention. Much of media writing is sales, news, and entertainment for a wide range of people, so its appeal has to be effective. The following activities are aimed at developing student awareness of and skills in effective writing for the media.

2. *Activity.* Teach students to write a news story by using the following suggestions. What the writer must do is to find out what actually happened in a news event and then write the story based on those facts. Although the writer may have an opinion on the matter, he or she must write impartially using the third person (*he, she,* or *it*) and stating the facts accurately. Ask students to bring in a news story from their local newspaper to analyze for its characteristics of objective, unbiased reporting of events.

3. *Activity.* Reproduce and distribute to students Reproduction Page 5-4, the fact or opinion exercise. Read aloud the story in the brief paragraph, then ask students to decide, based on the story, which statements are fact and which are opinion. Discuss their answers. All factual statements have to be supported by the story. Have students analyze the sentences in their news stories (Activity 2) to classify them as fact or opinion statements.

4. *Activity.* Explain to students that there are three main patterns to be found in a news story:

- the inverted pyramid
- the time-order story
- the multiangle story

The inverted pyramid story presents the major points of the story in the opening paragraph (the lead). The details are presented in order of decreasing importance. Draw an inverted pyramid on the board for students to visualize this pattern. In the time-order story the first paragraph is a summary with the following details presented in chronological order of occurrence. The multiangle story is usually written by several reporters concerning the same subject but from different viewpoints. The several viewpoints may be presented together in a summary lead; or they may be given separately in chronological order or in order of importance playing up the most controversial or biggest angle.

Ask students to form small groups. Have each group read aloud their news stories and identify which pattern each news story fits into. Tell students to be able to defend their choice by explaining the patterns. Have students attach their news story articles to a piece of paper, identify the pattern used in a title at the top of the paper, and explain the choice of pattern in a brief explanation at the bottom of the paper. Collect the papers and mount samples of them on a bulletin board in the room.

5. *Activity.* Assign a news story article for students to write. This assignment may be in the nature of a research project in any content field. The research may be in gaining facts and information about a problem or event, whether current or historical. Have students follow these steps to develop their story:

a. Uncover all the facts available.

b. Write a lead (an opening paragraph based on one of the three patterns studied in Activity 4).

c. Plan and write the body of the story based on the chosen pattern.

d. Use short paragraphs that contain one topic and start with important words.

e. Name the authorities involved.

f. Stop when all facts have been stated.

Have students write their own news story after they have gathered all their facts (through interviews, encyclopedias, reference books, and so on). Ask each student to identify the pattern used and to develop the story according to the pattern. As an aid to their own writing, have students refer to the bulletin board for professional newspaper examples of the patterns they choose. Collect the stories and hold them for later use.

6. *Activity.* Present this information to students on writing an editorial. The editorial is the personal, subjective voice of the reporter. An editorial writer follows certain general principles:

a. The subject is made interesting with clear and brief wording.

b. The writer's opinions are supported with examples and lead to a logical conclusion.

c. The writer focuses on only one point, giving facts that support the point.

Reproduce and distribute to students Reproduction Page 5–5, which presents an editorial column and a news article. Have students read both, decide which is the editorial, and have them compare the two according to the word choice, tone (emotional expression), style and formality of presentation. Ask students to judge whether the editorial is effective in getting across the writer's views and in convincing the reader with facts and examples that his views are valid. Ask students why the editorial column is signed by the writer and the news story is not.

7. *Activity.* Reproduce and distribute Reproduction Page 5–6, the human-interest newspaper article. Ask students to read it and to discuss what happened in the story. Have students rewrite the story as though it had happened to them personally. The boys can be the man in the story, while the girls should write from the woman's experience. Tell students to use the first-person point of view, the *I*, and to elaborate greatly on the experience from a personal angle. Ask students to read aloud their human-interest stories to the class and discuss what makes them interesting and colorful. Define the human-interest story as one that portrays an event that happened to a person or persons that is of interest to other people.

8. *Activity.* Reproduce and distribute Reproduction Page 5–7 to students. The lead, or the opening paragraph, has been cut out of the article. Ask students to read the entire article and then to write an interesting opening lead. A good lead includes all the five *W*'s: who, what, where, when, and why. It is also designed to capture the reader's interest so that he or she continues reading. Tell students to follow these guidelines in writing their opening leads. When these are written, ask students to read them aloud to the class and discuss them according to the guidelines. Then have students read the original lead and decide how theirs compare to it. Are theirs more effective or is the original? Why or why not?

9. *Activity.* Reproduce and distribute to students Reproduction Page 5–8, the newspaper obituaries. Ask students to read them and to decide what kind of information is included. For example, the ceremony time and place is announced first. The person, age, and town of origin are given immediately. Where the person died is stated, and then family background, biographical data, and survivors are mentioned.

Where donations and contributions may be sent is provided at the end. Usually, cause of death is not stated, but unusual causes are probably included. Ask students to write their own obituaries following the kinds of information they found included in the examples. Tell them to follow the format closely but to include other information if they wish to. Tell students to have fun with this exercise and to be creative in the data they supply about their distant, future demise. Collect what they write and display some examples on a classroom bulletin board.

10. *Activity.* Reproduce and distribute Reproduction Page 5-9, the advertisements, to students. Ask students to read the ads and to create a story to explain why the item in each ad is being sold. For example, perhaps the seller of the wedding dress was jilted at the altar on her wedding day and is now selling her dress. Perhaps the Mercedes Benz is being sold by a millionaire who drove it across Europe and because of a dock strike could not get it back to the USA; what the buyer doesn't know is that he or she must get the car in France to buy it. Discuss these imaginative possibilities. Have students divide into six small groups and have each group write one paper on one of the ads. Have the group develop the story behind the ad in great detail, using descriptive words for the items listed for sale. Have each group read aloud the paper it produces.

11. *Activity.* Reproduce and distribute to students Reproduction Page 5-10, the house they must sell. Ask students to write an appealing ad for the house in less than seventy-five words, using abbreviations and all the information given. Read aloud their ads and decide what makes an ad effective. Discuss advertising appeals to emotion, logic, and ego.

12. *Activity.* Reproduce and distribute Reproduction Page 5-11, the comic strip. Have students read it aloud in the characters' dialect. Ask students to write endings to the comic strip using dialogue suitable to the characters' personalities. Ask students to end the episode appropriately with a humorous punch line. When the students have written endings in either one or more comic strip frames, ask them to share their writing with the class. Then have students compare their endings with the original to determine which they like best and why.

13. *Activity.* Ask students to watch an episode of a soap opera they select on television. Have them in class write a short script that ends one of the scenes and that will keep the audience hanging in suspense for tomorrow's episode. Ask students to read aloud their scripts and discuss them for suspense, interest to audience, and characterization.

14. *Activity.* Ask students to read the sports section of their Sunday newspaper. Ask them to write down all of the verbs they find that lend the articles color. Discuss the verbs and expressions they find for slang, jargon, connotation, and alliteration.

15. *Activity.* Return students' ungraded news stories to them to reread and to rewrite in the light of all they have learned about writing for the media. Ask students to consider three aspects in their rewriting: their word choice, the appeal they make to the reader, the interest-getting devices they use, the development of facts and detail, and the pattern of writing they follow. Have students rewrite their news stories in class. Ask them to exchange their papers with a classmate and to read them for errors. Pass them back and correct the errors found. Collect the rewritten papers and grade them based on the criteria specified in this activity.

Topic III: Understanding and Practicing Technical Writing

1. *Teacher Presentation.* Explain to students that technical writing is purposeful and practical writing that is needed in most subject areas and in various jobs. This kind of writing deals mainly with presenting facts accurately, concisely, and objectively. The technical writer often uses narration and description but must be very careful to describe accurately only what happened without displaying personal reactions and feelings. The writer convinces by reason and logic and must explain information with exact details, definitions, and data. The technical writer defines, uses description to represent phenomena, explanations to analyze a subject or to portray steps in a process, and synthesis to summarize an idea. Further, technical writing involves reporting data with words and visuals, writing biographical sketches, and citing sources. The technical writer uses not only paragraph forms, but also uses graphics such as charts and diagrams to present the data and the results. The following are exercises designed to teach students to write technically.

2. *Activity.* Teach students to write a technical definition by using the following suggestions. The first step in writing a definition is to know as much as possible about the object that is being defined. This may involve using reference materials such as a dictionary or encyclopedia to learn specific terminology to use. However, the definition should be stated in simpler language than the term defined. The first sentence in the definition should state what is being defined. Next, the definition is expanded using examples, details, comparison to a more familiar thing, and analysis. The sentences should be clear, concise, and accurate in information. Some principles for writing technical definitions are the following:

   a. Definitions should state what the term means directly and clearly.

   b. Definitions should not include the opinions of the writer.

   c. Definitions should be explicit, not ambiguous.

   d. Definitions should be expanded with examples, comparisons to a familiar thing, details, background, and analysis.

   e. The language used for the definition should be simpler than the term being defined.

   The following is an example of a well-written technical definition:

   > A gel is a form of matter intermediate between a solid and a liquid. It consists of polymers, or long-chain molecules, cross-linked to create a tangled network and immersed in a liquid medium. The properties of the gel depend strongly on the interaction of these two components. The liquid prevents the polymer network from collapsing into a compact mass; the network prevents the liquid from flowing away. Depending on chemical composition and other factors, gels vary in consistency from viscous fluids to fairly rigid solids, but typically they are soft and resilient or, in a word, jellylike.[2]

   Assign a technical definition that students may write. Ask them to research what it is they will define and then to visualize it clearly as they define it with specific terminology. The following are suggestions for technical-definition topics in different subject areas:

---

2. Toyoichi Tanaka, "Gels," *Scientific American* (January, 1981), p. 124.

Mathematics: Write a clear definition of an isosceles triangle and compare it to other triangles.

Social studies: Using at least three examples, write a definition of a monarchy.

Home economics: Write a definition of "cream" as used in a recipe.

Music: Write a definition of romantic music comparing it to the colors it suggests.

English: Define *metaphor* and *simile* and give examples to illustrate them.

3. *Activity.* Teach students to write a technical explanation by using the following suggestions. This form of writing is the one most used in school and later on because throughout our lives we must explain things, events, feelings, reasons, and processes. Who will be reading the explanation will be the consideration for how detailed it is and how explicit it will have to be. The reason for writing the explanation is similarly important. Explain to students that audience and purpose for writing must be considered carefully in writing an explanation. The following principles should guide students to writing an effective explanation:

a. First, clearly define what you are going to explain.

b. Describe the setting, equipment, and preparations needed.

c. Indicate any principles behind the operation or process.

d. List major steps in logical order.

e. Give a step-by-step explanation of every action or condition.

f. Conclude with a summary or evaluation.

g. Include visual drawings to aid the explanation.

The following is an example of an effective technical explanation of a process:

Clutch fans are more complex and there are sophisticated tests for them, including measurements of engagement speeds and temperatures. As a practical matter, however, when a clutch fan's clutch fails and causes overheating, the problem usually can be easily isolated.

First look for a fluid leak in the center at the bearing. Minor seepage isn't significant, but if you see a real accumulation on the shaft hub, it's bad.

Next, put a hand on a fan blade and try to turn the fan slowly. You should feel smooth, even resistance. If you don't the fan clutch is partly locked internally. Although it isn't causing overheating, it is wasting power . . . and precious gasoline.

Next, try to spin it as hard as you can, using just one hand and only on the blade. If the fan turns five revolutions or more, the clutch is gone.

Replacing a defective clutch is simple. Just unbolt it from the water pump pulley. It's held by bolts on Ford and Chrysler products, by studs and nuts on GM cars and some imports, such as Toyota. If you're only removing the clutch for some other service, be sure to keep it vertical, so there's no chance of silicone leaking out.

Whatever fan clutch service you do, make sure you finish up with a belt inspection, tension check and adjustment, if necessary.[3]

Assign a technical explanation for students to write. Here are some suggestions for writing an explanation in different content fields.

---

3. Paul Weissler, "Taking Care of the Cooling System," *Mechanix Illustrated* (July, 1980), p. 87.

Social studies: Explain the events leading up to the beginning of the Vietnam War.

Science and math: Explain the procedure for converting from the Fahrenheit to the Celsius temperature scale.

Home economics: Explain how a person's clothing makes a statement about the person. Discuss different age groups.

Music: Explain the process of sound production in reed instruments.

4. *Activity.* Present the following suggestions to students for learning to write a technical description. The purpose of description is to provide a verbal picture to a reader of the object, person, or event that is being described. The reader must be able to get a clear picture in his or her mind so that it is not misunderstood. These principles should be followed in order to write an effective technical description:

a. Start by defining what is to be described.

b. State its purpose, its use, and its value.

c. In detail describe what the object looks like.

d. Use drawings to help the reader understand.

e. Write to the intended reader by considering the reader's specific requirements and background in the subject.

f. Explain why the object operates as it does.

g. Break the object into parts and explain each major part.

h. Summarize by explaining how the object goes through a cycle of operation.

The following is a well-written example of technical description:

> There are certain infectious diseases of plants that cannot be associated with any of the usual causative agents such as fungi, microorganisms or viruses. The only notable thing about a plant afflicted with one of these diseases seems to be that small molecules of an unusual form of the genetic material ribonucleic acid (RNA) can be isolated from its tissues. Such molecules cannot be detected in a healthy plant of the same species; if they are introduced into a healthy plant, they proliferate and give rise to the characteristic symptoms of the disease. In other words, these RNA molecules, which are called viroids, are the causative agent of the disease in question. They are the smallest known agents of infectious disease.
>
> Viroids are much smaller than viruses and much simpler. Whereas a typical virus consists of genetic material (either RNA or DNA) surrounded by a protein coat, a viroid is nothing more than a very short strand of RNA. To date viroids have been identified with fewer than a dozen specific diseases, all of which afflict higher plants, but there are indications that they may also cause animal disease, perhaps including some rare nerve diseases that affect human beings.[4]

Assign a description for students to write in class. Have students refer to resource materials in order to become thoroughly familiar with the thing or event they are to describe. Here are some suggestions for writing technical descriptions in different content fields.

---

4. T. O. Diener, "Viroids," *Scientific American* (January, 1981), p. 66.

Science: Write a description of a single-celled animal.

Music: Write a description of a tuba using your music appreciation book for reference.

Math: Write a clear, concise description of a geometric plane.

Social studies: Look at a picture of pioneers migrating westward. Write a description of that picture.

Industrial arts: Write a description of a coping saw tool for someone who needs to operate it.

5. *Activity.* Teach students to write a summary of materials they have read by referring to the following suggestions. A summary of information must be clear and concise because much meaning is compacted into a small amount of writing. The basic principles involved in writing a summary are these:

a. A summary (or précis) is no more than a third of the length of the original material.

b. Include only the major ideas of the original. Don't repeat examples, illustrations, or repeated information.

c. Use your own words; don't copy long phrases or whole sentences.

d. Write from the author's viewpoint. Don't use phrases such as "the writer means" or "the passage says."

e. Do not add your own ideas, but stick to the author's major points.

Ask students to write a summary of something they had been assigned to read. Have them read the passage carefully to get a grasp on the main idea and to look up any words they do not fully understand. When they write the summary, have students revise it because it will probably be too long. The following are some suggested assignments for writing a summary in different subject fields.

Math: Write a summary of the article in your math book of people who have developed basic math theories.

Home economics: From Chapter 3 write a summary of factors in a family situation that experts agree help a child develop normally.

Social studies: Write a summary of the Bill of Rights with reference to the Amendments to the Constitution.

Music: Write a summary of the baroque style of music presented in Chapter 7 of your music appreciation book.

6. *Activity.* With reference to the following suggestions, teach students a variety of ways to report their data collected for a study or survey. After the data are collected, certain principles should be followed. First, the data should be organized in a logical way. Put related data together in the same table or chart. Visual aids such as charts, tables, and figures should be designed not to replace the written selections but to increase the understanding of them. Be sure to label visual aids clearly and relevantly. The foremost purpose in reporting data is to inform the reader, so clarity and reliability of information are essential.

Table 5-1 shows a simple horizontal-vertical chart, which is an easy way to display many small items of data.

Table 5-1. *Cost comparison for CU's set of calls*[1]			
Company and plan	*At day rate*	*At evening rate*	*At night/ weekend rate*
AT&T (Direct dial)	$19.49	$12.66	$7.80
ITT City Call	15.86	10.24[2]	3.20
ITT City Call I	Not offered	6.39[3]	3.20
MCI Execunet	14.92	5.97	5.97
MCI Execunet Supersaver	Not offered	5.97	5.97
Southern Pacific Sprint V	15.13	6.36	6.36
Southern Pacific Sprint Ltd.	Not offered	6.36	6.36
Western Union Metro I	14.74	6.89	5.14
Western Union Off-Peak Metro I	Not offered	6.89	5.14

1 Calls of 30 seconds, 5 minutes 1 second, and 10 minutes from New York to each of three cities—
Philadelphia, Chicago, and Los Angeles.
2 If made 5 P.M.–8 P.M.; $6.39 if made 8 P.M.–11 P.M.
3 Service available only 8 P.M.–11 P.M.
Copyright 1981 by Consumers Union of United States, Inc., Mount Vernon, NY 10550. Reprinted
by permission from *Consumer Reports*, March 1981.

Another easy visual technique is the pie graph which shows data from parts in percentages of a whole group (see Figure 5–1).

Assign students the task of displaying data from a reading assignment each has. The following are suggestions for assignments in different subject fields.

Social studies: prepare a graph of dates for the battles that the North won in the Civil War. Or graph the number of casualties in these wars: Revolutionary War, War of 1812, Civil War, Spanish-American War, World War I, World War II, Korean War, or Vietnam War.

Physical education: Plot out your skill development in the number of pushups you can do over the semester.

Math: Graph the hand sizes of every student in this class in metric measurements.

Science: Plot the data from the paleolithic evidence on the size of cheek teeth in the horse.

English: List all the adjectives you hear in a Rolling Stones record. On a bar graph, indicate the frequency of repetition of each adjective. Compare the frequency of the use of the same adjectives in a Billy Joel record.

7. *Activity.* Teach students to write a biographical sketch of a famous person in the content field. The problem is to read and gather information on the person and then to provide a sketch without copying or summarizing the author. These are some suggestions for writing a biographical sketch:

a. Read one or several sources carefully on the person you select.

b. List in informal outline all the chronological data and important information that are to be included.

c. Arrange the information in a time-order sequence, most-important to least-important contributions, or other logical order that you want to use in your writing.

d. Write the biography so that it is interesting and readable, using clear sentences that give the factual information without opinions or comments.

e. Keep in mind the purpose of the assignment, which is to write a short biographical and factual account about a person.

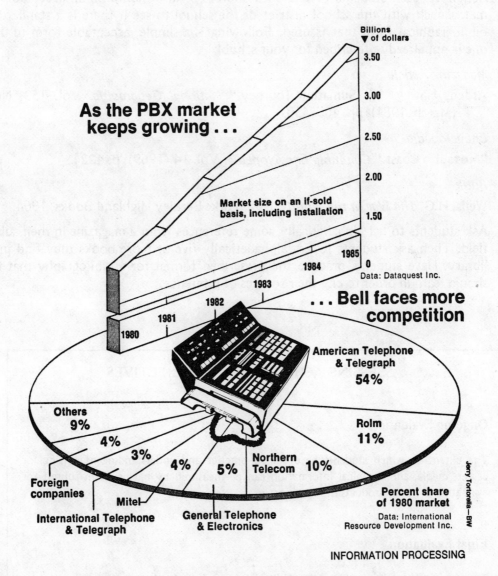

Figure 5-1. The Pie Graph. Reprinted from the April 13, 1981 issue of *Business Week* by special permission, © 1981 by McGraw-Hill, Inc., New York, NY 10020. All rights reserved.

Ask a student to look up a person's name in the encyclopedia and to read that short selection aloud to the class to give them an example of a well-written biographical account free of opinion and subjective comment.

Have students write a biographical sketch of a famous person who has made a contribution in the subject field. The following are suggestions for writing a biographical sketch in different subject areas:

Social studies: Write a biographical sketch of Benedict Arnold.

Physical education: Write a biographical sketch of Terry Bradshaw or Peggy Fleming.

Art: Write a biographical sketch of Salvadore Dali.

Science: Write a biographical sketch of Isaac Newton.

8. *Activity*. Teach students to cite their sources of information in an acceptable format. Check with the school district or the school to see if there is a standardized bibliographical form that is used. Following is a simple, acceptable form to use if one is not already prescribed for your school:

Magazine Article

Arden, Hawey. "A Sumatran Journey." *National Geographic.* Vol. 159, No. 3 (March, 1981), pp. 406–430.

Encyclopedia

"Mosquito Coast." *Columbia Encyclopedia.* Vol. 14 (1969), p. 4224.

Book

Wells, H.G. *The War of the Worlds.* New York: Berkley Highland Books, 1964.

Ask students to list alphabetically some references from a magazine in their subject field. Then ask students to list alphabetically five or more books they find in the library. Have students practice the prescribed format for a bibliography that they should learn in order to cite their sources of reference.

ASSESSING ACHIEVEMENT OF OBJECTIVES

Ongoing Evaluation

The extent to which students have gained practice and understanding of writing for career, media, and technical information can be measured by having them submit for evaluation the final products of Activities.

Final Evaluation

For an overall evaluation of students' ability to use technical writing techniques, assign an in-class writing assignment on a subject in the content field that requires factual reporting. Evaluate the writing with the following criteria in mind:

1. The terms used are clearly defined for the reader.

2. The purpose for writing is immediately made clear to the reader.

3. The reporting of the facts is objective without giving the personal opinions of the writer.

4. Enough facts are presented to develop the subject fully and clearly for the reader.

5. The factual information given is accurate and reliable and can be verified.

6. The information is given in the writer's own words, not copied from the source.

7. The words used to present facts are as exact and as precise as the writer can make them in the effort to inform the reader.

8. The purpose of providing factual information to inform the reader is fully and clearly accomplished.

RESOURCES FOR TEACHING SPECIALIZED AREAS OF COMPOSITION

Below is a selected and annotated list of resources useful for teaching the subject matter in this chapter. Resources are from books and are for both teacher use and student use.

Cunningham, Donald H., and Estrin, Herman A. *The Teaching of Technical Writing.* Urbana, Ill.: NCTE, 1975. This is a collection of articles written by many different authors including MacIntosh on aspects of teaching technical writing. As a resource for the teacher, it provides some answers to what technical writing is, what students need to learn to write scientifically and technically, and what industry requires of the technical writer. This paperback book is of interest to teachers who desire more background in some of the philosophical and practical concerns involved in teaching this type of writing.

Estrin, Herman (editor). *Technical and Professional Writing.* New York: Preston Publishing, 1976. This paperback book is a series of essays by different writers on aspects of technical writing such as precise word usage, clarity and brevity in sentences, and addressing the reader or audience. This book is recommended for teachers for their greater understanding of what is of value and what should be emphasized to students in teaching them to write technically. Especially important is the insight into language it presents and its use for the content area teacher's understanding.

Gilman, William. *The Language of Science.* New York: Harcourt, Brace & World, 1961. The book discusses the particular style and language of scientific writing in an informal, conversational way that is understandable and usable in the classroom. Suggestions are made for improving problems of ambiguity, clarity, and precision in word usage and style. Chapter 11 presents ways to develop an effective lead in technical writing that elaborates on the ideas given for writing leads in media writing in this present chapter. This book is recommended for science teachers who want background in teaching the language of science.

Maimon, Elaine P., et al. *Writing in the Arts and Sciences.* Cambridge, Mass.: Winthrop Publishers, 1981. Written by teachers from several different departments (English, history, biology, psychology, and philosophy), this textbook instructs in writing across the curriculum. Particularly, Chapters 9 through 14 deal with writing different kinds of papers in the sciences, such as case studies, laboratory reports, and data findings. Examples are given, review questions are included, and exercises for students follow each chapter. This textbook is recommended for high school and college students who are learning to write technical papers and composition in all fields.

Olin, Walter E.; Brusaw, Charles T.; and Gerald, Gerald J. *Writing That Works.* New York: St. Martin's Press, 1980. This is a paperback textbook designed for student use. Each of the chapters instructs the student in the process and procedure of technical prewriting, writing, and revising and in using different kinds of technical formats. The book instructs in writing business letters, reports both informal and formal, and in creating visual graphs and illustrations. Examples are included for clarity, and student exercises follow each chapter to give practice in the concepts. The textbook is highly recommended for technical writing instruction.

Tracy, R.C., and Jennings, H.L. *Handbook for Technical Writers*. Alsip, Ill.: American Technical Publishers, 1961. This paperback, spiral-bound book defines technical writing and its function as making "the unfamiliar familiar" in presenting facts in "clear, concise and straightforward writing." The book presents the elements of technical materials with examples, discusses technical writing style and mechanics, and gives specialized terms and definitions in a glossary.

This book is recommended for students who are learning to write technical materials and for teachers who teach technical writing as a resource book.

Weisman, Herman M. *Basic Technical Writing*. Fourth Edition. Columbus, Ohio: Charles E. Merrill, 1980. Designed as a textbook for students, this hardback book covers the fundamentals of basic technical writing. In detail it instructs in writing definitions, descriptions, process explanations, and analyses. It includes a reference index to usage, pronunciation, and grammar necessary for learning technical writing. The book contains problems and exercises for students as well as illustrations and examples of effective writing. This is highly recommended as a textbook.

6

Teaching Vocabulary and Spelling

CONTENT OVERVIEW

Vocabulary is the nemesis of every content field. To teach a subject is to teach new terminology and unfamiliar concepts to students who bring to class partial, whole, or no background in the field to be learned. In order for learning of new concepts to take place, bridges have to be built by the teacher from what students already know to what is to be learned. Those bridges are built of words that represent understanding and perceptions common to teacher and student.

Teaching vocabulary can be dull. But teaching vocabulary can also be great fun and very stimulating. All depends on the approaches used. The following chapter suggests three different approaches to making the teaching of vocabulary fun and very worthwhile.

The first approach is designed to provide language experiences for students in their transition from what they know already to what the teacher wants them to know. It is designed to help teacher and students discover what in their backgrounds can be used in the new learning. This approach also provides a sharing of experiences in language that will result in a greater commonality of understanding between students and between teacher and students.

A second approach to teaching vocabulary involves teaching context clues in usage of language in both oral and written forms. Understanding new words through context means recognizing syntactic (sentence-order), semantic (word-meaning), and structural (word-part) clues. These clues can be taught to students to increase not only their recognition of new vocabulary, but their awareness of language usage.

The last approach can be the least interesting of all if it is not presented with enthusiasm, fun, and in varied ways. This approach to teaching vocabulary involves teaching morphemes, units of meaning such as prefixes, roots, and suffixes. A psychological phenomenon occurs when people are introduced to a new way of considering what they have always just taken for granted: they start to identify it everywhere. Take, for example, the word *conduct*, a common, ordinary word used daily. When one is taught the parts of the word—*con* meaning together, and *duct* or *ducere* meaning to lead—then the newly identified parts are recognized everywhere in *induct, reduction, conductor*, and so forth. This vocabulary approach is very exciting and opens a whole new window to understanding new words and appreciating language. This approach is almost mandatory in just about every content field and especially in the following: mathematics, sciences, social studies, English, home economics, and vocational arts.

There are three major approaches to teaching spelling at the secondary and adult levels. The first deals with visualization and memory based on different sensory experiences provided for diverse learning modalities. The second approach is phonetic analysis and syllabication, which are important to hearing the sound and rhythm of the language. The last approach is the most sophisticated, that of word analyses of morphemes, related word families, and structure.

Teacher attitude toward spelling can have a tremendous effect on production of the students and their interest in careful communication. Anxiety is universal, but it can be met with a helpful, constructive, and positive approach by the teacher. When a student asks, "How do you spell that word?," approach the question diagnostically. Ask the student to pronounce the word and then to spell it as the student thinks it is spelled. The spelling will be mostly correct; locate the troublesome parts and determine if the misspelling is because the student does not pronounce the word accurately and therefore does not hear the correct spelling. Determine if the misspelling involves a morpheme (see Topic III in this chapter) that the student has not learned. Determine if the misspelled part is troublesome for other reasons, but find out *why* the student cannot spell it. Write it correctly for the student, then compare the two spellings, making sure the student understands the misspelled part. Have the student rewrite the word correctly and then with eyes closed spell it from memory. The teacher's attitude, thus, is not one of condemnation, impatience, or negativity. Rather, the attitude is helpful, constructive, and valuable to a student's growth and understanding.

OBJECTIVES

As a result of the learning experiences in the chapter, students should be able to:

1. Develop associations between vocabulary they already know and new concepts they are to learn through free associations, analogies, and semantic mapping.

2. Clarify ideas in their writing by using synonyms and classifications.

3. Understand logical order in composition, introductions, sequencing, and conclusions.

4. Develop sensitivity to language usage in creation of humor.

5. Research related ideas, gather supporting details, and synthesize relevant information preparatory to writing.

6. Present ideas more clearly in their writing by recognizing how context clues can be used to aid the reader.

7. Realize levels of usage of words they choose.

8. Recognize patterns and structures in language.

9. Appreciate the flexibility, great variety, and versatility of the English language.

10. Establish effective, individualized approaches to learning to spell new words.

LEARNING EXPERIENCES

Topic I: Using and Developing Language Experiences

1. *Teacher Presentation.* Explain to students that the teacher needs to know the backgrounds that each brings to the class so that the experiences and language development of the students can be used as a base and built on with new concepts to be taught them. Ask students to complete an interest and attitude inventory constructed for them according to the subject area and the information you seek. Figure 6–1 shows suggested questions and types of format for discovering interests, experiences, attitudes, and language backgrounds of students. The suggestions are to be modified and adapted to the specific needs and requirements of each content area teacher for teaching purposes. These are time-honored, successful, and valuable methods. Not only are they informational, but they may be used diagnostically to detect possible problems of students. Students perceive these instruments as expressions of their personal selves that the teacher cared enough about to obtain. It is highly recommended, when students share their personal selves with the teacher, that the teacher do so as well. It is a human sharing and involvement. So when the students fill out the Inventory, the teacher is urged to do so also, and to discuss commonalities and differences of the group in order to build bridges of experience and communication.

2. *Activity.* Before a class discussion or a reading assignment, present a free-association exercise of some of the emotionally "loaded" words to be used or encountered. Present orally each word one at a time and have students individually write down the very first word that occurs to them in association with the word presented. This associated word reveals the student's possible connotation, bias, conception, or experience with the word and is what shapes his or her comprehension of it. The following are examples of emotionally "loaded," experiential words to watch for in students' reading and writing.

love	school
blood	noon
war	deserter
fire	draft
mother	sin

List associations students voluntarily share on the blackboard. Discuss possible implications of the associations and guide students' understandings toward what you want them to learn or newly comprehend.

3. *Activity.* Vicki Tanner, a teacher at Rawlins High School, in Rawlins, Wyoming, suggests a variation of the free-association exercise in the game of Password. A word is written on the board while two students sit or stand with their backs to the board. Another student sees the word and gives word associations of it (up to four words) to the students who try to guess the word. These associations are discussed as to their validity, relevance, and effectiveness for experience with the concept.

I. Check things that interest you.
___ cars   ___ music   ___ sports   ___ art
___ camping   ___ swimming   ___ pets   ___ school
___ family   ___ motorcycles   ___ a job   ___ sewing
___ travel   other _____

II. Television
1. How many hours do you watch on weekdays? ____ weekends? ____
2. Which shows do you watch the most?

_____

_____

_____

III. Newspapers
1. Which do you take regularly in your home?
2. Which parts do you read the most?
___ news stories   ___ ads
___ sports   ___ funnies
___ editorials   ___ advice columns (Dear Abby or Ann Landers)
___ theater   ___ horoscope
                  other _____

IV. Personal Concerns
1. Name a short-term goal important to you at this time.

_____

2. Name a long-term goal important to you at this time.

_____

3. If you could do anything you wanted to (had money, time, and talent), what would you do?

_____

V. Attitudes
Check the blank that is closest to your feelings for each question.
SA (strongly agree) *A* (agree) *U* (undecided) *D* (disagree) *SD* (strongly disagree)
SA   A   U   D   SD
___ ___ ___ ___ ___ 1. I like to read.
___ ___ ___ ___ ___ 2. I like to watch television.
___ ___ ___ ___ ___ 3. I like this class in _____ .
___ ___ ___ ___ ___ 4. I enjoy expressing my ideas in writing.
___ ___ ___ ___ ___ 5. I will use what I learn in this class.
___ ___ ___ ___ ___ 6. I will need this subject after I leave school.
___ ___ ___ ___ ___ 7. I like school.

For industrial arts: Check what you think should be the goals for this shop.
___ Should teach students about jobs.
___ Should teach how to plan and build a project.
___ Should teach how to use machines in a safe way.
___ Should teach students how to read and write technical literature.
___ Should teach people to get along with others.

For art: Circle yes or no to the following questions.
Yes No 1. I would like to know how an artist plans a drawing.
Yes No 2. I would like to learn to judge art.
Yes No 3. I would like to learn how to express my ideas in art.

Figure 6-1. Interest and Attitude Inventory

4. *Activity.* The interview is suggested by Dr. Bob Pavlik of Cardinal Stritch College, Milwaukee, Wisconsin, and is modified in Reproduction Page 6-1. Have students interview the teacher, who has become an abstract word. For example, in science an abstract term to be taught is *ecology.* As students ask the teacher the interview questions the teacher becomes or personifies this word and fills in relevant details so that students come to understand and experience the concept.

5. *Activity.* A variation on using Reproduction Page 6-1 is to form students into groups with a new word for each group to research and prepare answers for. The class then can interview the prepared groups, whose answers make clear the meaning and background of the new concept.

6. *Activity.* Using Reproduction Page 6-1, pair students off so that one is the interviewer and the other is the interviewee for a new vocabulary word. The interviewee must be prepared for the interview so that she or he can answer the questions in order for the interviewer to learn the word. The pairs may alternate as interviewees and interviewers. The interviews may be conducted in front of the class as well so that the class will learn the word.

7. *Activity.* Tell the class the story of "Goldilocks and the Three Bears." Using Reproduction Page 6-2, have students compare each character in the story to a known thing—a kind of tree, for instance: Papa Bear is an oak tree, Mama Bear is a weeping willow, Baby Bear is a sapling, and so on. This is a warm-up activity for content material analogies. For example, in music, different tones may be compared to known colors or rooms. Styles of music may be compared to different kinds of houses. Analogies provide students with visual associations and mnemonic (memory) devices for retaining information. In history the characters of the Civil War may be compared to different mountains: Robert E. Lee may be Mt. Everest, and General Grant may be Pikes Peak, and so forth. In health subjects, different diseases may be compared to various invading armies and the body's defense system likened to a resisting naval force in the blood, for instance. Analogies can be useful in every content subject to help students make comparisons of new concepts that are unfamiliar with old concepts that are known.

8. *Activity.* Dale Johnson and David Pearson, in *Teaching Reading Comprehension* (see Resources at end of chapter), suggest an exercise they call "mapping." Their purpose for mapping is to develop reading comprehension, but the activity may also be used to develop vocabulary and to provide for expansion of concepts to be used in writing. In their experimentation with mapping, they found that people's knowledge of concepts is organized, not random. Thus when a new word is introduced to students, they will guess at its meaning in a systemized manner rather than in a random way. Students will associate a new word with ones they know according to three kinds of relationships: an *example* of it, a *property* of it, or the *class* of things it belongs to. The word *cat,* for example, if written on the blackboard as a new vocabulary word, would be associated by students with *animal* (its class), with *meow* (its property), and with *Persian* (an example).

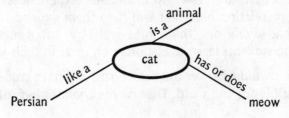

Semantic (word meaning) mapping of new vocabulary words is a whole-class activity with everyone sharing in the associations that can be elaborately mapped according to the three types of relationships. Students will be fascinated and surprised at how much they already know about the new word. The value of this activity to writing is that it teaches students to expand and elaborate on concepts and words. In descriptive writing especially, students should be aware of the different directions they may take, those of giving properties of, examples of, and classifying. Communicating through writing is elaborating, making associations of new ideas with known concepts. Thus in presenting new ideas in writing, students should be taught to give associations and comparisons; this mapping activity will give them practice in expanding and systematically organizing information.

9. *Activity.* A variation of mapping is to write a new vocabulary word on the blackboard along with headings for the three types of relationships—class, property, and examples. Students then list as many associations as they can make under each heading until they work out the actual meaning of the word. This is an inductive rather than deductive process. So instead of drawing the mapped relationships, the associations would simply be listed, the lists acting as organizers of the new concept to be learned. The following is an example:

New vocabulary word: *lithographer*

Class	Property	Example
biographer	stone	sculptor
monolith	writing	typesetter
photographer	picture	writer

These associations will eventually lead students to discovering the meaning of the new word to which they have brought known relationships.

10. *Activity.* Using Reproduction Page 6-3, have students in small groups decide on analogous relationships between sets of concepts. The relationships will be determined by the type presented in the heading, such as "Part–Whole." In making their decisions, students should be encouraged to disagree according to the logic they have followed in getting their answers. Experience with analogies can prepare students to analyze relationships and to use logical processes of thinking in their own writing by making them sensitive to meanings and functions of words. The relationships are read as follows: "Borderland is to country as water is to land . . . or as rock is to soil," and so on. Through logic and elimination the choice is made. Students should gain valuable experience with new concepts by defending their logical choices. Show students examples of non sequiturs and illogical relationships in their own writing. Analogies provide experiences in understanding language as preparation for writing and in actual writing.

11. *Activity.* Reproduction Page 6-4 gives students experiences with synonyms and antonyms, concept relationships that will help them expand ideas in their writing. Understanding that saying one thing in several ways often makes meanings clearer in writing will help students learn to elaborate on ideas in their writing.

12. *Activity.* Write the word *man* on the blackboard and have students provide as many synonyms as possible for the word. Discuss the *connotations* of each word students

provide, the experience behind and association with each synonym. The following are possible connotations for the word *man:*

male	husband	groom	boyfriend
father	brother	gentleman	beau
son	uncle	guy	buddy
grandfather	chap	widower	fellow

Another word that has a simple *denotation* (dictionary meaning), but is rich in connotative meanings is the word *thin.* Have students describe a thin girl. The following are possible connotations of the word *thin:*

skinny	emaciated	stringbean
svelte	bony	slender
trim	beanpole	rail

Which are complimentary in description and which are unflattering? Where is the appropriate usage of each one of these words?

13. *Activity.* Reproduction Page 6–5 was suggested by Shirley Bau, a graduate education student. It is a rebus vocabulary game, which provides hints to students pictorially to help them guess a word. The game's purpose is to develop word sensitivity and experience in working with concepts literally displayed with humor. For example, the first one, $\frac{\text{play}}{\text{play}}$ —————, is a display of the word *doubleplay.* Students can make up their own rebus game of words or concepts which give them trouble. It may also be used as a memory device for certain troublesome words or phrases. Clichés may be emphasized in this game so as to be avoided or recognized in student writing.

14. *Activity.* A vocabulary game that provides experience in classifying, organizing, and generalizing concepts is a class game, grouping words into classes or categories. The game is played with classifications put onto cards that are passed out to students. Four classifications for each concept are on the card. The game is played in the following way:

a. Divide the group into two teams.

b. First member of team 1 picks a card and reads the four items. First member of the opposing team (team 2) must say precisely (in one word only) what is the class or category name of the four items.

c. If he misses, the second member of team 1 gets to try. If she is right, team 1 gets one point. If she is wrong, the second member of team 2 tries to answer. If he is wrong, it is discussed and the right answer is found.

d. First member of team 2 picks a card and asks the second player on team 1 to name the class. If he misses, then the second player on team 2 gets to score one point for his team if he answers correctly. Play alternates until all cards have been used.

e. The team with the most points wins.

f. Teams can make up their own four items and class for further play.

Classification cards can be made up in any content area for the concepts to be mastered. Examples are the following:

- In *English:*

  pentameter

  trimeter

  dimeter

  heptameter

      Class: poetic meter or rhythmic feet

- In *science:*

  geology

  geography

  biology

  physiology

      Class: areas of science

- In *social studies:*

  democracy

  autocracy

  socialism

  communism

      Class: types of government

- In *mathematics:*

  pentagon

  quadrilateral

  octagon

  triangle

      Class: types of polygons

- In *art* and *music:*

  composition

  balance

  rhythm

  harmony

      Class: elements of design

- In *home economics:*

  baste

  whip

  blanket

  slip

  Class: types of hand stitching

15. *Activity.* Cartoons are a rich resource for vocabulary-building activities. The following is a sequence puzzle using comic strips. This experience teaches students logical order in their introductions, conclusions, and development of ideas. It also teaches recognition of the main idea and sequential arrangement of supporting details.

Sequence Puzzle

Envelopes containing cut-up comic strips are given to a student or a small group of students. The puzzle is to put the comics into their proper order so that a story is told and there is a punch line at the conclusion. Students should be able to justify the sequence they select and to identify which comic strips introduce the main idea and which conclude it or sum up. One student can check the sequencing against another student's.

16. *Activity.* Cartoons provide a marvelous wealth of experiences with aspects of language such as connotations, levels of usage, malapropisms, circumlocutions, and literal denotations. Cartoons develop an awareness of how language is used, manipulated, and distorted to achieve a humorous effect. Students can learn vocabulary development through cartoons by understanding what it is in the cartoon that makes them laugh. Their understanding will transfer to their own use of language and sensitivity to it in their writing. The teacher in every content field can find examples from the daily newspaper.

17. *Activity.* Understanding relationships between words is a valuable vocabulary exercise. The relationships can be researched and elaborated on to any depth possible. Ask students to research (in a dictionary, encyclopedia, or technical book) the relationships between the three words in each group below:

a. Cyrus   Darius   Xerxes

b. Harpy   Minotaur   Triton

c. McKinley   Rainier   Washington

d. Rachel   Rebecca   Sarah

In providing details of the relationships, students should be encouraged to glean as much information as possible that relates the words. This vocabulary exercise teaches students to research related ideas, to gather supporting details, and to synthesize relevant information.

Topic II: Understanding and Using Context Clues

1. *Teacher Presentation.* Explain the following kinds of context clues that students can locate in their reading and can use as reader aids in their own writing. Clues

given from context must be taught students in a vocabulary development program in every content field. New words should never be taught in isolation as in a list but always given a contextual setting in order to develop skills of understanding clues to meaning and usage. New words are remembered better if they are presented in context because meaningful associations are made and retained for the word. So teaching context clues is a valuable necessary approach to teaching classroom concepts and developing lifelong vocabulary skills.

Clues given in context are of three kinds. The first are *semantic clues,* clues to the possible meaning of the new word from other information presented with it. The second are *syntactic clues* of word order in a sentence. And the third are *structural clues,* such as endings or inflections of words that suggest their usage (for example, *ly* for an adverb).

Many times the meanings of new words are directly explained by a writer or a speaker through several techniques. The first direct method would be to give a definition following the usage of the new word.

Example: The pterodactyl lived in prehistoric times. The ptetodactyl was a mesozoic reptile characterized by winglike limbs.

Another direct method for presenting new vocabulary with contextual clues is usage of appositives, a short restatement following the new word and set off by commas.

Example: The pterodactyl, a mesozoic reptile with wings, lived in prehistoric times.

Here the clues are recognized in the description following the word, but students need to be taught to use this device in learning new words and in presenting new words to their audience in their own writing.

Another direct method for understanding context clues is use of parentheses that contain rephrasings or synonyms for the new word.

Example: The pterodactyl (a winged reptile) lived in prehistoric, mesozoic times.

Teach students to place the clue right next to the word it defines or explains or else the clue will not function. In other words, to be most effective and to communicate most clearly modifiers are to be placed next to the thing they modify in a sentence.

The last direct explanation technique used to convey meanings of new words is the use of *id est,* abbreviated *i.e. Id est* is Latin for *it is,* and the term provides a restatement or synonym for a new word. Usually it gives a more precise term for a generality.

Example: The pterodactyl was a winged reptile which lived in prehistoric times (i.e., mesozoic era).

or

Winged reptiles (i.e., the pterodactyl) once lived in prehistoric times.

Recognizing and using clues in their own writing to convey meaning are essential skills to be taught to students.

2. *Activity*. Have students find the following commonly known words in any good standard dictionary. Each word has many *different* areas of meaning. Have students provide contexts (sentences) that will make clear the different areas of meaning given in the dictionary for each of these words:

frame	open
strike	pink
out	point

This is a fascinating vocabulary development activity that will surprise students who think they already know what these words mean. The surprise comes in learning that each word has up to sixty different meanings and that the meaning intended depends on how it is used, its context.

3. *Activity*. List the following sentences on the blackboard. Have students give a brief description of *pool* as it is used in each sentence. See if students can identify the part of speech each usage of the word is.

a. The brook formed a pool at the bend.

b. He lay in a pool of blood.

c. Let's go to the pool for a swim.

d. The wheat pool succeeded in sustaining the price of wheat.

e. He had the winning team in our baseball pool.

f. The balls clicked sharply on the pool table.

g. At the present time, it is not possible to pool the research findings of scientists all over the world.

h. We three should pool our money to buy her a gift.

Contextual clues to the meaning of *pool* in each sentence are given by the way the word is used, which involves its position in the sentence, its part of speech (noun, verb, or adjective), and the modifiers used with it. For example, in the first sentence *pool* is the object of *brook* and is restricted to the concept of how the brook formed itself. In the second sentence *pool* is limited in meaning to its modifier, the prepositional phrase *of blood*. Lastly, *pool* is limited in sentences (d) and (e) to the modifiers that precede it, *wheat* and *baseball*.

4. *Activity*. Ask students to become lexicographers or dictionary makers. By using all the information presented in each sentence, students can write out a ten- to twenty-word definition for the following nonsense word.

a. He was exceptionally skillful with a shrdlu.

b. He says he needs a shrdlu to shape the beams.

c. I saw Mr. Jenkins yesterday buying a new handle for his shrdlu.

d. The steel head of Jenkin's shrdlu was badly chipped.

e. Don't bother with a saw or an ax; a shrdlu will do the job faster and better.

This vocabulary exercise trains students to develop meanings for new words in their writing by providing explicit detail. It teaches students to provide a context that is meaningful, clear, and developed so that their audience will understand the new word they are explaining. Further, it gives students an opportunity to synthesize information and to combine it logically in a sentence.

5. *Activity.* Write the following sentences on the board. From the information presented in each sentence, students can make up a definition in less than twenty words of *wanky.* Tell students to be careful to use all the details provided and to combine them into a meaningful definition.

a. He seems perpetually wanky.

b. Some people feel most wanky in the early morning.

c. If you want to get over that wanky feeling, take Johnson's Homogenized Yeast Tablets.

d. Everybody feels more or less wanky on a hot, humid day.

e. . . . the wanky, wanky bluebell.

   That droops upon its stem.

f. I am not cross, just wanky.

Discuss the definitions provided and the clues students used in each sentence to gain the meaning. How is *wanky* used in each sentence, what part of speech is it, and what kinds of modifiers are there around it? In their own writing, students should understand how it is they communicate meanings using clues (see Activity 2).

6. *Activity.* Cloze exercises have many uses in diagnosing reading problems, determining the readability of texts, assessing comprehension, and as a tool for other kinds of testing. They may also be used very effectively to teach semantic and syntactic relations in contextual settings. To fill in each blank requires that a student read the total passage and decide on a logical fill-in based on words surrounding it, its position in the sentence, and its inflectional endings or part of speech. The word *cloze* stems from the psychological term *closure* meaning "to close in a gap." In the original Cloze Test, every fifth word was deleted from a 250-word passage that students had to fill in with the exact missing word. The suggestion here for vocabulary development is not to use the Cloze Test, however, but rather cloze exercises constructed in any way the teacher desires. Blanks may be for adjectives, nouns, proper nouns only, specific adverbs, and so forth, depending on what is to be emphasized in the text or the vocabulary. Cloze exercises draw attention to emphasized words and foster memory retention of them.

   Reproduction Page 6–6 is based on a suggestion by Dr. Irene Reiter of the Philadelphia Public Schools and is an example of cloze exercises that emphasize specific words in content materials. Passage 1 is from the novel *Red Badge of Courage* and deletes colors in the blanks. Colors as symbolism are crucial to recognize and understand in the book, so they would be important to emphasize. Passage 2 deletes proper nouns and dates from a secondary social studies textbook. Passage 3 deletes adjectives, specific types of cells, and is from a secondary science text. The last passage, out of a secondary math textbook, leaves blank information about angles. Students would have to read contextually to gain semantic clues to filling in logical information for each blank. This type of exercise is valuable in each content area to build background knowledge, provide experience, and develop contextual building of concepts.

7. *Activity.* Advanced organizers help students see relationships among technical vocabulary words and related concepts. However, before using advanced organizers, prepare students with some background. Use the advanced organizer as a tool for review of learned concepts, as a study guide in learning and researching concepts, or as a notetaking device when concepts are presented. In all three suggested activities, however, give guidance in order for students to build the necessary background of understanding required to do the exercise. The "advanced" organizer should really be called a *concept guide* because it is to be used *during* learning and as a review, rather than solely in advance because student background is needed.

The concept guide may be used in any content area and adapts itself well to beginnings and endings of new study units where many new vocabulary words are presented. Figures 6-2 and 6-3 are examples of concept guides prepared by teachers in different content areas.

8. *Activity.* Using Reproduction Page 6-7, discuss with students how meaning in writing is conveyed through structure of sentences and through forms of words. The structure of sentences concerns the order of words in the sentence, the meaningful groups of words (phrases and clauses), and structure words that provide relationships in sentences. The forms of words involve inflectional endings such as *s* for a plural or *ly* for an adverb, and so forth.

In question 1, have students understand the subject and the verb of each clause in the stanza. *'Twas* means "it was" and is the subject and verb of the first clause. *Toves did gyre* and *gimble* are the subject and compound verb of the second clause. *Borogoves were* and *raths outgrabe* are the compound subjects and verbs of the last clause. Students can understand the subjects and verbs even though there are nonsense words because of the structure signals given.

In question 2, lexical meaning is dictionary meaning, and all the recognizable English words have lexical meaning such as *was, and the, did,* and so on. In question 3, words that provide structural meaning are *and, the* and *in.* Question 4 pertains to English sentence structure with the noun or pronoun before the verb *(It was),* the adjective before the noun, *(slithy toves),* and prepositional phrases *(in the wabe)* next to what they modify *(gyre and gimble).* In exercise 5, where actual words are to be substituted for nonsense words, have students fill in logical words by paying attention to the word endings provided. Fun, too, is to tell students to use words that have the same number of syllables as the nonsense words being replaced. This keeps the rhythm of the poem and restricts their choices.

The great instructional value of this vocabulary exercise is that it helps students develop sensitivity to language use through structure. It helps them understand use of semantic and syntactic clues in conveying meaning, for although the nonsense words have no meaning themselves, the stanza does have meaning and can be understood through context clues. In their own writing and use of language, students can be taught to be sensitive to these clues to meaning.

9. *Activity.* Using Reproduction Page 6-8, have a student in the class read aloud the story of Bretty Bairford. Ask students to write out answers about the story to the four questions below. Discuss their answers and ask how they were able to understand the story even though it has so many unknown or nonsense words in it. Point

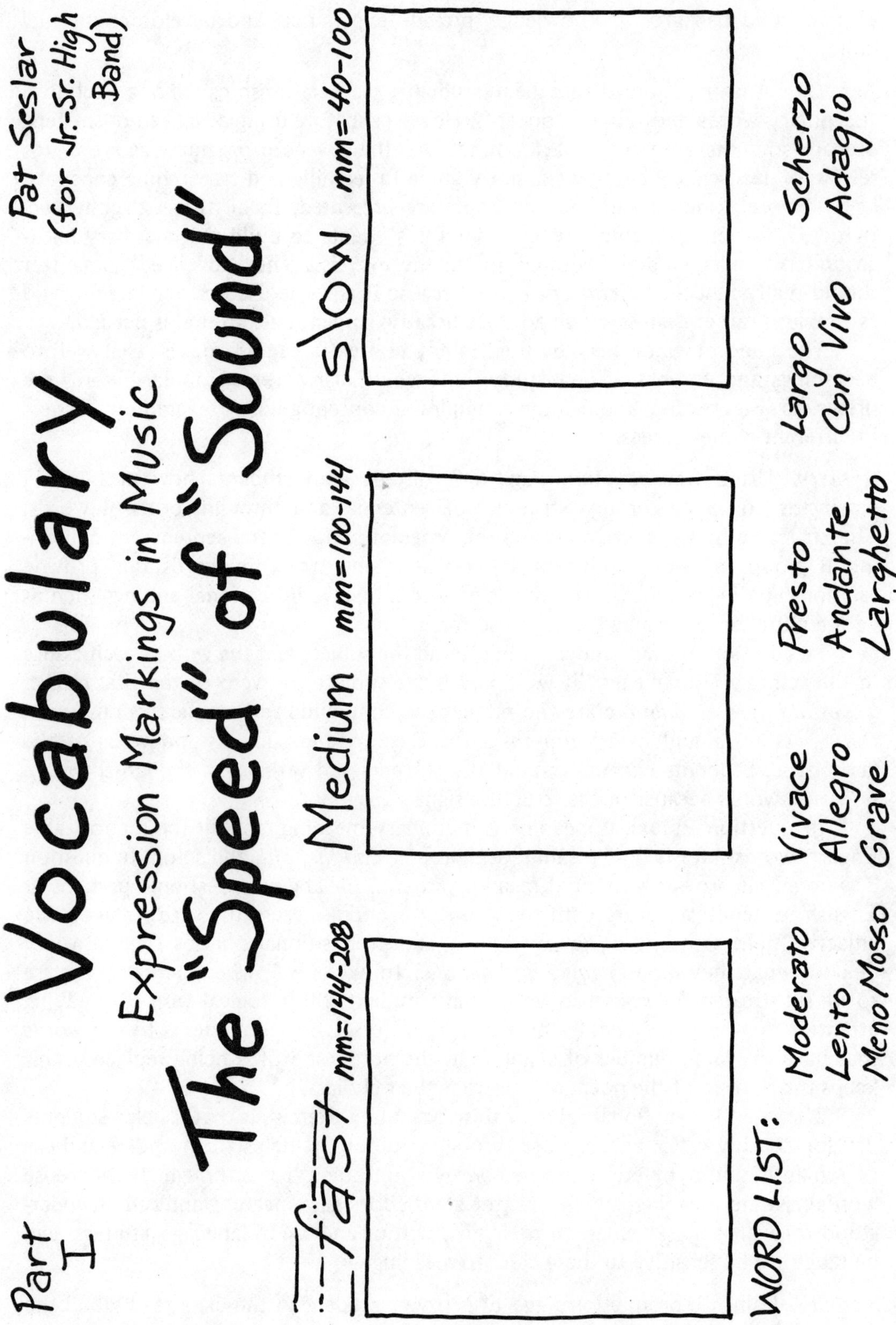

Part I

Vocabulary

Pat Seslar
(for Jr.-Sr. High
Band)

Expression Markings in Music

The "Speed" of "Sound"

Fast mm=144-208

Medium mm=100-144

Slow mm=40-100

WORD LIST:

Moderato
Lento
Meno Mosso

Vivace
Allegro
Grave

Presto
Andante
Larghetto

Largo
Con Vivo
Adagio

Scherzo

Figure 6-2.   Example of an Advanced Organizer, or Concept Guide

Below is a list of terms:

acute	interior	obtuse	triangles
equiangular	isosceles	remote interior angles	types of angles
equilateral	named by angles	right	
exterior	named by sides	scalene	

Is there some way that you could rearrange the terms to that there would be a pattern developed that would depict an interrelationship among the term?

SURE THERE IS...........

Place one term from the list in each shape in the form provided below. The most general term should head each column.

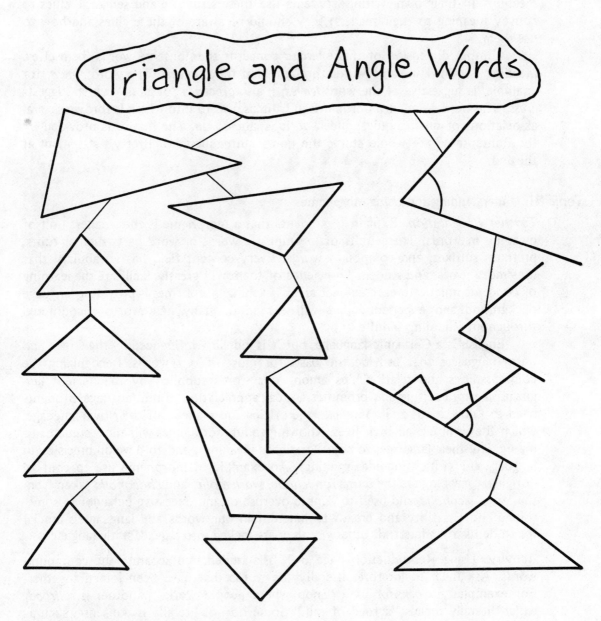

Figure 6-3. Another Example of a Concept Guide

out to students that there are words and phrases that they can recognize: *once upon a time, he cried, "come and see,"* and so forth. Have them identify the recognizable words. Ask students to find the subjects and verbs of each proper English sentence. How can they identify the subject? Because of its place in the sentence, because it follows adjectives and precedes verbs, and because its form is that of a noun and has pronoun references *(he)*. The verbs are recognized through their placement in the sentence after the nouns and through their inflected endings, such as *ed* to denote past tense.

Discuss with students the point of the vocabulary exercise, which is that meaning is gained from clues given in context, that words in sentences have relationships to each other, and that our English language structure in its patterns gives us meaning. In their own writing, students use these structure and semantic clues to convey meaning to their readers; they should be aware of these clues and how to use them.

Another dimension of this exercise concerns the nonsense words themselves. Meaning is gained in some words through what they suggest. The word *reaves*, for example, is suggestive of the word *leaves;* it also precedes "of gless," which suggests *grass.* The word *quiant* is a portmanteau (suitcase) word into which is thrown several associations of quaint, quiet, queer, curious, and so on. The humor is provided by the nonsense of the whole story, the non-sequitur illogic of Bretty's statement at the end.

Topic III: Understanding and Using Morphemes

1. *Teacher Presentation.* Explain to students that a morpheme is the smallest unit of meaning in words. These units of meaning are words or word parts such as roots, prefixes, suffixes, and compound words. Every content field has vocabulary that uses morphemes, and student knowledge of them will greatly facilitate the learning of concepts unique to each subject area. Teaching morphemes is providing language background and experience that will extend to many new words encountered throughout schooling and life.

   English is a Germanic language, but it is indelibly influenced by the Greek and Latin languages that provide the basis for most of our words. Recognizing the commonalities and relationships among our words supplied by the ancient languages is very exciting and promotes a great appreciation of our language. Students need to know about and appreciate the origins and makeup of their own language, which they will use all their lives. Knowing about morphemes will allow students to manipulate their language, to coin "original" meanings, and to develop precision in language use (which includes spelling). An example of morpheme use to coin an "original" meaning are the terms *foodaholic, workaholic,* and *chocoholic* taken from the word *alcoholic* and used to denote overuse of and excessive behavior in something. The versatility and creativity inherent in our words and language is crucial for students to understand: otherwise they are locked into a dead, static language.

2. *Activity.* Using Reproduction Page 6-9, ask students to separate the compound words. Ask them to interpret literally the words that have been joined together. For example, a *workshop* is a "shop where people work." Another is *railroad,* which literally means "a road of rail." Some do not literally make sense, such as *butterfly,* "a fly of butter." How did those two words come to be joined? Have students locate compound words in their own textbooks and interpret them lit-

erally. In their own writing, students should be asked to find and to use some compound words.

3. *Activity.* Have students make up compound words by joining two common words to invent a "new" word that has logical literal meaning. Or have students reverse the compound words and see how the literal meaning has changed. Some compound words, such as *roadrail* and *shopwork*, will not change their meaning that much. But some will change greatly, such as *papernews* and *cakepan*. The emphasis changes when the words are reversed because the main word is the second one and is described by the first.

4. *Activity.* Using Reproduction Page 6–10, explain to students how compound words are formed. Through discussion have students supply the answers to the first word in each category. Form small groups and have the groups think of compound words completing the examples given under each category. Share the examples in a general class discussion.

5. *Activity.* Have students think up as many compound words as possible, write the words on tagboard paper, and cut them into pieces. These compound word pieces can then be played as a game in a group to see who can form the most number of compound words within a certain time limit. The student who forms the most number is the winner of the compound-word-parts game.

6. *Activity.* Another game is the compound race game, which is played with the entire class. A leader lists on the board three or more words, each of which can be used as part of a great number of compound words, such as *house*, *some*, or *book*. Students write these on their papers as headings and then in the five minutes allowed list all the compound words they can think of using those three words. The student with the most number in each list is the winner.

7. *Activity.* Using Reproduction Page 6–11, present the *Prefix* and *Root* columns to students. Ask them to define each master word literally. For example, *detain* literally means "to hold down or away," which is somewhat the meaning we attach to the word today. Have students think of other examples they know for each root given so they can tie in their known vocabulary with these morphemes. Have students make up new words by joining prefixes and roots to make logical sense. For example, *monospect* could be a logical, "new" word meaning "to look once," and *monocept* could be "to seize alone." This is playing with the versatility of our language, manipulating it, and enjoying it.

8. *Activity.* Using Reproduction Page 6–12, have students fill in the blanks for each well-known root. Discuss the meanings of these words according to the literal meaning of each root. For example, the literal meaning of *dent* is "tooth," so it logically follows that an *idention* is so called because of its "toothy" appearance.

9. *Activity.* With Reproduction Page 6–13, have students think of other examples of words they know using the number morphemes. In math, English, art, science, and music, especially, these number morphemes can be specifically applied to vocabulary study.

10. *Activity.* Ask students to think of all the "seed" words they can think of, words that contain *cede*, *sede*, and *ceed*. When they have written all of them down and checked their spellings carefully, have the students write the words on colorful

construction paper, one color for each of the three roots. When the words are cut apart into different shapes, they can be displayed as a mobile hanging in the room that can serve as a reminder for students to learn the "seed" words and to use and spell them correctly.

11. *Activity.* Using Reproduction Page 6-14, have students construct sentences (context) for some of the words given for each root. Have them think of other examples of words they know for each root. Students in groups can be assigned to look up one of the roots in a good dictonary and to write down all of the related words given. Then each group can share its findings for its root with the rest of the class.

12. *Activity.* Using Reproduction Page 6-15, ask students to define the meanings of the prefixes given by understanding their effect on the words listed with them. For example, the word *active* becomes negative when *in* is attached to it; therefore, *in* must mean "not." When *in* is affixed to *land,* however, it does not have a negative meaning but denotes a direction. Through the uses of the prefixes given, students can understand their meanings and develop a sensitivity and awareness of prefix function in altering meanings of words.

13. *Activity.* Reproduction Pages 6-16 and 6-17 present negative prefixes that must be understood if students are to grasp the meaning of a word to which one is attached. Awareness of these negative prefixes—*a, an* and *un*—can be fostered with these exercises. Encourage students to use the words given as any part of speech. For example, if they want to change the noun *atheism* to the adjective *atheistic* in their sentence, allow them to do so. Ask students to find this prefix in their reading assignments or in their own writing and to report on what they find.

14. *Activity.* Using the words having prefixes listed below, construct a forty-six-card prefix rummy game for two to four students to play at a time. Write the prefix above the word on each card.

ac	*inter*	*in*	*re*
accord	interfere	introvert	redo
accede	interrupt	inverted	restore
accept	intertwine	intimate	return
acclaim	intermission	introspective	rebuild
ad	*co*	*dis*	*trans*
advise	cocaptain	dislocate	transport
admire	copilot	distort	transgress
adventure	cooperate	dismantle	transform
advent	coeducation	disease	transcontinental
un	*en*	*pre*	
unmarried	entire	preteen	
unflavored	entrap	predict	*wild card*
unpredictable	enslave	preposterous	*wild card*
unstable	envelope	pretend	

Write the following rules on one of the cards for students to follow:

1. Shuffle the cards.

2. Deal five cards to each player.

3. Put the deck face down with top card turned up.

4. Players draw and discard (face up) in turn until one has three of a kind (or four of a kind) of each prefix.

15. *Activity*. Play the prefix race game with the whole class. The class is divided into two teams. The teacher writes a common prefix (for example, *un, non, pre, bi, re*) on the board. The first member of team 1 writes a word using that prefix on the board. Then the first member from team 2 writes a word using the prefix. Each team alternates until one team can no longer think of any other word or until they have duplicated a word. The opposing team then scores one point. The team with the most points at the end is the winner.

16. *Activity*. Using Reproduction Page 6–18, read the directions to students to locate suffixes in each word and then to match them with other roots given in the list. After students have worked silently on them, discuss what they have formed and share with the class.

17. *Activity*. Using Reproduction Page 6–19, have students add the given suffixes to the list of words. In part 2 have students locate all of the suffixes in each word. For example, *departmentalism* has the suffixes *al* and *ism*. Point out the pronunciation of *mischievousness* (four syllables), which is frequently mispronounced as if spelled *vi-ous*. Recognizing these suffixes will help pronunciation and spelling mainly because students will be made aware of each part of the longer words.

18. *Activity*. Reproduction Page 6–20 shows how the suffix *logy* can be used with various roots to form new words. Have students draw a line from the science to its definition and discuss their guesses.

19. *Activity*. Using Reproduction Page 6–21, stress with students the importance of recognizing *less* as a word ending because it makes the meaning of a word a negative. Have students fill in or check the blanks to answer. Have them locate words using this suffix in their reading and in their own writing.

20. *Activity*. Using the words having suffixes listed below, construct a forty-six-card suffix rummy game for two to four students to play at a time. Write the suffix above the word on each card.

ence	*ous*	*able*	*ment*
emergence	vigorous	movable	settlement
influence	boisterous	portable	advertisement
difference	religious	sinkable	establishment
resurgence	precious	usable	advisement
tion	*ful*	*ance*	*ly*
location	bountiful	appearance	usually
mention	grateful	reliance	merely
evaluation	beautiful	allowance	surely
diction	thankful	disappearance	quickly

ize	*less*	*ness*	
realize	careless	sadness	
tantalize	spiritless	kindness	*wild card*
cauterize	tasteless	brightness	*wild card*
sympathize	helpless	darkness	

Write these rules on one of the cards for students to follow:

1. Shuffle the cards.

2. Deal five to seven cards to each player.

3. Put the deck face down with the top card turned up.

4. Players draw and discard in turn until one has three of a kind (our four of a kind) of each suffix.

Topic IV: Improved Spelling Through Visualization and Memory

1. *Activity.* For "eye spelling," have the students look at the entire word, then close their eyes to visualize the word in the memory. Tell the students to picture each letter separately and then to picture the word as a whole. Students then open their eyes and look again at the word. Repeat with eyes closed until the students feel confident they have mastered the word. If possible, have students devise mnemonic (memory) devices for difficult parts of a word. For example, *principal* can be remembered by *pal* at the end, *principle* as a *rule* with similar *le* endings, and *stationery* by *paper* (the *er* association).

2. *Activity.* "Ear spelling," or training in careful pronunciation as the students see the word, is crucial. Be sure to stress and even exaggerate the sounds of new spelling and vocabulary words presented to students so that they associate phonemes (sounds) with graphemes (written symbols). Consider with students the following list of *ough* words that have the same graphemes but not the same phonemic sound; they are sounded very differently from each other:

cough	"awf"		bough	"au"
enough	"uf"		hiccough	"up"
slough	"oo"		dough	"o"

3. *Activity.* "Tongue spelling" is another approach. Have the students pronounce the whole word. Then ask them to sound out every individual letter sequentially, rolling the word off their tongues. This method will force students to pay heed to every letter in the word and to hear as well as tongue the word.

4. *Activity.* "Finger spelling" can be effective at the secondary level. Ask the students to trace the entire word with the index finger to have the tactile experience of "feeling" its lines and formations. Tell the students to exaggerate in the mind the "feeling" the word.

Topic V: Improved Spelling Through Phonetic Analysis and Syllabication

1. *Activity.* For a new spelling word or a word misspelled in students' writing, have students correctly pronounce the word aloud and then find other words that rhyme with the word or with the part that is troublesome. For example, the spelling word *statue* given to students may be rhymed with *hue, rue, sue, glue,* and so forth, and the troublesome part *ue* would be associated and remembered.

2. *Activity.* Give the pronunciations of the new spelling words that are in view on the blackboard. Have students pronounce each word as you point to each syllable. Have students exaggerate the sounds to really hear them.

3. *Activity.* Have students write a list of one-syllabled words on the board and then a list of two-syllabled words. Finally, ask students to write words they can think of that are multisyllabled. With the entire class, break the multisyllabled words into syllables. Syllabication follows three usual rules that students should learn:

   a. Divide two consonants when they separate two vowels (for example, *spel-ling, hop-ping*).

   b. With one consonant separating two vowels, allow the consonant to go with either vowel, whichever seems best (for example, *ma-jor, min-or*).

   c. A consonant plus *le* at the end of a word becomes a syllable (for example, *cra-dle, sim-ple*).

4. *Activity.* Once students have seen the new spelling words on the blackboard, have heard the teacher pronounce them carefully, and have spoken them, the words can be broken into syllables and scrambled for students to reassemble. Scramble each word by syllables separately, so that students do not suffer confusion. For example, the spelling word *syllable* would be scrambled *ble, la, syl* so that students would assemble it with an awareness of the sounds in each syllable and how they are represented visually.

5. *Activity.* There are multisyllabled words in every content field. Take eight difficult words that have three syllables each. Construct bingo cards with all of the syllables arranged differently on each card (five to seven cards make one set). In a group of students, each with a bingo card and paper markers, read the entire word, sounding the syllables clearly. Students place markers on each syllable as it is pronounced. Read each of the eight words in the same manner until a student scores bingo. Several lists can be constructed for several sets of cards, enough for an entire class. The following are suggested, general words:

List A	*List B*
dif-fer-ent	fi-nal-ly
gro-cer-y	plan-ta-tion
po-ta-to	en-ter-tain
re-mem-ber	im-por-tant
um-brel-la	mes-sen-ger
mo-las-ses	in-ter-rupt
il-lus-trate	cu-cum-ber
pro-mo-tion	tor-pe-do

6. *Activity.* Have the students write some multisyllabled nonsense words on the blackboard; then divide the nonsense sounds into syllables. Guide students to recognizing the syllabic divisions according to the three syllable rules (see Activity 3) and to associating sounds with visual representations. Nonsense words are valuable to use in developing phonic sensitivity because the meaning is not the important consideration in the word.

Topic VI: Improved Spelling Through Morphemes and Structure

1. *Activity.* Using Reproduction Page 6-22, guide students to the usage and spelling of words that end in *able*. There are three types of changes indicated for words that use this suffix. Define the suffix and apply it to the correct spellings.

2. *Activity.* With Reproduction Page 6-23, have students review common suffixes used in English. Ask students to underline all the suffixes they can find in the "big" words listed using the suffixes presented. Pronounce each word for the students, exaggerating the syllabic divisions between the morphemes in order to hear as well as see the word parts.

3. *Activity.* Using Reproduction Page 6-24, have students review the common prefixes found in English. Pronounce each word carefully in the list of "big" words and ask students to listen for the prefix and underline it as they hear and see it. Ask them to write five more words they know using the prefixes given. Discuss and share the words they give with the entire class.

4. *Activity.* As a review of morphemes, have students add affixes to the common roots given on Reproduction Page 6-25. Guide them to creating the longest meaningful words they can devise using the prefixes and suffixes previously studied. Students' fears and anxiety over the very long word at the bottom of the page will lessen when they realize that they already know most of the word and that its length should not frighten them. Help them define the word using prefix and suffix definitions.

ASSESSING ACHIEVEMENT OF OBJECTIVES

Ongoing Evaluation

The extent to which students have learned how to develop their vocabulary and their spelling skills can be measured by having them submit for evaluation the final products of Activities.

Final Evaluation

For an overall evaluation of students' understanding of how to develop their vocabulary and their spelling skills, assign a composition and evaluate it based on the following questions:

1. Are new concepts defined through associations with synonyms and analogies?

2. Are connotative words that students use appropriate as used for the subject matter? Would any word be more effective if it were substituted with another word?

3. Is there a diversity in the context use of new words with use of appositives, parenthetical explanations, or other clues?

4. How many words can be found in the composition that have three or more syllables? Count them and see how many contain affixes.

5. How many errors in spelling does the composition contain?

6. Can the spelling errors be classified as to kind, such as morphemic, phonetic, or faulty visualization of a difficult word part?

7. In their rewrite and revision of the composition, are spelling errors recognized and corrected by the students? Is improvement shown in their spelling skills?

RESOURCES FOR TEACHING VOCABULARY

Below is a selected and annotated list of resources from journals and books.

Burmeister, Lou. "Morphemes Commonly Used in Specific Content Fields." *Reading Strategies for Secondary School Teachers.* Reading, Mass.: Addison-Wesley, 1974, pp. 298–308. Detailed lists are given of important morphemes and their meanings found in major content areas. These lists are an excellent source for morphemic study to which every content area teacher can refer. Other words can be added to the examples given by students from their backgrounds to make meaningful associations with the morphemes.

Burmeister, Lou. *Reading Strategies for Middle and Secondary School Teachers.* Reading, Mass.: Addison-Wesley, 1978. Excellent textbook for teaching reading in the content areas. Chapter 6 is particularly valuable, though, for teaching vocabulary concepts to be used in writing. Word denotations, connotations, morphology, syllabication, and other approaches to teaching vocabulary are clearly and fully detailed. The book is a valuable resource for teaching language in all content fields.

Dale, Edgar; O'Rourke, J.; and Bamman, H. *Techniques of Teaching Vocabulary.* Palo Alto, Calif.: Field Educational Publishers, 1971. The approach to conceptual development in the subject area is through systemized analyses of words to get clues to their meaning and to provide maximum transfer. Testing exercises to find student

knowledge and background are included so that this background can be built on. Included is a section on spelling and pronunciation that relate to vocabulary development. All content area teachers will find this book valuable in its approaches and its practical suggestions.

Dulin, Kenneth La Marr. "New Research on Context Clues." *Journal of Reading.* 13 (October, 1969). The article is about a study of tenth graders' use of five identified contextual devices in their reading comprehension. Analysis of variance measures showed that teaching context clues is a valuable practice, although some are more effective than others. Use of appositives, the most commonly used vocabulary device, was found to be least effective, so others such as cause-effect relationships and contrast should be used more frequently. Valuable in this article are the lists of contextual aids to which teachers may refer when teaching vocabulary and writing skill development.

Johnson, Dale D., and Pearson, P. David. *Teaching Reading Vocabulary.* New York: Holt, Rinehart & Winston, 1978. The book approaches the teaching of vocabulary through three main avenues, which the authors term *direct instruction* (sight words and meaning vocabulary), *generalizable* and *transferable* (phonics, structure, and context), and *reference sources.* Included are many activities, games, and guidelines for implementing all of the approaches in the classroom. The many instructional activities provided are adaptable to all content areas not only to teach comprehension of reading but to expand language use for writing.

Keller, Howard H. *New Perspectives on Teaching Vocabulary*. Washington, D.C.: Center for Applied Linguistics (June, 1978). The pamphlet presents three approaches to teaching vocabulary to second-language learners: (1) studying roots; (2) recognizing etymological/mnemonic devices; (3) using topical vocabulary checklists. The value of each of these approaches is that they provide a system of vocabulary study for the student. Suggestions for implementing the study systems could be adapted to any content area, not only in foreign langauge study.

O'Rourke, Joseph Patrick. *Toward a Science of Vocabulary Development*. Hawthorne, New York: Mouton Publications, Div. of Walter DeGruyter, Inc., 1974. The writer proposes use of a scientific method in vocabulary instruction, which he maintains is often taught in an unstructured, incidental manner. This scientific method should be based on a relationship between children's conceptual development and language development. The writer proposes vocabulary development through a classification-concept approach that extends the student's "natural potential to use language." Classifying words to show meaningful relationships involve seven kinds of context clues, morphemes, and "webbing" of synonyms, among others he proposes. His argument for meaningful classifications is valid and useful for all content areas.

RESOURCES FOR TEACHING SPELLING

Below is a selected and annotated list of resources useful for teaching the subject matter in this chapter. Resources are from journal articles and from books.

Dunkeld, Colin, and Hatch, Lynda. "Building Spelling Confidence." *Elementary English*. (February, 1975). The article argues that overemphasis on spelling mastery and a belief that spelling is an end in itself can delay writing development in children who lose courage because they are poor spellers. Almost all classroom spelling programs fail to select spelling words on the basis of writing needs and to provide application in written work. The authors suggest a system for selecting and learning words that involves self-choice by the students of words misspelled in their own writing.

Ediger, Marlow. "Objectives in the Language Arts Area of Spelling." *Elementary English*. (February, 1975). The article proposes certain objectives for students to emphasize in spelling and suggests some learning activities to achieve them. Although geared for elementary-level students, some ideas may be adaptable to secondary spelling.

Geedy, Patricia S. "What Research Tells Us about Spelling." *Elementary English*. (February, 1975). The article presents several different approaches to teaching spelling and what research indicates about their effectiveness. Greatest agreement is on selection of words according to immediate needs and on frequency of need in children's writing. Linguistic approaches, the Fernald kinesthetic approach, and the multisensory modalities approach are all discussed regarding their effectiveness.

Hanna, Paul; Hodges, R.; and Hanna, J. *Spelling: Structure and Strategies*. Boston: Houghton Mifflin, 1971. The book sets forth theoretical and historical backgrounds of knowledge and logic on which spelling principles are based. Then the principles are applied to a developmental spelling curriculum predicated on eight purposes the authors propose concerning phoneme-grapheme relationships and varying learning modalities (ear, voice, hand, and eye). Although directed toward elementary instruction, the linguistic and psychological theory is of interest in developing a systematic spelling program in secondary curriculum.

Manolakes, George. "The Teaching of Spelling: A Pilot Study." *Elementary English* (February, 1975). The article details the interesting results of a study of children's spelling achievement. The findings indicated that children have certain error patterns, that words that are commonly misspelled have certain "hot spots," and that phonetic generalizations taught children may not be justifiable. Such findings raise questions about current methods of teaching spelling.

Monson, Jay A. "Is Spelling Spelled Rut, Routine, or Revitalized?" *Elementary English.* (February, 1975). The article challenges teachers' attitudes toward teaching spelling and suggests some ideas for "revitalizing" the "rut" that teaching spelling often gets into. The author's ideas range from some word games to a cross-curriculum spelling notebook. There are some implementable, practical methods for teaching spelling in more interesting ways.

Rosler, Florence. "Sunrise, Sunset; Pretest, Retest." *Elementary English.* (February, 1975). The most effective method for teaching spelling is to integrate its study into the entire language arts program of listening, reading, writing, and speaking. The author details a day-by-day approach to achieving this integration with various media, classroom grouping, and testing methods.

Rowell, C. Glennon. "Don't Throw Away Those Spelling Test Papers . . . Yet!" *Elementary English.* (February, 1975). The article is concerned with the instructional value and follow-up possibilities in the weekly spelling test papers. Instead of throwing spelling tests out, use them to diagnose kinds of student errors and methods for their correction. Errors can indicate patterns of spelling problems to which correctional practice can be directed.

7

Teaching the Paragraph

CONTENT OVERVIEW

The paragraph that is traditionally taught in school, the "minicomposition," was introduced in 1866 by Alexander Bain, a Scottish logician.[1] It is a formal kind of paragraphing based on logic with a topic statement, a supporting middle, and a concluding sentence. It deals with just one major idea and is unified. All the sentences cohere to the major point. In other words, this kind of paragraph has a specific structure, a unity of sentences, and a coherence of text. Unity pertains to singleness of idea, and coherence concerns relationships of ideas in the whole composition. This kind of paragraph is most commonly found in expository writing but is taught in school for other modes as well.

In regard to paragraph structure using a topic sentence, a 1974 study by Richard Braddock of twenty-five essays published in current magazines (such as *The Atlantic*, *Harper's*, *The New Yorker*, and so forth) revealed that only 55 percent of the paragraphs had explicit topic sentences. Our current teaching of composition often stresses that every paragraph a student writes should contain a topic statement, but in reality this structure exists in professional writing only slightly more than half of the time. It is traditional since Bain's time to teach this structure, but in longer discourse of several paragraphs perhaps other structures should be considered and studied. Even though this chapter focuses on teaching the traditional paragraph structure, Braddock's findings should serve as a note of caution that more research is needed to understand other structures and how they should be taught.

OBJECTIVES

As a result of the learning experiences in this chapter, students should be able to:

1. Practice traditional structure of the paragraph using a topic sentence, detail development, and a conclusion.

---

1. Alexander Bain, *English Composition and Rhetoric* (London: Longmans, Green, 1866).

2. Understand the functions of certain paragraph types in longer composition writing.

3. Develop unity of sentences in a paragraph with a controlling statement and key terms.

4. Build elaboration of the topic through use of the controlling statement in a paragraph or several paragraphs.

5. Understand cohesion of text and the ties that provide it.

6. Practice using reference, connectors, repetition, and unstated information (ellipsis) ties in different kinds of writing to provide cohesion of text.

7. Understand what factors create a text, a group of sentences that have unity and cohesion.

8. Appreciate how writing has variety and flexibility when the writer knows options for using language.

LEARNING EXPERIENCES

Topic I: Understanding and Creating Structure in Paragraphs

1. *Teacher Presentation.* Explain to students the idea of the paragraph as a "mini-composition." A paragraph has a particular structure that has an opening or introduction, details that follow to develop the idea, and a conclusion that summarizes and restates the main idea. This structure works best with a composition of a single paragraph, but once it is learned, this structure can be extended to the logical development of longer compositions of several paragraphs. Draw a diamond on the blackboard for students to see. Point out to them that, just as the diamond figure has a shape and a structure, so does a paragraph; just as the diamond has symmetry and balance, so does the paragraph. The *top* of the diamond is similar to the *top*ic of the paragraph, which is then expanded with details, examples, or reasons, analogous to the enlargement of the diamond shape. The bottom of the diamond is similar to the top and completes the structure, just as the conclusion completes the paragraph by restating and summarizing the topic. With this visual image, students may more readily grasp the abstract idea of logical structure.

2. *Activity.* Assign a full-sentence topic in the subject area that requires reasons to develop it. Examples in different content areas would be the following:

Science: Leaves manufacture food.

Social studies: The Colonists came to the New World.

Mathematics: A negative times a negative is a positive.

Have students copy down the topic sentence. Below it, ask students to list three or four reasons to develop the main idea. Have them begin each reason with *because.* Have students practice writing a conclusion by summarizing in one sentence the topic and reasons. Students will have practiced topic development but not actually written a paragraph yet. Ask students to read aloud their list of reasons and their concluding sentence. Discuss these for their effectiveness.

3. *Activity.* Assign a topic in the subject area that requires examples to develop it. Examples in different subjects follow:

Mathematics: Zero times any number equals zero.

Social studies: Many revolutions have been fought because of high taxation.

Art: Stipling as an art form may be found in several communication media.

Tell students to copy down the full-sentence topic and then to list three or four examples under it. Ask them to use introductory words for their examples, such as *the first example,* secondly, lastly, and so on as they list the examples. Have them practice writing a concluding sentence by summarizing the topic sentence and the examples. Ask students to read aloud their listed examples and their concluding sentence. Discuss why some conclusions are more effective than others, and write on the board a well-written one that students provide. Ask students to copy it down on their paper.

4. *Activity.* Assign a full-sentence topic in the content field that requires details to develop it. The following are examples for different subjects:

Social studies: Many events led to George Washington's trip to the Ohio River Valley.

Science: Several characteristics distinguish animal cells from plant cells.

Mathematics: There are many types of polygons.

Have students copy down the topic sentence; then list the details to develop it below the sentence. Discuss with students what kinds of connectors could be used—such as *also, besides, for example, in addition,* and so forth—to tie the details together in a composition. With students, construct a concluding sentence that summarizes the main topic and the details. Discuss with students that the purpose of a conclusion is to reinforce the main points in the mind of the reader. It brings the topic to a logical close and reminds the reader of the major ideas.

5. *Activity.* Have students practice writing topic sentences through the inductive method. On the board, list three reasons, examples, or details from the subject area. Ask students to write a topic sentence that would introduce the body of the composition. Have students read their topic sentences aloud and discuss their effectiveness. The topic sentence should introduce the main idea and be general enough to include all the points to be made. Have the class choose the topic sentence they want to use. Ask students to copy it down and list the supporting points below it. Then ask students to practice writing a concluding sentence. Read these sentences aloud.

6. *Activity.* Give students practice in writing concluding sentences. Ask them to use their topic sentence from Activity 5 and the three reasons, details, or examples you presented on the blackboard to construct a concluding sentence that will restate the topic and summarize the main points. Have students write the composition in one paragraph using these five sentences: the topic sentence, three sentences giving details, examples, or reasons, and the concluding sentence. Remind students of the analogy of the diamond to paragraph structure and symmetry.

7. *Activity.* Have students read aloud their five-sentence paragraphs and discuss the structure. Is their topic sentence clear and does it introduce the main idea? Do the

details, examples, or reasons develop the main point and are these connected logically with transition words such as *for example, first, also,* and so on? Check the
students' concluding sentences for how well they serve the summarizing function.

8. *Teacher Presentation.* In longer writing of more than one paragraph, the structure
is such that each paragraph is seen to serve a particular function. The structure is
similar to the single paragraph in terminology, yet the extent of development and
expansion is much greater. Thus longer compositions have an introductory paragraph, middle or sometimes transitional paragraphs, and concluding or summarizing
paragraphs. Present and explain to students the following definitions and examples
of different kinds of paragraphs and the functions they serve in longer paragraph
forms. The examples of the different kinds of paragraphs come from secondary
textbooks representing various content fields.

H. Alan Robinson defined the introductory paragraphs as broad in nature,
serving as purpose setters for the reading to follow.

Introductory Paragraphs in Content Area Textbooks

Example: You might think there isn't much to the idea of crossing streets, bridges, and
so on, but as a matter of fact there is a famous problem in mathematics that
involves the idea of "crossing" and hardly any other idea at all.[2]

Example: Geography is many things. It includes our natural surroundings, the resources
and needs of the world's nations, and the relationship between people and the
land they live on. Mostly, geography is the study of the kinds of landforms
and climates that form our physical environment, how they are arranged on
the earth and how they influence the way we live. In this book we will study
how people are distributed over the earth, how they make their living from
it—and how they change it.[3]

Transitional paragraphs conclude or summarize one idea and introduce another,
often through the use of questions.

Transitional Paragraphs in Content Area Textbooks

Example: Why were railroads important? The development of railroads brought many
changes. Rail transportation was much swifter than that provided by turn-
pikes and canals. People, therefore, could move more freely from one section
of the country to another, and products could be exchanged faster and in
greater quantity. By promoting commerce and industry railroads encouraged
the growth of cities. [Goes on to describe how railroads tied East and West
together.][4]

Example: If Indians pursued them, the Indians chose a good place of ambush, waited in
utter silence, and then pounced upon the Colonists and killed them. This
Indian use of ambush and guerilla tactics contrasted with European tactics of
open warfare and frontal assaults. [Goes on to say Colonists adopted Indian
methods.][5]

---

2. E. Moise and Downs, *Geometry* (Reading, Mass.: Addison-Wesley, 1975).
3. Saul Israel, Douglas L. Johnson, and Dennis Wood, *World Geography Today* (New York: Holt, Rinehart & Winston,
1976), p. v.
4. Raymond J. Wilson and George Spiero, *Liberty and Union* (Boston: Houghton Mifflin, 1972), p.   .
5. Lewis P. Todd and Merle Curti, *Rise of the American Nation* (New York: Harcourt Brace Jovanovich, 1977), p. 68.

Summarizing and concluding paragraphs serve as comprehension aids and as a means of review. Some of these paragraphs repeat major ideas, redefine terms, refer to important ideas given earlier or some combination of the three. The signals given in writing for the conclusion are the transition words used, such as *to sum up*, *it is easy to see*, *from this*, and *note that*.

Concluding Paragraphs in Content Area Textbooks

Example: Note that we have defined the interior of an angle as the intersection of two half-planes. One of these is the side of *AC* that contains *B* and the other is the side of *AB* that contains *C*.[6]

Example: From this brief description it is easy to see that the United States has very close economic ties with the Orient. In addition, we have close political and military ties with most of the non-Communist nations in the region. The Orient is becoming more and more important to the American people. This will become evident as we study each country in this vast and rich area.[7]

9. *Activity.* Have students identify the introductory types of paragraphs in their own textbook reading. Ask them to list the words and expressions that indicate a subject is being introduced, such as *in this book*, *the following*, and so on.

10. *Activity.* For their own writing, have students use the words and expressions they have identified in their reading to clearly introduce to readers the purpose of their writing. Pair off students to read one another's papers to find the stated purpose. If the purpose is not stated clearly, discuss with the class how it can be improved in the rewriting.

11. *Activity.* Ask students to identify transitional paragraphs in their textbook reading. Have students identify ideas that are linked as the transition is effected from one point to another. Lead students to understand that they must examine the paragraphs before and after the transitional paragraph in order to understand the points that are linked. The transitional paragraph introduces a new subtopic for the whole section, and the subtopic follows the transitional paragraph.

12. *Activity.* In their textbook reading have students identify summarizing and concluding paragraphs. Ask them to state the major concepts that are repeated from the whole section in the concluding paragraph. Ask students to locate in the section where the repeated major concept is originally presented. Does student understanding match the writer's conclusion? Discuss the logic involved in writing concluding paragraphs.

13. *Activity.* Have students identify words and expressions they find in summarizing and concluding paragraphs, such as *it is seen from the above*, *from this*, *to sum up*, and so on. How do these words signal the reader as to the writer's intentions?

14. *Activity.* In their own writing, have students be aware of expressing clarity of their purpose in the kinds of paragraphs they use. Ask students to label introductory, transitional, and concluding paragraphs. Project examples of student paragraphs on a screen to the class to teach effective writing of the kinds of paragraphs. Discuss purpose, signal words, and clarity for the readers of their writing.

---

6. E. Moise and Downs, *Geometry.*
7. Israel et al., *World Geography Today*, Chap. 31.

Topic II: Understanding and Developing Unity in Paragraphs

1. *Teacher Presentation.* Present and explain to students the concept of unity in their compositions. Unity pertains to singleness of idea, that all the points support one central idea. One paragraph is separated from another because each has one central point to make. All of the sentences in a paragraph, therefore, should develop and relate to that one main point. If they do not, then the paragraph is not unified. Unity is achieved when all the sentences talk about the one main idea within a paragraph. Each sentence can develop the sentence that states the main idea, or else sentences can further explain each other. Many paragraphs have the first or the last sentence state clearly the main idea and all the other sentences descend from that major sentence.

2. *Activity.* An excellent, classroom-tested device for teaching unity in expository paragraphs is the *controlling statement* (see Resources at end of chapter) by Mrs. Leslie Zorko, assistant professor at University of Wyoming. The controlling statement is the viewpoint that the topic is going to take. It controls the direction of student writing and unifies all the sentences toward that direction. The composition consists of three parts, as in the following:

1. idea	subject to be written about
2. viewpoint	what there is to say about the subject

3. key terms—two or more
   a.
   b.
   c.
	reasons or support for the idea and viewpoint

Write on the blackboard an idea to be developed in the subject area. An example in science would be the following:

erosion

Ask students to provide a viewpoint for this idea. Write on the blackboard a viewpoint students might express, such as the following:

Erosion causes land formations.

erosion	idea
causes land formations	viewpoint

Explain to students that the viewpoint restricts the general idea of erosion and that it provides a direction for the paragraph that the other sentences can take for unity. The key terms can answer the question *Why?* and can begin with a unifying word *because,* as in the following examples:

because the wind is a powerful eroding force that shapes land

because rain is another force of erosion that changes the land

because different soils react to erosion to cause varying formations

Ask students to use the topic sentence (idea plus viewpoint) to make a complete sentence for each *because* phrase, as in the following:

Erosion causes land formations because the wind is a powerful eroding force that shapes land.

Erosion causes land formations because rain is another force of erosion that changes the land.

Erosion causes land formations because different soils react to erosion to cause varying formations.

3. *Activity.* Ask students to combine the three sentences of Activity 2 into one longer topic sentence. Tell them to leave out some repeating words and use commas where needed. Have each student read aloud the sentence he or she creates. Discuss how the three ideas are combined into one topic sentence. Write some of the sentences on the board and point out redundancy and punctuation problems.

> *Example:*   Erosion causes land formations because the wind, the rain, and different soils
> create varying formations.

4. *Activity.* Reproduce and distribute Reproduction Page 7–1. Assign an idea (a noun) in the content area. Ask students to create a viewpoint of their own for the idea and to write it on the Reproduction Page. Have them list three key terms all beginning with *because* (reasons) to develop the topic (idea plus viewpoint). Ask students to write out a five-sentence paragraph using the first as the topic sentence, the next three to provide reasons to develop the topic, and the fifth sentence as the conclusion to sum up the paragraph. Discuss how the paragraph is unified in that all sentences develop one main point and have a singleness of idea.

5. *Activity.* Mrs. Zorko, who developed the controlling-statement technique, suggests that this device can lend itself easily to learning how to outline. Reproduce and distribute Reproduction Page 7–2. Explain the organization of the topic sentence.

Popsicles	idea
are refreshing	viewpoint
because they are cool	key terms
because they are flavorful	
because they are colorful	

Have students outline their paragraphs from Activity 4 in the same manner using the format of Reproduction Page 7–2. Ask two or three students to write their outlines on the blackboard to share with the class. Discuss the organization, unity, and logic of the paragraph when it is presented in outline form. If the ideas do not fit easily into outline form, then unity or organization may be missing in the paragraph and the student should analyze it to find the problems.

6. *Activity.* Reproduce and distribute Reproduction Page 7–3. In class discussion help students develop the format for answering an essay question on a test in the subject areas. The idea and viewpoint are already given to students in the question. They

must supply the key terms (the *becauses*) to complete the topic sentence. Once students understand the format for developing an essay question, they can fill in the details and elaborate on them as fully as they know how.

7. *Activity.* Reproduce and distribute Reproduction Page 7-4. Have students practice writing the idea plus viewpoint plus key terms for each "essay question." Discuss and write some examples on the board. In the subject area, present other essay topics to students and show them how the controlling-statement technique may be used to develop a unified composition of topic sentence, details or reasons, and a conclusion. Tell students that a longer composition of several paragraphs may have the same unity as a single paragraph in that the first paragraph may state the topic in more detail, the following paragraphs may develop each point more specifically, and the last paragraph may serve as a conclusion. The same structure is maintained and there is unity from paragraph to paragraph throughout the longer composition.

8. *Activity.* Unity may be achieved by using a certain order of details in a composition. Reproduce and distribute Reproduction Page 7-5. Instead of using *because* to introduce the key terms that give reasons, other kinds of order may be used, such as spatial, comparison, or procedural. Ask students to write a five-sentence paragraph in the subject area using a topic sentence (idea plus viewpoint), three sentences using three key terms in a specified order (given on the Reproduction Page 7-5), and a conclusion sentence. Have students read aloud their paragraphs. Discuss how the order used helps to provide a unity for the topic.

9. *Activity.* Reproduce and distribute to students Reproduction Page 7-6. Form small groups and have each group discuss the probable order to be used in each type of essay question for different content areas. Have them discuss and support their choices with the entire class.

10. *Activity.* Have each small group from Activity 9 write three key terms on a topic (idea plus viewpoint) in the subject area using a particular order. List several ideas (nouns) in the subject on the board and have each group choose an idea and develop a viewpoint for it. Then ask each group to list three or more key terms for the topic and to indicate the order used for the key terms. Collect each group's work, pass the papers to a different group, and have the groups critique each other. Have students summarize what is meant by unity in a composition.

Topic III: Understanding and Developing Cohesion in a Composition

1. *Teacher Presentation.* Review with students the concept of the paragraph as a diamond figure that has structure, expansion of ideas, and symmetry in its design. Discuss with students what they have learned about unity in a paragraph, which refers to singleness of idea and how it is achieved with a controlling statement and key terms. Now introduce to students the concept of **cohesion** in a paragraph, which refers to the relationship of the sentences to each other in the paragraph. Cohesion means the sentences "stick together" because they are connected by meaning and use certain devices to tie them together. When sentences are tied together into a meaningful whole, this becomes a **text**, a structured group of sentences that have unity and cohesion. Explain to students that there are several kinds

of ties in writing that link sentences together (see Halliday and Hasan in end-of-chapter Resources) but four of them are most common: reference (of pronouns to prior nouns), connector words, repeated words, and unstated information (ellipsis). All these cohesive ties exist in writing in all the content areas, but the unstated information is more dramatically recognized in math, home economics, and vocational arts, where procedural writing is used most. The following explains and applies the concepts of cohesive ties to the teaching of writing in all subject areas.

2. *Activity.* Discuss with students the following examples of reference as a cohesive tie in text.

> *Example:* Andrew Johnson was a self-educated man. Without any formal schooling, he had spent his boyhood as a tailor's apprentice. Later his devoted wife had helped him to improve his meager writing ability. While still a young man, he was elected mayor of his community, a small mountain village in eastern Tennessee. This was the beginning of a political career that took him in 1857 to the Senate of the United States. Although he owned a few slaves, Johnson disliked the large planters who were so influential in the South, and he had resisted the secession of Tennessee in 1861.[8]

The use of reference links every sentence in this paragraph into a cohesive unit clearly dealing with one topic only, that of Andrew Johnson's life. Every sentence refers to Johnson through the pronouns *he* or *him.* There is no ambiguity or confusion as to which noun every pronoun refers to. The use of *this* in the fifth sentence is also a reference tie to the preceding statement, "he was elected mayor," the main clause of that sentence. This tie requires the reader to use inferential skills because it is much more implicit in its reference than the pronouns *he* and *him,* which are explicit.

3. *Activity.* Reproduce and distribute Reproduction Page 7-7. Have students write out the referent for the pronouns given in the two passages. Explain to students that their skill in identifying references affects their reading comprehension as well as clear communication in their own writing.

4. *Activity.* Reproduce and distribute Reproduction Page 7-8. Have students match pronouns and nouns according to number and gender.

5. *Activity.* On Reproduction Page 7-8, discuss with students how reference of pronouns to their antecedents makes a text coherent. How are relationships set up between one item and another, and why are the relationships valuable? Explain that they associate ideas and tie points together.

6. *Activity.* In their own writing, have students identify references and associations of ideas. Have students change the number and/or gender of pronouns they have written and then read the text aloud. Discuss how meaning is distorted and lost for the reader.

7. *Teacher Presentation.* Discuss with students the concept of using connector words as cohesive ties in composition. The following examples illustrate this.

---

8. Lewis P. Todd and Merle Curti, *Rise of the American Nation* (New York: Harcourt Brace Jovanovich, 1977), p. 359.

Example: Although in 1914 American sympathies were divided, the great majority of Americans hoped for an Allied victory. However, most Americans supported the President's policy of neutrality and prayed for an early end to the war.[9]

Example: Appetizers are the tasty tidbits designed to tantalize the appetite before a meal. Serving them is simple. As a first course before dinner, arrange them on salad or dessert plates and place on service or dinner plates. If you plan to pass them with beverages in the living room before the meal, arrange on large trays or platters. Group all of a kind together. Pass them once or twice, then let guests help themselves.[10]

8. *Activity.* Using Reproduction Page 7-9, have students locate the connector words used in passages in their own textbooks. Have them determine the function of the connective tie according to the types listed on the chart. What does the connector do? Does it add information, develop logical order, or provide a contrast?

9. *Activity.* Using Reproduction Page 7-9 again, have students explain how the sentence in which the connector is used relates to its preceding sentence. How do the connectors tie the two sentences together in meaning?

10. *Activity.* On Reproduction Page 7-10 have students fill in the listed connector words that make sense in the text given. Discuss the reasons for their choices as to their understanding of the function of the tie.

11. *Activity.* Have students fill in connector words they think of in the recipe directions on Reproduction Page 7-11. What functions do the words provide? Is meaning made clearer when the ties are used?

12. *Activity.* Using Reproduction Page 7-12, have students identify the connectors used and the function each has in relating one sentence to another in meaning.

13. *Activity.* Have students identify and practice using connector words in their own writing. Ask them to explain the functions of the connectors they use.

14. *Teacher Presentation.* Present the concept to students that repetition of words can be a cohesive tie. Read the following passage aloud to students and have them identify the repeated words from sentence to sentence:

Example: The Babylonians used extensive libraries of clay tablets, with many kinds of number facts recorded on them, to solve problems. Babylonian scribes made wedge-shaped symbols for numbers on soft clay tablets. The tablet became a permanent record after it was allowed to dry and harden. Clay tablets were used instead of the papyrus scrolls of Egypt, and they were, in fact, made from the same basic material as that used in the construction of homes and public buildings. The several hundred tablets discovered that relate to mathematics are frequently "text tablets" that state problems as well as their step-by-step solutions, or "problem tablets" that contain long lists of problems to be solved. The libraries, or "tablet houses" where the tablets were catalogued and stored, also served as the training place for scribes.[11]

9. Ibid., p. 531.
10. *Better Homes and Gardens Cookbook* (Des Moines, Iowa: Meredith Pub. Co., 1953), p. 62.
11. Franklin Math Series, *Mathematics: Man's Key to Progress* (East Millstone, New Jersey: 1969).

The repetition used ties one item back to another and is related to it. The repetition comes in repeating the original word or by using a synonym or near synonym. This repetition serves as the cohesive agent in the text and provides its texture or unity.

15. *Activity.* Using Reproduction Page 7-13, have students identify all synonyms and the original noun to which the synonyms refer in each of the passages. For example, *Californians* in the first passage has five repetitions and synonyms (five blanks), and Chicago has six (six blanks for students).

16. *Activity.* Have students find in their own textbook writing examples of repeated words and use of synonyms. Have them write these down. Ask students to supply from their own imaginations five more synonyms to add to the ones given.

17. *Activity.* On Reproduction Page 7-14, have students write a parody of the poem given by providing a synonym of the same syllable length for every underlined word. Have students recopy the poem in its entirety as they provide their own words in order to experience its style, rhythm, and meter.

18. *Activity.* In their own writing, have students underline the repetitions of key words and concepts they make from sentence to sentence. Have them provide synonyms for the nouns they use, and discuss subtle changes in meaning that synonyms provide. See Chapter 6 for further vocabulary exercises in developing sensitivity to synonyms.

19. *Activity.* Divide students into groups. Ask each group to write out explicit, step-by-step directions on how to make a peanut-butter-and-jelly sandwich. Ask them to write down every decision involved (wheat or white bread, strawberry or blueberry jelly, and so on) and every step to be undertaken. This precision of detail should impress on students how elliptical is their approach to everyday tasks. They assume steps already known; but in writing directions to a reader who doesn't know (how to make a peanut-butter-and-jelly sandwich), the writer cannot assume all the hidden steps are known, so they must be communicated.

20. *Activity.* Using Reproduction Page 7-15, have students fill in all the unstated steps a person would have to know in order to bake the pecan pie. Have students begin from the very beginning, such as "get butter from the refrigerator and sugar from the pantry," on to "measure the sugar, break the eggs into a bowl," and so forth. Have students write out each step so that they have practice in communicating a process and stating directions to a reader. Help students to recognize the complexity of giving explicit information and communicating in a procedural style.

21. *Activity.* Using Reproduction Page 7-16, have students write out every detail that a person must understand in order to complete the equation problem. Impress on students how much understanding and knowledge in the problem that the writer assumes the reader already knows.

22. *Activity.* In their own writing, have students be explicit in giving directions for a process, such as how to drive a car or make a report of an experiment in science. Have them fill in steps for the inexperienced reader they should write for.

ASSESSING ACHIEVEMENT OF OBJECTIVES

Ongoing Evaluation

The extent to which students have mastered concepts of paragraph structure, unity, and cohesion can be measured by having them submit for evaluation the products of Activities.

Final Evaluation

For an overall evaluation of students' abilities to use the concepts of paragraph structure, unity, and cohesion, assign a five-paragraph composition based on the following principles to be evaluated by students and teacher:

1. Does the introductory paragraph contain a clear idea plus viewpoint?

2. Does each of the three middle paragraphs express a key term that develops and elaborates on the idea plus viewpoint?

3. Is there a summarizing paragraph that refers to the idea plus viewpoint and to the key terms?

4. Can cohesive ties be identified within the paragraphs and between the paragraphs? Are students able to identify the ties they have used to provide cohesion, such as reference, connector words, and repetition, particularly?

5. In revising their compositions, are students able to rewrite according to the principles of structure, unity, and cohesion? Is there a difference between the initial drafts and their revisions in their employment of the principles learned?

6. In discussion, can students express the *purpose* of the principles learned regarding structure, unity, and cohesion, and do they appreciate how these principles help them to communicate more clearly?

RESOURCES FOR TEACHING THE PARAGRAPH

Below is a selected and annotated list of resources useful for teaching the subject matter in this chapter. Resources are from journal articles and from books.

Braddock, Richard. "The Frequency and Placement of Topic Sentences in Expository Prose." *Research in the Teaching of English*. (Winter, 1974), 287–302. The study "disproves" the century-old teaching that every expository paragraph has a topic sentence and that the topic sentence is usually the first sentence. His findings in analyzing twenty-five contemporary essays in magazines were (1) that only 55 percent of the paragraphs written by professional writers had explicit topic sentences and (2) that there were different types of topic sentences such as the *assembled*, the *delayed-completion*, and the *inferred*. The article is well worth reading for understanding some of the complexities and subtleties of writing paragraphs.

Christensen, Francis. "A Generative Rhetoric of the Paragraph." *College Composition and Communication*. 16:3 (October, 1965). The article deals with the *cumulative* paragraph, built on a sequence of sentences structurally related. Many examples are provided to illustrate the concepts presented. Sequencing in coordinate and subordinate structure is elaborately defined, detailed, and exemplified.

Cohan, Carol. "Writing Effective Paragraphs." *College Composition and Communication.* 27 (December, 1976). The article proposes teaching the paragraph by considering that the topic sentence implies a question to be answered by the rest of the paragraph. Once the question is posed, students are ready to provide the supporting answers to the question. Useful concepts in many content area expository writing assignments are given. The article details the procedure to be used.

Halliday, M.A.K., and Hasan, R. *Cohesion in English.* London: Longmans Group, 1976. This book presents a fascinating study of textual semantic relations useful in teaching writing as well as reading. The semantic relations provide the clues to understanding text and are the elements that link ideas together. Five such elements of cohesion presented are reference, substitution, ellipsis, conjunction, and lexical repetition. Each is explained in detail, including examples and the theoretical concepts behind them.

Robinson, H. Alan. "Paragraph Functions." *Teaching Reading and Study Strategies.* Boston: Allyn and Bacon, 1978. The book details in Chapter 7 the functions and descriptions of different types of paragraphs. The paragraph function is dependent on the writer's intention. Although Robinson addresses the problems of reading different types of paragraphs, the definitions and exercises for teaching paragraph functions are easily transformed to writing problems. The difficulties lie in the communication problems involved for both reader and writer. Excellent suggestions are presented for the secondary content area teacher, along with examples, strategies, and other references.

Stern, Arthur A. "When Is a Paragraph?" *College Composition and Communication.* 27 (October, 1976). This article details an experiment with students in deciding when to paragraph based on intuition and preconceptions about paragraphing. Discussions proceed on notions of paragraphing proposed by various spokespeople: Bain, Christensen, Becker, Rodgers, and Braddock. The approach to teaching the paragraph is based on content rather than on structure.

Zorko, Leslie. *Composition with a Controlling Statement.* Laramie: University of Wyoming, Center for Research, Service and Publication, 1981. This teacher-resource booklet explains in great detail how to teach the controlling-statement technique for paragraph writing to secondary students. The many helpful examples are actual student writing samples that were obtained when this technique was taught in the classroom. Included are ideas for single- and multiple-paragraph compositions, outlining, and term papers. The content area teacher will find this a valuable reference book.

8

Sentence Variety

CONTENT OVERVIEW

The teaching of writing concerns teaching putting language together, putting words together into meaningful sentences and sentences together into comprehensible texts. Students have a strong sense of their own language and are able to make meaning with what they say or write. The task of the teacher of writing is to instruct students in the options open to them to vary their expression for best use of their already developed sense of words, sentences, and larger texts. One way to teach the options and to build on student knowledge is to provide sentence-combining practice for students. Not only is it interesting and can be fun for students, but it allows them to manipulate and experiment with their own language, creating patterns and meanings that allow them to express themselves with more complexity and richness of texture. Teaching students to give their sentences texture involves teaching them the process of addition or modification of the basic information they want to express. This addition or modification process can be of several types: coordination, subordination, and embedding of related phrases, clauses, and word modifiers in sentences. In other words, sentence-combining practice helps students to learn sentence variety, which is necessary for their growth in composition. It will help them grow syntactically—in understanding sentence structures—and semantically—learning how meanings are affected by use of words in context. Students can measure their own growth when they are taught a system of sentence weighting, a numerical weighting that indicates degree of elaboration and modification.

OBJECTIVES

As a result of the learning experiences in this chapter, students should be able to:

1. Understand that sentence parts may be manipulated in order to create variety in expression and to develop style.

2. Develop greater elaboration of ideas in sentences by building *texture* or adding to the *text*.

3. Use the processes of coordination, subordination, and embedding to develop texture in their writing.

4. Combine related ideas into one sentence for more fluency and more mature sentence construction.

5. Realize that language manipulation creates changes in emphasis and in meaning in texts.

6. Move around the phrases, clauses, and word modifiers in sentences so that they may manipulate the language.

7. Recognize that there are different kinds of describer parts for different ideas in a sentence and that placement of these parts is important.

8. Use the cues to combine sentences for practice and for learning sentence variety.

9. Transfer what they learned from cued exercises to open exercises that provide no cues.

10. Apply the concepts of sentence combining to their own whole-text compositions.

11. Edit and revise their own writing in terms of elaboration and complexity in expression.

12. Understand their own language much more thoroughly through actually using it and manipulating it rather than by solely analyzing it grammatically. *

Optional

13. Evaluate the degree of complexity and elaboration in sentences with the sentence weighting system.

14. Develop greater maturity and fluency in their own writing by monitoring the growth indexed with sentence weighting.

LEARNING EXPERIENCES

Topic I: Understanding and Developing Texture in Sentences

1. *Teacher Presentation.* Explain to students that there are many different ways to create a sentence as a basic subject, but it can be presented with much elaboration or with none. Students can write a sentence with texture giving it richness and density because much development of the basic subject has been provided. Most of their sentences have a "thin texture" (to use a term coined by Francis Christensen) because the idea is not given elaboration. These exercises will give them practice in developing texture or adding to the text, to enable them to develop variety in expression. Understanding how to create sentence variety will allow students to develop style and effectiveness.

2. *Activity.* Teach students the process of coordination as a method for developing texture. Write the following sentences on the blackboard for students to read:

John went to the store.

He bought a loaf of bread.

Ask students to combine the related ideas in the two sentences into one sentence. Tell them that these are two very simple sentences that you want them to combine so that the one resulting sentence will sound more mature. Have students read aloud what they produce. There will be a variety of ways the sentences can be combined, and they will probably all be correct English sentences. The task here, however, is to understand how to coordinate the idea, so ask students to rewrite their sentences, combining the ideas with the coordinator *and*. The simplest coordination is to connect one subject and two verbs with *and: John went to the store and bought a loaf of bread.* Another type of coordination students may produce is that of connecting two clauses (two subjects and two verbs): *John went to the store, and he bought a loaf of bread.* The idea of *coordination* is to join two ideas and make them equal (*co* means equal). The sentence that results from the two sentences being combined has more texture because more information is provided for the basic subject. The process of coordination is one way to develop texture.

3. *Activity.* Teach students the process of subordination as a method of developing texture. This process is fun because it has so many interesting varieties of ways it can be used. Sentence combining in this process will be much more diverse. Using the two sentences from Activity 2, ask students to write them as one sentence but not to use *and* to connect the ideas.

John went to the store.

He bought a loaf of bread.

Students have many options open to them. Probably all of the sentences they form will be correct English. The process will involve making one sentence subordinate (*sub* means under) to the other, which means it will describe or add information to the main sentence. Some varieties students may produce are the following:

John went to the store to buy a loaf of bread.

When John went to the store, he bought a loaf of bread.

To buy a loaf of bread, John went to the store.

All of these sentences show subordination of one of the original sentences to the main sentence. The first two sentences subordinate one sentence into a describer phrase, and the third sentence subordinates one sentence into a describer clause. The main point in this exercise is to have students enjoy all the possibilities of sentence manipulation and to experiment with rearranging sentence parts. Students should be encouraged positively in their creations. Subordination is another technique students should understand for creating texture.

4. *Activity.* Teach students the process of embedding as a method for developing texture and sentence variety. To embed is to take relevant describers and place them next to an idea they describe. Add a third sentence to the two in the above activities that students have been using.

John went to the store.

He bought a loaf of bread.

It was whole wheat.

Ask students to combine these three related sentences, which are childish sentences, into one longer, more mature-sounding sentence. Tell them to have fun putting the sentences all together and assure them that there is no one "correct" way to combine them. Their responses should be diverse. Some possibilities are the following:

John went to the store to buy a loaf of whole wheat bread.

When John went to the store, he bought a loaf of whole wheat bread.

Whenever John bought a loaf of whole wheat bread, he went to the store.

John bought a loaf of bread, which was whole wheat, when he went to the store.

Discuss changes in *emphasis* and in *meaning* when different sentence parts are shifted around. These changes are important to consider in order to make meaning clear in writing. The embedding occurred when the describers in the third sentence were positioned next to the thing they described, the bread. The embedding was of single word modifiers in the first three sample sentences, but it was in the form of a modifying clause in the fourth sentence. Each modifier, though, is placed next to the thing it modifies in order to make the best sense. Have students understand that embedding of describers adds texture to a sentence because it develops the idea more fully for the reader.

5. *Activity.* Ask students to find examples of these processes of creating texture in sentences in their own textbooks. Have them copy out on paper the sentences that use coordination, subordination, and embedding of describers. Copying the sentences will give students practice in writing them and in "experiencing" them tactilely for reinforcement. Ask students to read the sentences aloud to the class after they have written them so that then they hear how effective sentences sound. Have students identify in each of the sentences read aloud which of the three processes was used to develop the idea, to create the texture, and to express an effective sentence.

6. *Activity.* Ask students to find examples of sentences that use these three processes in their own writing. Have them refer to test papers or compositions they wrote earlier. Tell students to underline the sentences they find and discuss which processes they used. Have students locate simple-sounding, short sentences in their writing. Tell them to try combining some of the sentences in their own writing to make them more complex and to create denser texture. Have students read aloud first their short sentences and then their combined sentences, and discuss with them which is the more effective expression. How does combining sentences change the style of their writing?

7. *Activity.* Have students exchange their papers with each other in pairs. Ask the students to read through the entire composition first, then locate sentences that they think could be rewritten into a combined form to be more effective. Tell students to copy out the original sentences and then to rewrite them using the three processes of coordination, subordination, and embedding. Have students discuss with each other the rewritten sentences and all the possibilities for combining them. Discuss with students their discoveries about language manipulation.

8. *Activity.* To sum up, discuss with students the concepts they have learned and practiced. Have them define the concept of texture, of adding elaboration and information to ideas in a sentence. Discuss the differences between a thin and a dense texture for development of ideas in a sentence and why elaboration is needed

for reader comprehension. Is there danger of confusing the reader with too much information in a sentence? The writer must be careful to give enough but not too much information in the sentences. Practice in sentence combining can help students discover how much elaboration is effective.

Topic II: Practicing Sentence Combining

1. *Teacher Presentation.* There are several approaches to teaching sentence combining. One is called the *open* system, and another is termed the *cued* approach. The open system is not cued or directed as to how the combining is to be performed. The student is free to combine in any way that appears logical and allows experience in language manipulation, organization, and options for expression. I believe the cued system should first be presented to young, developing writers to give them guidance in learning options that they may later use in the open exercises, which are more difficult without prior guidance. Explain to students that in order to learn to write effectively and to develop an individual style, they should be aware of how style is created. Learning and practicing sentence combining should open their eyes to awareness of style. The following activities proceed from the cued system to the open approach. Since composition involves the principles of addition and extension of ideas, the exercises will be geared toward creation of longer discourse forms such as whole paragraphs so that students may get a feel for sentence variety within the whole text and the compaction of ideas within different sentences. What is to be emphasized in the cued system is the practice in language manipulation and *not* the terminology used. Secondary students should be familiar with most of the grammar terms used, but the terms are not the point; the practice is.

2. *Activity.* Have students read a full paragraph together in their textbook. Select a sentence and ask students to rewrite it in some other way. Have students read aloud their rewritten sentence and discuss how it changes the meaning and the style of what has originally been said. Is one version better than another? Why? Have students discover for themselves that sentences can be varied and expressed in different ways for different purposes. This exercise should raise their awareness that language can be manipulated if one knows how to do it. Students will discover that they know more about their own language than they thought.

3. *Activity.* Reproduce and distribute to students Reproduction Page 8-1, which uses repetition as a cue to combine. Do the examples with the students to show them how the combining is performed by using the repeated phrase and the signal word in the parentheses. Ask students for any questions or problems they may have understanding what they are to do. Assign the sentences for students to manipulate using the cues. Have students write out their own sentences following the combined one. Ask them to read aloud their sentences. Ask students if their own sentences were affected by the combining exercise, that is, if their own sentences were more complex than they usually write them. Does there seem to be a carryover effect?

4. *Activity.* Reproduce and distribute to students Reproduction Page 8-2, which teaches combining with phrases. Cue phrases are underlined and cue words are in parentheses. Do the example sentences with students for practice and for their clear understanding of what to do. Then, assign the rest of the sentences to students.

The last exercise is for students to develop into a paragraph of several (five or six) sentences. Have students read their paragraphs aloud to the class. Discuss the style and the development of their sentences. Can the sentences be improved further?

5. *Activity.* Have students practice further language manipulation by rewriting and revising some of their own sentences in the paragraph on Reproduction Page 8-2. Collect their paragraphs and evaluate their sentences according to development of the basic ideas with elaboration. Display some of their sentences for student discussion and analysis. Read aloud some of the students' paragraphs so that they may discuss sentence variety and effectiveness within the whole text. How do sentences sound in relationship to each other? Do some sentences seem too choppy and always begin with subject and verb? Can phrases be added or rearranged in sentences to provide some diversity? Discuss style and language variation with students.

6. *Activity.* Explain to students that because sentences have different parts to them, the parts may be moved around to different positions in the sentence to create emphasis and to vary the style. One sentence part is a *clause*, which is a group of words with a subject and a verb. There is a main clause, but there are three kinds of subordinate clauses, noun, adjective and adverb, which act as describers of the main clause. These subordinate clauses add information and elaborate on the basic idea. One kind of modifier clause is a noun clause. In the following sentence pairs, the cues provided in parentheses after the first sentence will be used to introduce the noun clauses taken from the second sentence when both sentences are combined. Write these sentences on the board so students may understand how to create noun describer clauses:

a. The jockey said SOMETHING. (that)

b. The horse had a lame leg and could not run.

Ask students to combine the two short sentences into one longer, more complex sentence by substituting the noun clause introduced by *that* for the word *something*, so that the sentence becomes: *The jockey said that the horse had a lame leg and could not run.* The noun clause adds information to the main idea and creates a complex, fluent sentence, an indication of a more mature writer. Ask students to create their own sentences using noun clauses and to place some of the modifying clauses at the beginning of the sentence for variety. Ask students to combine these sentences:

a. SOMETHING made the children wonder. (how)

b. The kite flew so high in the sky.

In combining these sentences, students will place the noun clause at the beginning, which will help them realize that clause parts of a sentence may be moved around for diversity.

7. *Activity.* Another kind of describer clause is the *adjective*, which describes a noun (person, place, or thing) and is positioned right next to it in order to make sense Present the following cued sentences to students on the blackboard for them to combine in order to learn how to use adjective clauses:

a. The traffic officer yelled at the driver. (who)

   The driver ran the red light.

b. The two books were misplaced. (which)

The two books were mystery stories.

c. The tea kettle was black with soot. (that)

The tea kettle sat on the back burner.

Have students read aloud their sentences and discuss positioning of the describer clauses. The describer should be placed right next to the noun it describes, but the different sentence parts may be moved around to make logical sense. Ask students to write ten more sentences of their own using adjective clauses beginning with *who, which,* or *that.* Discuss their sentences according to elaboration of the basic idea and the variety they create in manipulating sentence parts.

8. *Activity.* The last kind of describer clause is the *adverb,* which describes and adds information to verbs in a sentence. Present the following sentences to students to combine:

a. The car stopped. (after)

The engine conked out.

b. The ball game was postponed. (when)

The rain flooded the fields.

c. John avoids candy bars. (because)

He had three cavities last month.

Have students read aloud their sentences, and discuss placement of the adverb clauses. Some of the adverb clauses can be at the beginning of the sentence and still make sense. The clauses can be moved around to change the emphases because the beginning of the sentence would get the most emphasis. Discuss with students the concept of location of describers and how they may be manipulated for diversity, style, and emphasis. Ask students to write their own sentences to create a paragraph for one of the topics presented in the above sentences. Ask them to use adverb clauses in some of their sentences. Have students read aloud their paragraphs to the class and ask the class to identify sentences with adverb clauses.

9. *Activity.* Explain to students that other parts of the sentence that may be moved around to create variety and to give additional information to the main ideas are phrases. *Phrases* are groups of words that serve as describers of main ideas. There are four kinds of phrases—prepositional, participial, infinitive, and gerund phrases—but terminology is not the important matter in learning to use phrases. Rather, the focus in language manipulation and in composition should be on the practice of using sentence parts, not in labeling them. Because secondary students have probably heard the terminology before, it may not be threatening to them to use it in teaching phrases, but this is the choice of the teacher. Present the following sentences on the blackboard for students to combine using the underlined cues:

(Prepositional phrase)

a. The pitcher threw the ball.

The ball was thrown <u>to third base</u>.

b. The umpire called the pitch a strike.

(Write in a phrase describing the umpire)

(Participial phrase—used as an adjective)

a. The musician performed professionally.

The musician is <u>playing the cello</u> .

b. The dancer was applauded by the audience.

(Write in an *ing* phrase describing the dancer)

*(Infinitive phrase—*To *plus verb)*

a. The team reviewed the play patterns.

The patterns were <u>to be used in the next game</u> .

b. Jane decided SOMETHING.

(Cross out SOMETHING and add a phrase with *To* plus verb)

*(Gerund phrase—*ing, *used as a noun)*

a. Bob's best sport is SOMETHING.

He enjoys <u>playing soccer</u> .

b. SOMETHING made Susan feel guilty.

(Drop SOMETHING and add an *ing* phrase)

Have students read aloud their sentences and discuss them with the class. Ask students to write several sentences on one of the topics presented in the above sentences. Ask them to underline the phrases they use in their sentences. Collect the paragraphs and evaluate them on the use of phrases they use. Have students rewrite their sentences if they use too few phrases in order to expand and elaborate on their main ideas.

10. *Activity.* Ask students to suggest a noun (such as *student, chair, dog,* and so on) and write it on the board. Then ask students to supply as many describers of that noun as they can create. List those on the board under the noun as students give them. Remind students that these describers are adjectives that add information to the basic idea and should be used in sentences to expand ideas and provide variety. Similarly, ask students to supply a verb (such as *run* or *swim*), then list the describers of the verbs as students provide them. Remind students that these describers —adverbs—add information and create variety in sentences. Building sentences with describer clauses, phrases, and word modifiers is learning to compose—to write for reader comprehension and clarity of information.

11. *Activity.* Ask students to read a passage in their textbooks and find examples of the uses of describer clauses, phrases, and words. Discuss with students how sentences are built and that these describers are important to style of sentences and to fluency (so that the sentences just seem to flow). Ask students to identify what each describer describes. Have students copy out the passage onto their own papers for

practice in writing whole sentences that use describers and that are professionally written by the textbook author. Ask students to underline the describers they find.

12. *Activity*. With the background and practice students have had with the preceding cued sentences, present to them the open exercise on Reproduction Page 8-3. Reproduce and distribute to students Reproduction Page 8-3, which is a whole text grouped into suggested sentence clusters. The exercise is from William Strong's book, which emphasizes whole-text, open exercises. Ask students to combine orally the first four sentences, which are grouped together because they all relate to one main idea. Then have students combine the remaining clusters on their own, but have them collaborate in pairs or groups. Have them read aloud the whole text when they finish, and discuss different sentence arrangements students create. Write different sentence versions on the board and have students discuss which they like better, which are more effective, and why. When students are satisfied with the combined sentences, ask each student to write out the entire text in paragraph form to get practice in whole composition and to recognize variety in sentences. The paragraph will be similar to the following example.

Rock Concert

The singer was young and swarthy as he stepped into the red spotlight. His unbuttoned shirt bared his chest. The sounds of guitars, drums, and screaming girls ballooned around him. He nodded and winked to his guitarist, who responded with the beat. As the singer became animated, with legs like rubber, jerking body, and head thrown back, he wailed a shout into the microphone at his lips. His twisting movements were strobed with floodlights. His voice a loud garble, the auditorium swirled with "heavy" rock.[1]

There will be many variations by students on these sentence arrangements. The point here is for students to experiment with their language as they manipulate the sentence parts. Have students refer to the cued sentences they have practiced for ideas on ways to combine using clauses, phrases, and word modifiers. Discuss where punctuation may be needed to make sentences clear. The commas and periods will be included naturally by most students, so discuss why the punctuation is needed. For further exercises on open combining of whole texts, refer to William Strong's book (see Resources at end of chapter).

13. *Activity*. Ask students to write a second paragraph of five to six sentences for the paragraph they wrote for Reproduction Page 8-3 about the rock concert. Ask them to write it from the first person point of view using *I*, in other words, as though they were there watching the concert themselves. Have students read aloud and discuss their own creations in terms of sentence construction, amount of elaboration used, and variety of sentences. How do their sentences compare in length and use of description to the combined ones in the first paragraph? Have students exchange their papers with each other in pairs to discuss how their sentences may be rewritten or changed to be more effective. Have students rewrite the sentences they wish to change, combine, or add to with elaboration. Collect their paragraphs and evaluate their sentences according to the amount of description they use in sentences and to the complexity of their sentences.

---

1. From *Sentence Combining* by William Strong, p. 40. Copyright © 1973 by Random House, Inc. Reprinted by permission of the publisher.

Topic III: Evaluating Sentences

This section is optional and may be of interest only to teachers of English.

1. *Teacher Presentation.* Because composition is the process of addition and elaboration of an idea, it is logical that measurement of growth in writing would involve assessing the degree of elaboration used. The extent to which an idea is developed depends on how much information is given to the basic subject and verb, that is, how many describers or modifiers are used to build the information. Maturity in writing can be measured according to this assessment. To assess description and elaboration used, a system called *sentence weights* (see DiStefano and Howie in resources at end of chapter) may be used. It may be used by only the teacher to evaluate growth in writing, or it may be taught to mature high school and college students who are very knowledgeable and secure in English so that they may evaluate their own writing. A teacher would have to judge the students and decide whether or not they could grasp the system.

   Sentence weights provides an index to complexity of sentences and to degree of modification used for the basic subject and verb. A sentence without any modifiers is called a *base sentence.* The modifiers expand the base sentence with words, phrases, and subordinate clauses (see Topic II). The processes used to expand base sentences with modifiers are the embedding, coordinating, and subordinating processes explained in Topic I. Sentence weights give a numerical index to the degree of modification a writer uses and indicates the growth of composing. Numerical Sentence Weights are found by the following method:

   a. Find the base clause (that is, subject plus verb plus objects) and give the major words a weight of 1.

   b. Find all the modifiers of the base clause and weight them with a 2.

   c. Modifiers of the weight 2 words receive a weight of 3 and so on.

   d. Exclude prepositions and articles.

   e. Add all numbers together and divide by the number of words used in each sentence.

   The number established for the sentence is its indication of how extensively ideas are developed and, compared to a composition written before sentence combining is taught, can give a measure of the effectiveness of sentence-building practice. It is recommended that only a sampling, perhaps the first ten or so, of sentences in a student composition be evaluated per paper if an entire class set is being assessed. The sampling will be faster and will give an indication of the sentence weight index for the entire class.

2. *Activity.* The following sentences provide an example of how the processes of embedding, coordinating, and subordinating can increase the complexity and degree of modification in composition. Present these familiar sentences on the blackboard to students:

   John went to the store.

   He bought a loaf of bread.

   It was whole wheat.

Following the rules for weighting the sentences, number the base sentences and their modifiers thus:

1   1   2

John went to the store.

1   1   1   2

He bought a loaf of bread

1 1 2   1

It was whole wheat.

Ask students to add the numbers and divide the sum by the number of words used for the numbering:

$$\frac{1.27 \text{ average sentence weight}}{11 \text{ words } \overline{)\ 14 \text{ count}}}$$

Write this (or another) combined sentence on the board for students to weight.

2   2   2   3 1 1   1   4   3   2

When John went to the store, he bought a loaf of whole wheat bread.

The sentence weight for this more difficult sentence is the following:

$$\frac{2.1 \text{ average sentence weight}}{10 \text{ words } \overline{)\ 21 \text{ count}}}$$

The more complex sentence has a larger numerical sentence weight because its degree of elaboration and modification is greater than in any of the three simple sentences. The larger sentence weight number indicates a more complex sentence structure and expression of ideas.

3. *Activity.* Have students form small groups and numerically evaluate sentences from their own writing. As they work in groups, ask students to combine and develop some of their sentences with words, phrases and subordinate clauses. Then assess those sentences to see if there is an increase in sentence weights from their original writing to the revised composition.

4. *Activity.* Using their textbooks, have students numerically weight the sentences used in the book. Ask students to compare the sentence weights in their own writing to the weights they find in their textbook writing. If the weights are close, then the textbook is probably well matched to students' language abilities.

5. *Activity.* Present this passage to very advanced students for them to analyze for meaning and to weight sentence complexity. The passage was written by Arthur Schlesinger.

> This intransigence on Vietnam—the persistence of the illusions that the Vietcong were the spearhead of a planned Chinese offensive; that American withdrawal would beckon Moscow and Peking into a "vacuum of power," as if Hanoi did not have the most stable government in the area; that if we did not stand where we had no business being, our adversaries would suppose we would not stand where our vital interests were engaged; that unanimity behind the policy could have gained us a victory we could not win on the battlefield; that negotiations which asked the other side for unconditional surrender had any chance of success—was President Johnson's tragic failure, just as his authentic and

moving concern about racial injustice and poverty at home was his supreme strength. In domestic policy, his knowledge was great and his instincts were sure; in foreign policy, he was rigid, dogmatic and ignorant. The irony of his presidency is that he righteously sacrificed the things he knew best on the altar of the things he knew worst.[2]

ASSESSING ACHIEVEMENT OF OBJECTIVES

Ongoing Evaluation

The extent to which students have gained practice and understanding of writing with sentence variety can be measured by having them submit for evaluation the final products of Activities.

Final Evaluation

For an overall evaluation of students' ability to use sentence variety, assign an in-class writing assignment that uses description of something in the content field. Evaluate the writing with the following criteria:

1. There is effective variety in the sentences used, such as long sentences that contain compacted ideas and shorter sentences that express simpler ideas.

2. There is elaboration of the main ideas that provides sufficient information to describe them and that builds texture.

3. Not all sentences follow the simple subject-verb design, but some begin with modifying phrases, clauses, and words.

4. Clauses, phrases, and word describers are used to build elaboration of the main ideas.

5. Modifying clauses, phrases, and words are placed next to what they describe.

6. The ideas appear to flow smoothly because the sentences have fluency.

7. The sentence complexity is not so great that the main ideas are lost in extensive elaboration.

When the students' compositions have been evaluated based on these criteria, return them for rewriting. Indicate which sentences should be rewritten, combined, and changed on students' papers, and have them revise them. Ask students to recopy their entire composition when they have reworked their sentences. Have students exchange papers with a classmate who can critique it. Collect the papers.

Optional

Advanced students who have been taught the sentence-weights system may evaluate their own writing numerically. Have them find the average weight for each sentence, add up the weights, and divide by the number of sentences to produce a paragraph weight, as in the following:

$$\text{number of sentences} \overline{\left)\begin{array}{l}\text{paragraph weight}\\ \text{added average sentence weights}\end{array}\right.}$$

---

2. Arthur Schlesinger, *Life* (November 12, 1971): p. 13.

Have students compare their paragraph weights. Read aloud some of the compositions that have high weights to see if they are too complex and lack fluency. Read aloud some of the compositions that have low weights to determine if sentences are too simple and choppy and if ideas need greater elaboration. Discuss with students which papers seem to have an effective paragraph weight. Have students rewrite their compositions in terms of building more effective sentences. See if the paragraph weights differ in the rewritten composition.

RESOURCES FOR TEACHING SENTENCE VARIETY IN COMPOSITION

Below is a selected and annotated list of resources useful for teaching the subject matter in this chapter. Resources are from journals and books and are designed for both teacher and student uses.

Christensen, Francis. "A Generative Rhetoric of the Sentence." *College Composition and Communication.* 14:3 (October, 1963). The article, recommended for teacher background information, presents the "cumulative sentence" on which sentence-combining theory is based. Christensen discusses principles of composition: that it is a process of addition and that there are layers of structure to the sentence. The layers of structure represent "levels of abstraction" that can be numerically evaluated as in sentence weighting. He also defines the concept of *texture* as it affects writing style. This article provides a theoretical base for much of the current theory, practices, and research being conducted in teaching composition.

Crowhurst, Marion. "Syntactic Complexity and Teachers' Quality Ratings of Narrations and Arguments." *Research in the Teaching of English.* 14:3 (October, 1980). This study correlated sentence complexity to quality ratings in two modes of composition written by students in grades 6, 10, and 12. The quality for high complexity was found by teachers to be greater than for low complexity in argumentative writing for grades 12 and 10. There was no significant difference found in grade 6. For narrative writing there was no difference in quality between high and low complexity. This study raises questions about sentence complexity: how much should there be and where—in which modes—is it most effective? The teacher of writing may be interested in pursuing research into these questions.

Daiker, Donald; Kerek, Andrew; and Morenberg, Max. *Sentence Combining and the Teaching of Writing.* Conway, Arkansas: L & S Books, 1979.

This paperback book consists of selected papers from the Miami University Conference in 1978. It presents the theory of sentence combining in the classroom. This collection of essays is useful as background information for the teacher and as a research resource.

DiStefano, Philip, and Howie, Sherry. "Sentence Weights: An Alternative to the T-Unit." *English Education Journal.* (Winter 1979). This article details the use of sentence weighting and explains how it compares to Kellogg Hunt's measure of syntactic complexity, the T-unit. Teachers who are interested in pursuing research in this area of composition would find this article informative and expressive of a viewpoint that is relevant to readability as well as composition. It includes a lengthy bibliography for further reference on the topic.

Faigley, Lester. "Names in Search of a Concept: Maturity, Fluency, Complexity, and Growth in Written Syntax." *College Composition and Communication.* 31 (October, 1980). An interesting discussion and definition of terminology is presented for teacher background information in this article. All of these debatable terms are used in the present chapter, so for further elaboration on their meaning and use, Faigley's article is valuable.

Howie, Sherry. "A Study of the Effects of Sentence Combining Practice on the Writing Ability and Reading Level of Ninth Grade Students." Doctoral dissertation, University of Colorado, Boulder, 1979. This study examined over a period of fifteen weeks the effect of sentence-combining practice on the writing ability and reading level of ninth graders in a public school. An experimental group of two classes was compared to another group who did not receive sentence-combining instruction, and it was found that there was a significant improvement in their descriptive composition but not in expository composition. There was no difference in reading level between the two groups, which showed that reading was not affected by sentence-combining study. This study brought out several questions that need further research, such as effect on quality, audience and purpose, and attitudes of students in regard to teaching this aspect of composition. The teacher interested in further research would find this study of value.

Marzano, Robert, and DiStefano, Philip. *Di-Comp: A Diagnostic System for Teaching Composition, Grades 10–14.* Florida: Wylie-Padol Publishers, 2977. This workbook gives students practice in developing ten different skills that will improve their writing ability. Besides practice in vocabulary development, punctuation, spelling, correcting fragments and others, exercises are given for use of subordinate clauses, phrases, and word modifiers. Students are given two-sentence combining exercises using cues for specific sentence constructions. Students learn grammatical terminology for the specific structure they are creating because the terms are used in the exercises. Paragraph weights are also presented, and students are given explicit exercises to practice.

O'Hare, Frank. *Sentence Combining: Improving Student Writing Without Formal Grammar Instruction.* Urbana, Ill.: NCTE, 1973. This study is the most popular one for illustrating the growth students may experience with sentence-combining practice. O'Hare compared seventh-grade students who had sentence-combining instruction over an eight-month period to students who did not receive the practice. Using the T-unit measure, he found a significant growth in the clause length and the number of clauses used in the group receiving the practice. Their sentence complexity resembled that of twelfth graders, he found. Teachers interested in research in this area of composition would find this study of value to read.

O'Hare, Frank. *Sentencecraft.* Lexington, Mass.: Ginn & Co., 1975. This textbook for students presents sentence-combining exercises with cues or signals that give students guidance in combining sentences. This system does not allow students much flexibility in writing. However, it is excellent for training students in specific sentence construction without using formal grammar for either the teacher or the students. Included in the book are suggestions for a course in sentence combining in the classroom, prewriting advice, and a peer evaluation form for student use. This book is recommended for use as part of a composition program. There is both a teacher's guide and a student exercise book.

Strong, William. *Sentence Combining: A Composing Book.* New York: Random House, 1973. This textbook for students presents sentence-combining exercises that are "open," which means students are free to combine the sentences in the ways that seem most natural to them. Students use their own language knowledge and experience rather than signals or cues provided to them. In my opinion, the "open" exercises are more difficult than the cued ones and should be offered to students after they have been given guidance with cues. A major benefit of Strong's program is that whole texts are given to students for practice rather than two or three isolated sentences. Thus students gain experience in longer discourse forms, which is what they generally write. This book is one approach to teaching sentence variety and is recommended for use as part of a composition program.

9

Motivating Students to Write

CONTENT OVERVIEW

Students learning to write need direction and guidance to motivate them to write. Composition is the most difficult of human expression, and learning to master it requires interest, background preparation, and necessary skills. The directed-writing procedure in three steps gives the teacher a method of approach to developing prewriting experiences necessary to motivation for writing (see Chapter 2). Step 1 concerns building background in the topic to be presented in writing. Various stimuli may be used to develop this background and to uncover student interests. Step 2 helps to clarify purposes for writing and to identify the audience, the writing mode, and the necessary skills to be used. Step 3 is the actual writing experience itself, which can be accomplished through interesting and imaginative genres. Genres such as the journal, the diary, and letter use the first person *(I)* point of view and come from personal experience. Other genres such as the biography and the report use the third person *(he, she, it)* and are more impersonal. The genre can be the stimulus for students to write in the content areas if imaginatively presented. Since writing is most often a solitary activity, social group compositions can be a stimulus for students to learn to enjoy writing. A planned and guided writing procedure can help to take the anxiety out of writing for students and motivate them to write.

OBJECTIVES

As a result of the learning experiences in this chapter, students should be able to:

1. Establish adequate background in the topic so that they become confident and interested in what they are going to write.

2. Experience prewriting as a social activity in order to reduce anxiety and develop fluency in writing.

---

3. Experiment with and practice using language without restrictions and inhibitions in free-writing exercises.

4. Respond to various sensory stimuli as a catalyst for writing.

5. Recognize specific reasons for writing so that the activity is meaningful and important.

6. Realize that writing in different content fields is for different purposes and accomplishes different goals.

7. Understand that the audience for writing helps to determine the reasons for writing.

8. Use different genres of composition in creative ways to express ideas in the various content areas.

9. Write from a personal, first-person point of view and from an impersonal, third-person point of view and recognize the differences.

10. Enjoy the process of writing through directed and guided steps that motivate them to write.

LEARNING EXPERIENCES

Topic I: Building Background to Write

1. *Teacher Presentation.* Before a writing assignment, be sure to give students background preparation in order to build their understanding and their interest in the task. One way to give this background preparation is with the *oral composition approach*, which develops language fluency with, and ease in, expressing the topic. This group exercise can help all the students feel more comfortable in expressing themselves on paper because they have been given experience expressing themselves verbally. Divide students into small groups of three to five students. Ask one student in each group to start telling a story pertaining to a topic in the subject field; then each group member adds to the story until the last student concludes the story. Have each student write out his or her part of the story. Then have students rejoin their groups and edit the parts into one story. Ask each group to read its story aloud to the whole class. This activity leads students from oral composing to writing and editing on to oral presentation.

2. *Activity.* Ask students a question and have them respond with the answer in writing. Then, with their papers turned over, ask them to respond orally. The oral answers students give will probably be much more fluent and spontaneous. The verbal sharing of ideas will probably ignite other ideas as well. This exercise should prepare students for more complete development of their written composition because they will feel more comfortable after the oral discussion and will have shared some ideas on the topic. Ask students to write out their ideas and to expand or change what they have already written. Collect the original and the second writing to compare the two for elaboration, length, and development of ideas.

3. *Activity.* Assign a topic to a student, and have the student write down the thesis statement. Ask the student to give a four-to-six-minute talk on the topic to a small group or to the entire class, who then write down what they think is the speaker's thesis. If the thesis is clearly and consistently identified, then the student may believe that the topic was organized and developed with adequate details and examples. The student is ready to write out the topic at this point.

4. *Activity.* Another kind of activity to get students motivated to write is the free-writing procedure. Read a story or poem or show a picture to the class. As a first response (response A), ask students to free-write their impressions in an unstructured, unpunctuated form. Discuss their responses for oral practice in the topic. Ask a significant question about the stimulus, and have students free-write an answer to the question (response B). Discuss responses A and B and list key terms and phrases on the blackboard. Form one sentence from the lists, which becomes the controlling statement (see Chapter 7) for the topic. Ask students to free-write a response C using only personal experience and the first-person *(I)* point of view. The procedure is as follows:

Stimulus: story, poem, or picture

- Free response A

  Discuss response A

  Significant question

- Free response B

  List key terms and phrases from A and B

  Form one sentence from lists—the controlling statement

- Free-write from personal experience—response C

5. *Activity.* Explain to students that the free writing explained in Activity 4 is for fun, to experiment with and practice using language. It is impressionistic and without restrictions and can lead to creativity, to important ideas and to later, more structured composition. Tell students that this activity was a practice paper. Collect the papers, if desired (but not everything has to be collected). Use this background, experimental writing for an assignment of structured writing that may be collected and graded. Ask students to use this free writing as background for a written homework composition.

6. *Activity.* An excellent idea that combines both oral composing and visual stimuli comes from Dr. Richard Sinatra of St. John's University in New York. He calls this motivator for student writing "visual composition." The visual composition consists of several photographs or slides that are presented to students as a meaningful whole. The organization of the pictures will help dictate the organization of the students' composition, whether spatial, sequential, procedural, or other. Display or project the series of pictures to the students and elicit from them an overall impression of what it is they have just seen. Ask students to write their *dominant-impression sentence* (the theme) at the top of their paper. Now show the series of pictures again more slowly. Have students jot down some comments that relate each picture to their dominant impression. Have students write their initial draft of the

composition based on their notes and impressions of the main idea. Discuss with the class their choices of organization and development of their main idea. Ask students to identify their choice of mode of composition, whether procedural, topic or time-order, or narrative/descriptive (see Chapter 3). Ask students to identify the transition words and connectors they use to provide cohesion in their composition (see Chapter 7). After class discussion ask students to rewrite and edit their initial drafts so that their ideas are fully developed and they use transition words to make clear the development of the topic.

7. *Activity.* Have students read aloud to the class their edited and rewritten compositions. Because all in the class have experienced the visual stimuli, they will be able to critique the compositions and make suggestions regarding the development of ideas, mode used, vocabulary, and transition of ideas. Have students rewrite their papers in view of the suggestions offered. Collect the compositions and evaluate them according to the development of the dominant impression perceived by the writer.

8. *Activity.* Reproduce and distribute to students Reproduction Page 9-1, the suggested visual-composition arrangements for the content areas. Discuss with students the different modes of writing in the various subject areas and how picture arrangements lend themselves to the modes for different subjects. Ask students to bring in three to five pictures or slides they may have or are able to find that fall into the arrangements suggested on Reproduction Page 9-1. Ask students to share their picture arrangements with the class. Have students determine the arrangement, the development of the idea, and the mode to be used in writing a composition about each series of pictures. Have students give transition words appropriate for the sequencing they establish for each series of pictures. This oral experience and class sharing should be valuable in reducing anxiety about writing and give practice in language usage about the experiences shared in common by the class.

9. *Activity.* Select a newspaper or magazine picture and mount it on colored paper. Remove the original headline, title, or caption of the picture and glue it on the back of the colored paper. Present the picture to the class and ask them to provide the main idea of the picture based on the visual details. Ask students to write out the main idea of the picture in sentence form. Then have students develop the main idea by writing further sentences about the details of the picture. When they have finished their writing, compare the main idea they established for the picture to the original headline, title, or caption. Which one do students like best and which expresses the essence of the picture best? Have students provide logical reasons for their choices based on the details in the picture.

10. *Activity.* To build background for writing using an aural-visual stimulus, invite a speaker in to present a topic of interest in the content area. Speakers from the community, from business, and from civic organizations can serve as powerful motivators for students to express their reactions and opinions on paper. The oral interchange of students with a speaker can develop language facility and vocabulary in the topic, as well as provoke a strong viewpoint and opinion in the student writer. Have students respond on paper to the speaker. Some students can be encouraged to give their viewpoint orally to the class after their composition is written. Following the oral presentations and class discussion, ask students to rewrite their papers, expanding and clarifying their views in light of the further development of the topic.

Topic II: Developing Incentives for Writing

1. *Teacher Presentation.* Review with students the purposes for writing found in Chapter 4, which are to give an opinion, to write creatively, to persuade the reader, and to report facts and data. In "real" life, people write because they have a need, a specific reason for doing so. School writing is artificial mostly in that it is assigned without much understanding on the students' part as to why they have to write except to fulfill the assignment. Establishment of a clear purpose for writing can be a powerful motivator for students, an incentive to communicate something important. The writing task, therefore, should be recognized by the student as being important to accomplish some purpose. Discuss with students the purpose for writing in each writing assignment. This establishment of purpose is an important step in the directed-writing assignment as a prewriting motivator.

2. *Activity.* Ask students to decide what the purpose is of each of the following assignments in different content fields:

Science: write a laboratory notebook.
(Purpose is to keep a record of facts and data that can later provide details for a research paper.)

Social studies: write an essay comparing Socialism and Capitalism and identify where they exist.
(Purpose is to compare and contrast two different economic and government systems and to make a judgment as to where they exist.)

Art: write a descriptive analysis of an oil painting in the gallery.
(Purpose is to observe and classify what is seen in the painting.)

English: write an analysis of a sonnet by William Wordsworth.
(Purpose is to examine the parts and then give an overall interpretation.)

Music: write a defense of the view that modern jazz is an outgrowth of black spiritual music.
(Purpose is to defend a viewpoint that is substantiated with facts and to persuade the reader of its "truth".)

3. *Activity.* Assign several topics and have students write what they think are the specific purposes for writing on each topic. Ask students to write down all the reasons why each topic would be important to develop into a written communication. Ask the students to discover for themselves why you believe the topics were important to write out. (If students cannot pinpoint specific important purposes for writing on a topic, perhaps it may lack the importance you give it, or perhaps its importance must be clarified for student understanding.) Student identification of specific purposes for writing on an assigned topic should help in their own motivation and sense of importance of writing it.

4. *Activity.* After students have completed Activity 3, ask them to choose one of the essay topics they were assigned in the subject area and write it out in composition form. Discuss with students the purposes they pinpointed in each topic. Collect their compositions and compare what they wrote to what they listed as the purposes for writing it.

5. *Activity.* Return to students the essays they wrote in initial draft in Activity 4. Ask them to put a checkmark in the margin next to where they fulfilled the purposes for writing that they had originally listed. Have students exchange papers with each other in pairs to proofread and to double check that the purposes have been fulfilled. Ask students to rewrite their essays according to peer and teacher comments. Collect the essays and evaluate them according to how well the topic was developed and how fully the purposes for writing it were fulfilled.

6. *Activity.* Remind students that audience helps to determine the purpose for writing. The purpose of most writing is to communicate thoughts and ideas in written form. The reader to whom one directs the communication will help determine why one is writing. Return students' compositions to them and discuss with them who their audience was. How did the fact that their reader was the teacher help to determine their purpose for writing? Who else as the audience could they have directed their essays to?

7. *Activity.* Ask students to rewrite their essay from Activity 5, but to direct it to a different reader-audience such as to a peer (by using slang), to a "boss" they work for, to a child of six, or to a technical journal for publication. Does this different audience change the purpose for writing? Their purpose is still to communicate in written form, but the purpose is affected by the audience. For example, their purpose in writing to a friend is to communicate on the level of the friend in a personal, informal manner, but their purpose in writing for journal publication is to communicate on a formal, impersonal level to a wide audience. Remind students to keep in mind that a specific audience helps determine the purpose for writing and, in the "real" world, is probably the primary motivation for writing.

8. *Activity.* Ask students to read aloud their essays directed to the different audiences. Discuss with the class how the vocabulary, style, and syntactic complexity changes in the writing with the variance in the audience. Also discuss how the purpose for communication changes with respect to the level, extent, and distance of language used.

Topic III: Enjoying Different Genres of Writing

1. *Teacher Presentation.* In every subject area, writing can be made especially interesting for students when the form of composition is varied from the usual essay form. To write in an interesting genre can be a very creative, motivating force for student writing. An essay directed to the teacher written in proper composition form is the usual genre for school writing. Certainly students must be taught to write in this form, but it can be varied occasionally as a gimmick for motivating students to write. Making any school subject a personal experience is possible with certain genres of writing. Explain to students that the class is going to experiment with different and interesting forms of composition and that they should have a lot of fun with the process. Tell students that most lifelong needs for written communication do not involve essay writing and that they are going to have practice in other forms, some of which will be from the personal point of view and some from a more impersonal approach. The following activities will give students practice in other genres of writing in different content fields.

2. *Activity.* Assign an essay topic(s) in the subject area that will lend itself to writing from a personal point of view (using the pronoun *I*) and can utilize either a journal, diary, letter, or autobiography genre of writing. Such topics may be suggested by the following:

Music: Write a letter to Johann Sebastian Bach congratulating him on his newest musical composition, which you just heard performed.

Art: Write a diary that Vincent van Gogh might have kept during the later years of his life.

Social studies: Write a journal of your trip with the Donner Party to California.

Science: Write as a white cell explaining your attack on an infection in the body.

Math: Write your autobiography as Euclid living in Alexandria and developing his works in geometry.

English: Write a letter to George Eliot telling her why she should publish her novels under her real name.

Industrial arts: Write as a specific tool explaining your history, your uses, and your purposes in construction work.

Physical education: Write a diary over a two-week period as an Olympic athlete competing in the Olympic events.

Students will have to research their topic thoroughly before they can provide specific facts such as dates, times, places, and persons involved. Tell students to be sure to gather all their facts from resource books such as encyclopedias, dictionaries, textbooks, technical books, and so forth.

3. *Activity.* Have students read aloud their writing to the rest of the class, who can enjoy the creativity and can critique the amount of information given. Making any information personal in these genres can be stimulating and can greatly broaden students' life experiences as they put themselves in the places of the persons or things they write about. Discuss with students how they related to their topic in a personal way and how this experience increased their understanding and interest in what they wrote.

4. *Activity.* Ask students to rewrite their papers from a third-person point of view using *he, she,* or *it.* Tell them that this writing must be impersonal whereas the other was personal and that they must be the observer, not the participant this time. Have them write in the genre of a report, a biography or a narrative (telling a story). Tell students to change the point of view completely and to rework their sentences to make them more formal or distant.

5. *Activity.* Ask students to compare the first, personal writing to the second, impersonal writing. Which did they enjoy the most and why? What are the uses of the two different points of view in their school writing assignments and in lifelong writing? Have students analyze the points of view they find in the content area reading materials they use. Why is the third person used most often in textbooks and teaching materials? Can they find examples of second person *(you)* writing? Directions and procedural writing use second-person point of view.

ASSESSING ACHIEVEMENT OF OBJECTIVES

Ongoing Evaluation

The extent to which students have been motivated and interested in writing can be measured by having them submit for evaluation the final products of Activities.

Final Evaluation

For an overall evaluation of students' motivation and interest in writing, ask them to fill in a short questionnaire built on a Likert Scale indicating their level of interest in writing *before* the directed-writing assignment is used to motivate them. This will provide a preassignment assessment of attitude toward writing. Then administer the questionnaire *after* using the directed-writing assignment to get a postassignment evaluation of students' attitudes and motivation for writing. Compare the pre- and posttreatment measures to see if there is a change in attitude. An example of the evaluation instrument follows:

Check the statement that best indicates your attitude toward writing in this class:

__ Dislike all   __ Dislike some   __ Don't care   __ Like some   __ Enjoy all
    writing   writing   either way   writing   writing

For another assessment of motivation of students toward writing, assign an in-class writing assignment using the three steps of the directed-writing procedure.

Step 1: Build background using a sensory stimulus (visual, auditory, tactile, and so on) to promote interest.

Step 2: Have students recognize and articulate the reason or purpose for writing and the audience whom they are addressing.

Step 3: Provide options as to the genre of composition students may use and the points of view (*I* or *he, she, it*) they may choose.

Evaluate the composition in terms of the following criteria:

1. Enough information is provided on the topic to reveal adequate background preparation for writing.

2. The stimulus is responded to clearly and directly.

3. The reason or purpose for writing is made clear and is accomplished.

4. An audience is clearly identified, and the language is appropriate for it.

5. The genre of composition is suitable and appropriate for the purpose and for the audience.

6. The point of view, either personal *(I)* or impersonal *(he, she, it)*, is sustained throughout the composition.

7. There is a certain level of interest and enthusiasm in students shown in their discussions and in their writing.

RESOURCES FOR MOTIVATING STUDENTS TO WRITE
IN CONTENT AREAS

Below is a selected and annotated list of resources useful for motivating students to write and for teaching the subject matter in this chapter. The selections are from books and are designed for teacher resource and for student use.

Long, Russell C. "Writer-Audience Relationships: Analysis or Invention?" *College Composition and Communication.* 31 (May, 1980). This article provides a discussion for the teacher of writing on writer-reader relationships. It defines audience and cites theories of writer-reader roles. The article contends that an audience should be created by the writer in order to avoid a superficial view of a supposed reader. This conscious creation of an audience will provide a method for redefining writer responsibilities. This discussion is of value to teachers and researchers interested in pursuing this topic as an avenue to motivation.

Maimon, Elaine P., et al. *Writing in the Arts and Sciences.* Cambridge, Mass.: Winthrop Publishers, 1981. This textbook for students presents many genres of composition to be found in the different content areas. It covers in detail research papers, journal writing, the laboratory notebook, writing analyses, criticisms, and many more. Specific content areas and genres to be found in them are covered with examples, student exercises, and discussion.

Moffett, James, and Wagner, Betty Jane. *Student-Centered Language Arts and Reading, K–13.* Second Edition. Boston: Houghton Mifflin, 1976. Chapter 8 discusses "Writing Stimuli" and their presentation to students to motivate them to write. The use of pictures, music, and other sensory stimuli is advocated, as well as how to have students duplicate and bind their own writings in order to share them. The book is an excellent resource for teachers with its many implementable ideas and suggestions for the classroom.

Moffett, James. *Teaching the Universe of Discourse.* Boston: Houghton Mifflin, 1968. This book is highly recommended as a resource for all teachers of writing. It covers kinds of discourse or genres of composition in great detail. The emphasis of the book is on a student-centered curriculum, and it presents learning theories and teaching methods toward that philosophy. Although directed toward teachers of English, the book is valuable to all content area teachers of language and communication.

Murray, Donald M. *A Writer Teaches Writing: A Practical Method of Teaching Composition.* Boston: Houghton Mifflin, 1968. This book is an excellent resource for teachers interested in the philosophy, the skills behind, and the methods toward teaching writing that professional writers have found workable. The author discusses the "climate for writing" and how to develop a lesson plan for teaching writing in the classroom. The book is full of many practical ideas that teachers will find useful.

Sinatra, Richard. "Visual Compositions and Language Development." *National Association of Learning Laboratory Directors Journal.* 18:2 (Winter, 1981). This journal article explains the visual-literacy method of verbal development of students in the classroom. The visual-composition approach involves right-brain processing (most common with males, it is found) in the formation of images, impressions, and feelings about a pictorial study in a holistic, organized teaching strategy. The visual composition method is highly effective as a motivation to write in every content field.

Sinatra, Richard. "A Visual Approach to Sentence Combining for the Limited English Proficient Student." *Bilingual Resources.* 4:2 (1981). This article discusses the use of structured pictures to develop English language skills in the English-as-a-Second-Language student. Particularly useful for spatial-holistic right-brain usage, visual images stimulate language use in cultures that prefer this mode over the analytic, serial mode of language learning. The visual method of teaching composition allows for different learning styles and different cultural approaches to language development.

Sinatra, Richard, and Howie, Sherry. "Visual Compositions: A Way to Teach Explicit and Implicit Text Factors in Content Areas." *ERIC* ED 207 003 (Urbana, Illinois) (Spring 1982). Different modes of composition existing in different subject area textbooks are analyzed for their text factors. How to teach writing of those text factors in each subject is made easier with the use of visual compositions that can be structured to the factors. For example, visuals can be arranged in a cause-effect sequence likely to elicit that kind of writing response from students in a social studies class. Teaching writers when to be explicit in development of their topic teaches them to be more effective in their communication. Visuals aid in this teaching.

Stanford, Gene, and Smith, Marie. *A Guidebook for Teaching Creative Writing*. Boston: Allyn and Bacon, 1977. Particularly Chapter 2, "Stimulating Students to Write," is important for its activities, discussion, and principles of motivation of students in writing. There are many suggested approaches, including use of sensory stimuli, understanding purpose for writing, and writing for an audience. The teacher of writing will find this an extremely useful, practical book. Its reproducible pages are very helpful.

10

Evaluating Writing

CONTENT OVERVIEW

The ultimate objective of evaluation should be to teach students to assess their own writing. Evaluation should be aimed toward instruction of students in judging their own production. Evaluation terminology and methods should be simple, meaningful, and clearly understood by students *before* they write. Most often, assessment by teachers is an atomistic process that involves dissecting every element of composition, a method so overwhelming and frustrating to most students that they rarely bother to read or understand the "R–O," "frag," and "CS" (for run-on, fragment, and comma splice, respectively) that decorate their papers. Not only is this frustrating to students, but it is noninstructional, dooming them to repeat the errors every time they write. In order to teach students ultimate self-evaluation, other methods may be employed that can be less complicated and less threatening to learning writers. The key to all methods, however, is to clearly identify for students the terminology and criteria used. Alternative methods of assessment include the holistic evaluation and the use of a matrix of expectations. Both methods are efficient and meaningful on a comparative basis and may be used together or singly to rate large or small groups of compositions. A third method is peer evaluation, which must be carefully taught in order to be effective and to allow students to learn judgment. Lastly, self-evaluation—where students criticize, edit, redraft, and revise their own writing—is the goal of teaching writing for students' lifelong use. All of these methods can be tried by teachers and students for experimentation and variety in learning to evaluate writing.

OBJECTIVES

As a result of the learning experiences in this chapter, students should be able to:

1. Develop an awareness of criteria used for evaluating writing and the differences in the relative rankings *A* to *F*.

2. Experience a common understanding with the teacher of the symbols and abbreviations used in the atomistic evaluation of the writing.

3. Have a clear understanding of teacher expectations indicated by markings and grade rankings A to F *before* they write.

4. Judge, edit, and revise their papers according to their understanding of the criteria standards established with the teacher.

5. Understand relative rankings 1 to 5 based on specific expectations expressed in a matrix.

6. Grow in their critical skills in order to upgrade their writing according to the expectations in the matrix.

7. Develop more realistic expectations for their own writing growth and production.

8. Understand the distinction between evaluation and grading in developing their critical skills of judgment and analysis.

9. Have the opportunity to learn effective composition through critical evaluation of peers' writing.

10. Use specific and concrete comments in peer evaluation for positive growth of the writer.

11. Develop their own criteria standards for evaluating writing so that they become responsible and independent in their writing growth.

12. Realize that writing is thinking and that evaluating their own writing is an exercise in refining thought in any content field.

13. Apply their learned critical skills of evaluation throughout their lives to whatever they write.

14. Appreciate the opportunity to participate in the evaluation process.

LEARNING EXPERIENCES

Topic I: Understanding and Using Atomistic Evaluation of Writing

1. *Teacher Presentation.* The most common method of evaluating student writing is *atomistic evaluation*, picking out every error that the student makes on the paper. Every composition element, or atom, is minutely dissected and marked. The problems inherent in this method are numerous, both for the teacher, who must mark all the mistakes, and for the student, who must figure them out and learn from them. For a teacher to evaluate *all* errors on all papers takes much valuable time. The physical space on the student paper is usually not sufficient to write out all remarks, so abbreviations and symbols are used, which can be confusing and frustrating to students, who see their "creations" all scribbled on. If the symbols and abbreviations are not fully explained to students and mastered by them, then no learning or understanding of how to avoid future errors takes place. The greatest problem with

marking all errors is that students are given no clear criteria on which to base their writing *before* they write and to judge their writing after they have written. If atomistic evaluation is to be used, students should be given clear definitions of the rankings from *A* to *F* and of the areas that are considered for evaluation.

Discuss with students the areas of evaluation that are important in the grading of a composition. Areas students may suggest are grammar, punctuation, spelling, idea development, paragraph structure (beginning, development, and conclusion), vocabulary sentence structure, and so forth. Working with the students, break these areas into major criteria such as mechanics, content, and style and list all their suggested areas under these major headings. Discuss with them your expectations and definitions for the criteria and fully explain any symbols and abbreviations that are to be used in the marking of their papers. Be certain students understand fully the criteria to be used *before* they write so that they may aim their writing toward the criteria standards.

2. *Activity.* Reproduce and distribute to students Reproduction Page 10-1, which is suggested as a guide for student understanding and teacher use in teaching atomistic evaluation. You may want to modify, add to, or adapt to your own purposes the rating section and the areas of evaluation. Explain to students your expectations in each area and how success may be achieved with careful consideration of the rankings *A* to *F*. Tell students that because they understand the areas to be evaluated, teacher expectations in each area, and the rankings for the criteria, their writing should be geared toward what they want to achieve. Each student should understand what it takes to achieve a particular grade and that each is expected to critique the composition according to the specified guidelines. Make sure the grading matches student preparation and understanding.

3. *Activity.* Assign an in-class writing assignment after students have been advised of the criteria for which they will be responsible (as on Reproduction Page 10-1). Review with students the teacher expectations *before* they submit their writing, and have them reread their papers according to the criteria. Collect their papers and check them according to the criteria established, but do not assign a permanent grade at this time. Indicate a probable grade, and return the papers for editing and revision. Discuss what the papers revealed, the strengths and the areas to improve, and refer to the criteria sheet (Reproduction Page 10-1). Discuss with students how they may improve their papers and review with them the symbols and abbreviations used in the evaluation.

4. *Activity.* Ask students to rewrite their papers according to the discussion and review of the specific criteria established for them. Discuss with students what changes they have made from the initial draft to the revision and why they made the changes. Direct the discussion toward content, style, and mechanics and what students have learned about the rankings *A* to *F*.

5. *Activity.* Ask students to grade their own composition in view of the discussion in Activity 4 and with use of Reproduction Page 10-1 rankings. Have students write at the bottom of the page their reasons for the grade they assigned their own paper. Discuss with students the meaning of an *A* or a *C* grade. What additions or changes in the ranking system would students make? Share with students a clear understanding of their expectations, interpretations, and associations with the *A-F*

ranking system. Collect their revised compositions and grade them. Compare the grade they assigned their papers to the one you assign, and consider the reasoning of the students. Help students to understand why they were accurate or inaccurate in their own grading and in their reasoning. Hold individual conferences with students to discuss their own writing evaluation.

Topic II: Understanding and Using Holistic Evaluation of Writing

1. *Teacher Presentation.* Explain to students that in the "real world" they will be their own critics for whatever it is they have to write and that you are preparing them to be self-evaluators. One method of evaluation is the *holistic method*, which is a comparative ranking system that is efficient, fast, and effective. It is a method that helps the teacher in terms of accountability and time in grading many sets of papers. It also helps the students to understand how one paper compares to another and why their paper receives a particular grade compared to those of other papers. The method establishes clear-cut criteria for the ranking system when it is used with a matrix, which establishes credibility for which teachers and students can be held accountable in the grading. Holistic refers to evaluation of the writing as a whole greater than the sum of its parts of style, content, and mechanics. The writing is evaluated without marking errors and on the basis of comparison to the other papers in the group. The great advantage of the method is that it usually takes about a minute to assess each paper. It is most effective when students are aware of and understand the criteria used for the given assignment. Prototypes or examples of the rankings should be shown to students so that they come to understand the method and to upgrade their writing based on their understanding. The following activities will help teacher and students to employ this method most effectively in learning.

2. *Activity.* Assign an in-class essay in the content area for students. Collect the papers. Sort through the class set of papers, quickly identifying what appears to be an *A* paper, a *B* paper, a *C* paper, a *D* paper and an *F* paper. These five papers are the prototypes of the ranking system. Without revealing any student names (assign each paper a number and white out the name), display on an opaque projector the five compositions to students and discuss the teacher evaluation of each paper in terms of content, style, and mechanics. Specifically pinpoint the differences between the *A–F* rankings. Return student papers and have them rewrite their essays in accordance with the specific criteria set in the discussion. Collect the rewritten papers.

3. *Activity.* Sort through the rewritten compositions, reading quickly each one and making a swift judgment as to its grade ranking. Perhaps there will be no *F* papers, but sort them into five piles with pile 1 the superior papers, pile 2 the lesser ones, and on down to pile 5 the weakest papers. Number the papers with a code without revealing student names. Select five prototypes from each pile and again present them to students, thoroughly discussing each of the five. Then have students sort through the class set and designate the five piles based on the prototypes. This training for students should reveal to them your standards and criteria and the ranking system for the grades they receive. With such training and knowledge, which requires no more than two class periods, students may be able to upgrade their

writing and to judge their own production much more realistically. Furthermore, this process establishes teacher judgment as being fair, understandable, and less threatening to students. Student growth in writing and in evaluation should be substantial.

4. *Activity.* Another way to use the holistic method is to pinpoint a specific criterion for the evaluation of a composition and then to construct a matrix of expectations for that criterion. Reproduce and distribute Reproduction Page 10–2 to students. Ask students to analyze the given criterion for each assignment and then to write in the expectation for the criterion at each of the levels 1 to 5. In order to receive a 1 for a composition, what would students expect they would have to produce? Fully discuss student expectations for the rankings and establish teacher expectations for the students. Understanding expectations for each level should help students be more realistic in their own evaluation and in teacher rankings.

5. *Activity.* Assign an in-class essay in the subject area. Establish a specific criterion or objective to be achieved. Discuss with students the matrix applicable to the criterion *before* they write so that their understanding of the assignment is based on the criterion and the expectation of fulfillment of it at different levels. Holistically evaluate the class set of papers according to the criterion. Rank the papers by sorting them into five piles as they match the expectations at the different levels. Mark 1 to 5 on each paper according to its ranking. Return the papers to students, and discuss the rankings with reference to the prototypes, a representative paper from each pile. Ask students to rewrite their papers in light of the discussion and their increased understanding of the expectations. Reevaluate the papers, and compare the initial ranking to the revised paper's ranking. Both you and the students should see improvement.

Topic III: Understanding and Using Peer Evaluation

1. *Teacher Presentation.* A distinction must be made for students between evaluation and grading. To *evaluate* is to analyze, criticize, and judge, whereas to *grade* is to give a comparative ranking. Students will be involved in evaluation, not in grading each other's papers, in order to develop critical skills that may be applied to their own writing and realistic understanding of what is effective. Grading is subjective and threatening, and learning students are not ready for this burden and threat, nor is it necessary for their learning purposes. Therefore, carefully explain to students that their task is not to grade but to evaluate each other's writing in order to learn critical skills. This method of evaluation by peers should take place later in the school year after students have come to know each other and you have developed a level of trust within the group. Writing for evaluation by peers changes the purpose and audience for students, who almost always have directed their writing toward a teacher audience. So, not only do they learn evaluation with this method, but gain experience in audience focusing as well. Peer evaluation provides for individualized learning situations because students are accessible to each other on a one-to-one basis. Present this rationale for the peer evaluation method to students and discuss the values of this opportunity to learn effective composition through criticism. The following activities will help students learn this method.

2. *Activity.* Assign an in-class essay in the subject area. Instruct students to direct their writing to other students in the class who will be evaluating their writing. Collect the essays. Pair students who will evaluate each other's writing. The pairing should be for best learning purposes, so a more skilled writer may be paired with a less skilled one, or however the teacher believes the learning will be most effective. The evaluations can be conducted in three stages. The first is a silent reading of the papers. The second is an oral discussion of the general impression. The third stage is the written response on the paper itself in which the student is very specific and concrete in making observations and suggestions for improvement. Collect the evaluated papers on which students have written their comments. Discuss with students any unclear, vague, and imprecise comments and how they can be reworded to be most constructive and instructional.

3. *Activity.* Return the essays in Activity 2 to the original owners. Include teacher comments and evaluation and ask students to study peer and teacher comments for their instructional value in revising and rewriting their papers. Ask students to rewrite their papers in light of peer and teacher comments. Ask students to write at the bottom of their revised essays what it is they changed in their revisions. Tell students to name specific changes they made and to say what was valuable to them in the comments made on their papers by peers and teacher. Collect the papers and evaluate the comments students wrote about their own revision in order to detect their learning about the composing process.

4. *Activity.* Reproduce the distribute to students Reproduction Page 10–3, a rating scale to be used as an index for peer evaluations. Explain the content, style, and mechanics categories and how they are specifically rated from strongest on the left side of the scale to weakest on the right. All students are to do is indicate with a checkmark their evaluation of each specific item. This scale should give students very specific language to use in evaluating other students' and their own writing. Return the revised essays of Activity 3 to the pairs of students in the peer-evaluation exercise and have them exchange papers again. Once each has carefully read the other's paper, ask them to evaluate the papers using the scale. After students have evaluated the papers and discussed them with the authors, have them write commentaries at the bottom of the page to summarize the strong points and indicate how to further improve the papers. Collect the papers and evaluate students' comments as to how specific they are for instruction and guidance to the author. Discuss with students their critical evaluations and their growth in assessing effective writing. Remind them that they are on their way to developing independent skills for self-evaluation, which will be valuable for the rest of their lives.

5. *Activity.* Have students form small groups of five to seven people. Ask each group to make up their own composition rating scale for the subject area. Tell them to make an evaluation instrument that would be most appropriate to the content field in which they write. What in students' judgment should be specifically evaluated in the subject area? Ask them to design a format that would be most meaningful and useful in peer evaluation. Discuss with students their evaluation instruments and the specific points they believe should be evaluated. Appoint a committee or elicit volunteers to look at all the groups' evaluation instruments and to form one for class use out of the ideas the groups have suggested. This activity should help students to

become more responsible for their own writing and to grow in critiquing writing with specific criteria. Students may share the burden of evaluation, which has been the province of the teacher for too long.

Topic IV: Developing Self-Evaluation Skills

1. *Teacher Presentation.* Few students have been given the opportunity and experience of evaluating their own writing. Self-evaluation entails setting personal standards and judging strengths and weaknesses for revision purposes. Self-evaluation is also an exercise in logic and in developing independence in judgment and criticism. This method should be the one that stays with each individual the longest because it is the most personally meaningful. Self-evaluation emanates from within the individual and is thus most important and valuable to its creator. Most evaluation during a student's school life is imposed from outside by a teacher or an authority figure, but this method gives the opportunity for personal development of critical standards. Explain to students that they are ready now for development of self-evaluation skills, and give them the rationale for doing so. Tell students that writing is thinking, and critiquing that writing is yet a more complex process, but a necessary one for further intellectual growth and knowledge in the subject area. The following activities will give practice in developing self-evaluation skills.

2. *Activity.* Assign a composition for students to write in the subject area. Discuss in specific detail with students what your expectations are for the performance in the writing. Ask students to develop the idea orally, to talk about the content and what should be inclusive in it. Have students elaborate on what they think the topic means and what it involves. Ask students to write it out and expand the ideas they have just discussed, keeping in mind teacher expectations as well.

3. *Activity.* Have students review Reproduction Page 10–3 and apply the concepts set forth to their own writing of Activity 2. Ask students to make comments on their own papers regarding the content, style, and mechanics using the specific language of the scale. Tell them to write positive comments on what they think is written effectively as well as on areas they feel need improvement. Ask them to summarize at the bottom of the page the major strengths and weaknesses of their own papers. Collect student compositions and assess their comments. Write a reaction to the comments as to how accurately they evaluated themselves.

4. *Activity.* Return student compositions and discuss the self-evaluation of Activity 3 with students. Discuss student reactions to the exercise and review with them the values of learning self-evaluation. Have students express their reservations and fears in self-criticism. Probably their fears stem from lack of practice and opportunity to be independent self-evaluators. Also, although taking responsibility for one's own production is the way to grow, change, and learn, students may initially feel insecure with this growth because in the past they have always let the teacher do the grading. Remind students that not everything they do has to have a grade on it, but that this occasional exercise in self-assessment is necessary to their growth and learning development in writing. Ask students to compare their comments with your reactions on their papers, and then to rewrite the compositions in light of both evaluations. Collect and read the compositions.

5. *Activity.* Have a brief individual conference with each student regarding the rewritten composition of Activity 4. Discuss the changes the student made in the revision that were based on the self-evaluation and on teacher comments. Go over the major points of Reproduction Page 10-3 with the student to make sure each concept is clearly understood. Impress on each student individual responsibility for growth and critical self-evaluation in writing. Discuss confusions and uncertainties so that each student begins to gain confidence in analysis and critical thinking.

ASSESSING ACHIEVEMENT OF OBJECTIVES

Ongoing Evaluation

The extent to which students have gained practice and understanding of evaluating writing can be measured by having them submit for evaluation the final products of Activities.

Final Evaluation

For an overall evaluation of students' ability to understand assessment of composition, follow these three suggested procedures.

1. Assign an in-class essay based on a topic found in the content field. Ask students to analyze the assigned topic and to name the criterion for evaluating the topic. For example, if a descriptive topic were assigned, the criterion for judging how it was written might be the use of adjectives or describer words. When students have agreed on a criterion, ask them to develop a matrix of expectations (see Reproduction Page 10-2) for the criterion ranging from most effective to least effective so that the degrees of performance are established.

2. Ask students to write out the assigned topic in composition form. Tell them that their peers are going to evaluate their papers based on the criterion and degrees of performance they have just established. When students have finished writing, collect their compositions. During the next class period return the compositions to a student other than the original owner so that students will practice peer evaluation. Review the criterion and the matrix of expectations. Ask students to evaluate the paper based on the matrix and to write comments regarding the strengths and weaknesses they find in meeting the criterion. Ask the evaluators and the writers to meet together to discuss the evaluations and to return the papers to their owners.

3. Have students evaluate their own composition, and to write comments on it in regard to what they see as their personal strengths in writing and to what they want to improve. Ask students to be very specific in their comments so that they may realize a definite course of action for improvement. Collect their papers and write reactions to the peer and self-evaluations. The extent of student understanding of evaluation should be evident in the comments they write.

RESOURCES FOR TEACHING EVALUATION

Below is a selected and annotated list of resources useful for teaching the subject matter in this chapter. Resources are from journal articles and from books.

Beach, Richard. "Self-Evaluation in an Activity-Oriented English Classroom." *English Journal.* (March, 1975), 59–63. The writer presents a clear rationale for developing skills of self-evaluation in students mainly as an assumption of responsibility for their own learning and understanding of what they are learning. Problems inherent in the self-evaluation methods are discussed, such as the summary format, in which students may tend to be too general and abstract in their own assessments. Included in the article is a sequence to follow for teaching student self-evaluation. The practical ideas given will be useful to teachers who want to explore and implement this valuable method of assessment.

Cooper, Charles R., and Odell, Lee. *Evaluating Writing.* Urbana, Ill.: NCTE, 1977. This paperback book presents several approaches to "describing, measuring, and judging" student writing written by different authors. Holistic evaluation is thoroughly discussed and the various types developed in great detail for the benefit of the writing teacher who is interested in learning about and using this valuable method of assessment. There are several scales to use in the evaluation, such as "analytic," "dichotomous," and "primary trait scoring." Any or all of these may be adapted to the needs of the teacher who uses holistic evaluation. Excellent and extensive pages of references are included for further study of writing assessment.

Corbin, Richard. *The Teaching of Writing in Our Schools.* New York: Macmillan (NCTE), 1966. This small book (118 pages) offers a rationale for teaching writing, defines the nature of the writing process, and suggests practical ways to teach students to write. The book is aimed at parents and teachers in all content areas who wish to understand better the integration of language, reading, and composition. Particularly important is Chapter 8, which deals with grading procedures and includes a list of specific points to consider in evaluating compositions. Suggestions are given for grading alternatives such as use of lay readers, closed television projects, and group instruction. The book is useful to content area teachers in order to gain an overview of writing instruction.

Dyer, Daniel. "When Kids Are Free to Write." *English Journal.* (May, 1976), 34–41. The writer deals with the problem of what to assign students to write, what students' interests are in writing and how teachers can participate in the writing assignments. Dyer advocates the idea of "Friday Writing" as a gimmick to give students writing practice. The teacher spends the hour writing right along with the students, and each person writes on any topic desired. At the end of the writing session, everyone who wants to, including the teacher, reads aloud to the class what he or she has written. The writing is submitted to the teacher, who reads it, makes comments on the content, but does not grade it. The teacher of writing will find this a valuable suggestion, which is developed in detail and can be of practical use in the classroom.

Elbow, Peter. *Writing Without Teachers.* London: Oxford University Press, 1973. This book may be used by students as a background to help build independence in writing, with techniques such as "free writing" to generate ideas and with improvement of skills in self-evaluation. The book attempts to build confidence in writing through practice and personal experience. It advocates the individual writer learning to write rather than being taught to write. The content area teacher will find the philosophy and practical suggestions useful for reluctant writers.

Ellman, Neil. "Peer Evaluation and Peer Grading." *English Journal.* (March, 1975), 79–80. This short article stresses the goal of creating independence in learners by teaching the skills necessary for self- and peer evaluation. Specific guidelines are given to teachers to follow in establishing principles and practices of teaching these methods of evaluation. Teachers of writing will find these principles of value in building an instruction curriculum that aims at developing critical thinkers through peer assessment.

Lewis, Kenneth. "Putting the Hidden Curriculum of Grading to Work." *English Journal.* (March, 1975), 82–84. Lewis discusses the premise that teacher expectation is a critical teaching tool that is communicated to students in the form of grades. He argues for using evaluation rather than grading for the greatest growth of student understanding and participating in what is expected. Included in the article is a grading standards chart that teachers will find useful in developing their own grading standards. It is to be used in cooperation with the students, who will be given an understanding of the grading criteria so that they will work toward them.

Olsen, Turee. "Grading Alternatives." *English Journal.* (March, 1975), 106-108. The discussion of informal and formal methods of evaluation defines the two and reviews the informal alternatives to traditional scaled grading. Conclusions found in studies are given to weigh pros and cons of various methods such as pass/fail, credit/no-credit, and mastery learning. This article is of value to teachers of writing in its many references to related literature on grading methods and in its discussion of some of the informal alternatives.

Wagner, Eileen N. "How to Avoid Grading Compositions." *English Journal.* (March, 1975), 76-78. The writer presents several alternatives to microscopic or atomistic grading that is the bane of most teachers of writing. Such shortcuts are "random grading," "blanket grading," and "grading by selective criterion." Each of these methods is explained and their advantages discussed to give teachers a repertoire of grading procedures and relieve the drudgery of grading compositions.

APPENDIX A

Addresses of Producers of Resources

Addison-Wesley Publishing Company, Inc.
1 Jacob Way
Reading, Massachusetts 01867

Allyn and Bacon, Inc.
7 Wells Avenue
Newton, Massachusetts 02159

American Book Company
135 West 50th Street
New York, New York 11104

American Technical Publishers
12235 South Laramie Avenue
Alsip, Illinois 60658

Bay Area Writing Project
Tolman Hall
University of California
Berkeley, California 94720

Center for Applied Linguistics
3520 Prospect Street, N.W.
Washington, D.C. 20009

Educational Resources Information Center
(ERIC)
1111 Kenyon Road
Urbana, Illinois 61801

Ginn & Company
191 Spring Street
Lexington, Massachusetts 02173

Glencoe Publishing Company
8701 Wilshire Boulevard
Beverly Hills, California 90211

Harcourt Brace Jovanovich, Inc.
757 Third Avenue
New York, New York 10017

Holt, Rinehart & Winston
383 Madison Avenue
New York, New York 10017

Houghton Mifflin Company
2 Park Street
Boston, Massachusetts 02107

Indiana University Press
601 North Morton Street
Bloomington, Indiana 47405

L & S Books
Department of English
University of Central Arkansas
Conway, Arkansas 72032

Longmans Group, Ltd.
19 West 44th Street
Suite 1012
New York, New York 10036

Macmillan Publishing Company, Inc.
866 Third Avenue
New York, New York 10022

Charles E. Merrill Publishing Company
Division of Bell & Howell Company
1300 Alum Creek Drive
Columbus, Ohio 43216

Mouton Publications
Division of Walter DeGruyter, Inc.
200 Saw Mill River Road
Hawthorne, New York 10532

National Council of Teachers of English
1111 Kenyon Road
Urbana, Illinois 61801

Oxford University Press, Inc.
200 Madison Avenue
New York, New York 10016

Prentice-Hall, Inc.
Educational Book Division
Englewood Cliffs, New Jersey 07632

Preston Publishing Company, Inc.
100 Avenue of the Americas
New York, New York 10013

Random House, Inc.
201 East 50th Street
New York, New York 10022

St. Martin's Press
175 Fifth Avenue
New York, New York 10010

The University of Wyoming
College of Education
Center for Research, Service and Publication
Laramie, Wyoming 82071

Winthrop Publishers
17 Dunster Street
Cambridge, Massachusetts 02138

Wylie-Padol Publishers, Inc.
Indian Rocks Beach, Florida 33535

APPENDIX B

Sample Answers

for Reproduction Pages

Reproduction Page 3–2
Probable Essay Questions in Subjects

1. narration/description
   comparison and contrast

2. topic exposition or time-order exposition
   an argument must be given

3. procedural
   a step-by-step process

4. topic exposition
   an explanation is to be given supported with details

5. topic exposition
   an argument is to be given

6. narration/description
   description is to be given

Reproduction Page 4–2
Purpose for Writing

Selection 1: The purpose is to present facts.

Selection 2: The purpose is to use the imagination in creative writing.

Selection 3: The purpose is to use the imagination and entertain the reader.

Selection 4: The purpose is to present facts.

Selection 5: The purpose is to express a viewpoint.

Selection 6: The purpose is to persuade the reader.

Reproduction Page 5-4
Fact or Opinion

1. O	7. O	13. O
2. O	8. O	14. F
3. O	9. O	15. F
4. O	10. O	16. O
5. O	11. F	17. O
6. F	12. O	18. F

Reproduction Page 6-3
Analogies

1. c	8. b	15. a
2. c	9. d	16. c
3. a	10. d	17. c
4. d	11. b	18. b
5. d	12. d	19. e
6. b	13. b	20. a
7. e	14. a	21. c

Reproduction Page 6-4
Synonyms and Antonyms

1. D (antonym)	6. B (syn.)	11. B (syn.)	16. D (ant.)
2. A (synonym)	7. D (syn.)	12. D (ant.)	17. A (syn.)
3. E (ant.)	8. C (ant.)	13. C (ant.)	18. D (syn.)
4. E (ant.)	9. E (syn.)	14. B (syn.)	19. A (syn.)
5. B (syn.)	10. E (ant.)	15. C (ant.)	20. C (syn.)

Reproduction Page 6-5
Rebus Game

doubleplay

joke's on you

the seven seas

bicycle

think twice

crossword

split personality

star wars

mind over matter

six feet under ground

side by side

bilevel

three degrees below 0

Reproduction Page 6-10
Compound Words

Two Nouns	Adjective and Noun
bookcase	redcoat
houseboat	highchair
tablecloth	chessman
pancake	anybody
horseshoe	brownshoe

Verb and Noun	Verb and Adverb
sailboat	crackdown
driveway	knockdown
workhorse	turnoff
watchband	begone
throwback	castaway

Reproduction Page 6-12
Common Word Roots

I. DENT	II. CHRON	III. RUPT	IV. GRESS	V. PAN	VI. POTE, POSS
2	3	1	3	1	5
3	6	4	7	10	1
4	5	2	5	6	7
1	1	6	2	8	2
5	2	5	1	4	3
6	4	3	4	9	2
			8	2	6
			6	3	4
			9	7	9
				5	10

Reproduction Page 6-18
Suffixes

1. fooling	11. stocker	21. kindly
2. fooled	12. stocked	22. kinder
3. quicker	13. rocket	23. starter
4. quickness	14. rockless	24. started
5. ticker	15. rocker	25. wicket
6. ticking	16. rocking	26. wickless
7. ticked	17. rocked	27. helpless
8. tickly	18. friendly	28. helping
9. stocky	19. wooded	29. helped
10. stocking	20. teaching	30. helper

Reproduction Page 6-19
Suffixes

childish

courageous

darkness

graceful

helpless

illustration

imitation

mischievous

movable

noticeable

politeness

readiness

slowly

softness

sweetly

worthless

payable

blamable

brotherly

dangerous

political

lawless

amorous — full of love

reprehensible — able to be blamed

capable — able

ductile — easily led

foolish — like a fool

petition — act of petitioning

meaningless — without meaning

dutiful — full of duty

motivation — act of motivating

reservation — act of reserving

departmentalism — practice of using departments

brotherhoodism — theory or practice of brotherhood

exceptionally — act of excepting

masterful — full of mastery

mischievousness — full of the quality of mischief

adaptation — act of adapting

Reproduction Page 6-20
Suffixes

geology — earth's history and life

astrology — stars and how they affect humans

herpetology — reptiles and amphibians

archaeology — material remains of earlier people

etymology — origins of words

biology — life

entomology — insects

meteorology — the atmosphere, weather

ornithology — birds

anthropology — humans

psychology — human mind

zoology — animals

Reproduction Page 7–6
Types of Essay Questions

1. cause and effect
2. cause and effect, or time
3. procedure
4. procedure
5. comparison
6. comparison or space

Reproduction Page 7–7
Reference Ties in Meaning

1. boat
2. the men
3. hill
4. the sea or the sea's play (movement)
5. the sea or the sea's play

"Richard Cory"

1. people on the pavement
2. Richard Cory
3. Richard Cory
4. the people
5. the people
6. the people
7. Richard Cory

Reproduction Page 7–8
Cohesion in Reference

1. his
2. his or her
3. her
4. me
5. It
6. She
7. They
8. It

Reproduction Page 7-12
Ties for Meaning

Hereafter — indicates time.

That is — indicates a specific detail or example that explains the preceding sentence.

But — indicates a contrast to what has been said before.

if — indicates a condition that may not exist, is hypothetical.

Reproduction Page 7–13
Cohesion in Repetition

   1. Californians: race of people

                      not merely inhabitants

                      Southerners of the West

                      loyal to their city

                      go into detail

   2. Chicago: Hog Butcher

                 Toolmaker

                 Stacker of Wheat

                 Player with Railroads

                 Nation's Freight Handler

                 City of the Big Shoulders

Reproduction Page 8–1
Using Repetition to Combine Sentences

   1. A skier who finds rocks instead of snow is liable to get upset.

   2. The outlaw ran from the sheriff, who organized a posse.

   3. Although it is usually quiet during the week, the skating rink, which is the only one in town, is very busy on weekends.

   4. The heavy waves that crashed against our boat changed what had been a calm sea.

   5. I know a talented actress who starred recently in our school play.

Reproduction Page 8–2
Combining Sentences with Phrases

   1. It was a dark stormy night with rain soaking through my sweater, chilling me through and through.

   2. Joe, quick, agile, and strong, played a winning game of tennis with a dynamic serve and a powerfully driven forehand.

   3. The scavengers are diving off the reef searching for treasure buried deep in the ocean floor centuries ago.

APPENDIX C

Reproduction Pages

THE WRITING PROCESS IN FIVE STEPS

Step 1 Prewriting   Time:
    Brain pick for ideas
    Choose a topic
    Incubate to let hatch
        Establish purpose: persuade, inform, entertain, etc.
        Select mode: narration, exposition, etc.
        Determine audience
    Narrow the topic
        Write the topic sentence
    Choose supporting details
        Outline in order: time sequence, topical, story form

Step 2 Initial Draft   Time:

Step 3 Preparing to revise the draft   Time:
    Read initial draft aloud to hear it
    Have a peer read it to critique it

Step 4 Editing the draft   Time:
    Sentence construction: fragments, complexity, awkwardness
    Punctuation and capitalization
    Spelling (when in doubt, use dictionary)
    Word choice and usage
    Paragraph effectiveness
        Interesting opening
        Supporting middle
        Summarizing conclusion
    Appropriate title

Step 5 Finalizing the composition   Time:
    Handwriting legible, in ink
    Even margins
    Title centered and capitalized
    Author's name and date on paper

                                           Total Time:

Areas to improve:

PREWRITING
STUDENT WORKSHEET

Topic

Subject in general:

Narrow to a specific aspect of the subject:

Narrow again:

Purpose

What my intention is:

What effect I want this to have on my audience:

Audience

Who my audience is:

What their special characteristics are:

Attitude

How I feel about my topic:

How my attitude will affect the tone of my writing:

Experience

What I know about this subject:

What other information I need:

Where I will get further information:

Persona

The role or approach I should take toward my audience:

I am an equal, an authority, or a character:

Mode

The form of writing that is best—an essay, story, letter, poem, procedures:

I will use either narration, description, procedural, time-order exposition, or topic exposition:

FEELINGS THAT PERSONS HAVE—BUT OFTEN FAIL TO IDENTIFY

Abandoned	Cruel	Foolish	Jealous
Adamant	Crushed	Frantic	Joyous
Adequate	Culpable	Free	Jumpy
Affectionate		Frightened	
Agonized	Deceitful	Frustrated	Keen
Almighty	Defeated	Full	Kicky
Ambivalent	Delighted	Furious	Kind
Angry	Desirous		
Annoyed	Despair	Gay	Laconic
Anxious	Destructive	Glad	Lazy
Apathetic	Determined	Good	Lecherous
Astounded	Different	Gratified	Left out
	Diffident	Greedy	Licentious
Bad	Diminished	Grieved	Lonely
Beautiful	Discontented	Groovy	Longing
Betrayed	Distracted	Guilty	Loving
Bitter	Distraught	Gullible	Low
Blissful	Disturbed		Lustful
Bold	Divided	Happy	
Bored	Dominated	Hateful	Mad
Brave	Dubious	Heavenly	Maudlin
Burdened		Helpful	Mean
	Eager	Helpless	Melancholy
Calm	Ecstatic	High	Miserable
Capable	Electrified	Homesick	Mystical
Captivated	Empty	Honored	
Challenged	Enchanted	Horrible	Naughty
Charmed	Energetic	Hurt	Nervous
Cheated	Enervated	Hysterical	Nice
Cheerful	Envious		Niggardly
Childish	Evil	Ignored	Nutty
Clever	Exasperated	Immortal	
Combative	Excited	Imposed on	Obnoxious
Competitive	Exhausted	Impressed	Obsessed
Condemned		Infatuated	Odd
Confused	Fascinated	Infuriated	Opposed
Conspicuous	Fawning	Inspired	Outraged
Contented	Fearful	Intimidated	Overwhelmed
Contrite	Flustered	Isolated	

Pained	Rejected	Sorrowful	Thwarted
Panicked	Relaxed	Spiteful	Tired
Parsimonious	Relieved	Startled	Trapped
Peaceful	Remorse	Stingy	Troubled
Persecuted	Restless	Strange	
Petrified	Reverent	Stuffed	Ugly
Pity	Rewarded	Stunned	Uneasy
Pleasant	Righteous	Stupefied	Unsettled
Pleased		Stupid	
Precarious	Sad	Suffering	Vehement
Pressured	Sated	Sure	Violent
Pretty	Satisfied	Sympathetic	Vital/vitality
Prim	Scared		Vivacious
Prissy	Screwed up	Talkative	Vulnerable
Proud	Servile	Tempted	
	Settled	Tenacious	Weepy
Quarrelsome	Sexy	Tense	Wicked
Queer	Shocked	Tentative	Wonderful
	Silly	Tenuous	Worried
Rage	Skeptical	Terrible	
Rapture	Sneaky	Terrified	Zany
Refreshed	Solemn	Threatened	

EDITING: FIRST DRAFT

What do I want to say?

	Yes	No

PURPOSE:
    Was the original purpose clear in my mind?
        (If no, redefine your intentions.)
    Is the purpose stated clearly in the writing?
        Can I find it?
        Did my peer critic find it?
        (If no, write it in.)
    Does the title indicate the purpose?
    Is the mode of writing suitable to my purpose?
        Narration—tells a story
        Exposition—explains a point
        Demonstration—shows how to do something
        Instruction—gives directions
        Other—

AUDIENCE:
    Did I clearly define my audience to myself?
    Is the vocabulary appropriate?
    Is the sentence structure suitable for the age and educational
        levels?
    Is the tone appropriate?
        Businesslike
        Joking
        Authoritative
        Hostile or angry
        Other:
    Is length of description or information suitable to the
        background of the audience?
    Is there definite appeal to the interests of the audience?

	Yes	No

How Have I Said What I Want to Say?

CONTENT:
    Do my ideas "sound good" when I read them aloud to myself?
    Did I say what I wanted to say?
    Is it of value to the reader?
    Do I believe it is worth saying?
        (If no, tear it up.)

ORGANIZATION:
    Will the reader find a logical order in what I said—time,
        comparison, cause and effect, plot, or procedure?
        Other:
    Is my topic statement clear and recognizable?
    Is the topic supported with details and/or descriptions?
    Are there a beginning, body, and ending?
    Are there connectives to give the reader clues to my logical
        organization—*therefore, also, because, first, if,* etc.?
        Others:

SKILLS:
    Does my writing "sound good" when I read it aloud?
    Does every sentence express a complete thought?
    Are words misspelled?
    Is the punctuation effective?
    Do all pronouns have clear references?
    Is the handwriting legible and neat?

PROOFREADING GUIDE
FINAL DRAFT

Does my paper have:	Yes	No
1. a title?		
2. a clear introduction?		
3. a logical development?		
4. one central idea in each paragraph?		
5. any sentence fragments?		
6. a variety of sentence types?		
7. transition between ideas?		
8. appropriate word choices?		
9. agreement of subject and verb?		
10. clear reference of pronouns to their antecedents?		
11. verified (in dictionary) spellings of words?		
12. punctuation at the end of each sentence?		
13. commas: for items in a series? before the conjunction in a compound sentence? before introductory words such as *however, therefore,* etc.? before introductory phrases?		
14. sources of credits, a bibliography, etc.?		

MODES OF COMPOSITION

Narration/Description: tells a story using description, characters, a plot; compares and contrasts using coordinating conjunctions such as *but, or, yet.*

Story Components	*Structure*
goal	prose
characters	poetry
time	metaphorical language
place	creative use of language
incidents	plot
resolution	a point to make near the end
theme	

Procedural: relates a process step by step using words of transition.

Components	*Structure*
sequence	prose
imperative sentences (commands)	elliptical sentences (subject *you* is
unstated steps	eliminated)
abbreviations and symbols	sequence to be followed
referents	elements listed first and directions follow
product or final outcome	assume some reader experience

Time-Order Exposition: presents events in a time sequence with characters often mentioned; there is a problem to be solved and the sequencing is often cause and effect.

Components	*Structure*
cause and effect	prose
causality/motivation	sequence to be followed
final events most important	transition "ties" connect events

Topic Exposition: states an argument or clear topic; has supporting details and logical connections.

Components	*Structure*
no event sequence	prose
main idea or topic	clear statement of main idea
supporting details or examples	clear summary of topic
relationships connected logically	transition "ties" connect details
specialized vocabulary	concepts defined
often abstract information	relationships built for the reader between known and new concepts

PROBABLE ESSAY QUESTIONS IN SUBJECTS

Directions: Tell what mode of composition would be best suited for each essay question given in different school subjects: narration/description, procedural, topic exposition, or time-order exposition. State your reasons for your choice based on what you know about each mode's components.

1. Compare and contrast the English colonists with the Spanish colonists. Were their settlements similar?

   Mode _____

   Reasons _____

2. Who were Lewis and Clark? Why was their expedition important?

   Mode _____

   Reasons _____

3. Tell how you could cut a doughnut into twelve pieces with exactly three straight slices.

   Mode _____

   Reasons _____

4. What is Sandburg's evaluation of Lincoln's speech as shown in the last eight paragraphs of the essay you just read?

   Mode _____

   Reasons _____

5. "The writer could end the story at any point after any experience she related." Why is this statement true?

   Mode _____

   Reasons _____

6. Describe in your own words the images Wright creates in his short story.

   Mode _____

   Reasons _____

MODES OF TEXT IN DIFFERENT CONTENT FIELDS

Directions: For each of the passages below, decide which school subject it comes from and which mode of writing it represents: procedural, time-order exposition, topic exposition, or narration/description. Each school subject has its particular form and mode of expression in its written communication; being aware of each should help you in writing and reading the subject.

Passage 1

Bells pealed all over England. Bells rang in the 13 colonies, too. They were celebrating the British victories over the French in North America and all over the world. England had won from France all of Canada and all the land between the Appalachian Mountains and the Mississippi River. And England was the most powerful nation in the world. It was a great time to be an Englishman.

The time was 1763. The war was the French and Indian War. The colonists were proud of England's victory, because they had helped to win it. But this great victory soon began to cause trouble.

Passage 2

A small plane used 4.8 gallons of gasoline the first hour, 6.4 gallons of gasoline the second hour, and 5.9 gallons of gasoline the third hour. How many gallons of gasoline did it use in the three hours?

Passage 3

The mass of an object is what makes it necessary to push, pull, or lift the object in order to move it. Its weight is how much it pushes down on a scale. Two objects with the same mass have the same weight when they are weighed at the same place. In the metric system, mass units are usually used to report weight. Milligrams and grams are used to report very small weights.

Passage 4

It was the green heart of the canyon, where the walls swerved back from the rigid plain and relieved their harshness of line by making a little sheltered nook and filling it to the brim with sweetness and roundness and softness. Here all things rested. Even the narrow stream ceased its turbulent downrush long enough to form a quiet pool. Knee-deep in the water, with drooping head and half-shut eyes, drowsed a red-coated, many-antlered buck.

Passage 5

Many circumstances led to the war of 1812—among them land hunger, national pride, Indian relations, and the fur trade. But in his war message to Congress, President Madison emphasized two major reasons—the continued seizure of American ships and the impressment of American sailors.

Thus, as you know, Congress declared war on June 18, 1812, two days after the British Parliament had suspended the Orders in Council. Many Americans, among them Henry Clay, believed that the Kentucky militia could conquer Canada in three weeks. However, the war dragged on for more than two years. (From *Rise of the American Nation* by Lewis P. Todd and Merle Curti. Copyright 1977 by Harcourt Brace Jovanovish, Inc. Reprinted by permission of the publisher.)

Passage 6

There is evidence that about four billion years ago most of the earth's surface was covered with molten rock. The first rock of the crust was igneous rock formed as the molten material cooled. The igneous rock formed a thick layer covering the surface of the young earth. Since its formation, the igneous rock on the continents has been exposed to the agents of erosion.

The chief agent of erosion is running water. Water flowing over the surface can pick up small pieces of rock. Also, small amounts of many of the minerals in rock dissolve in the water. The small rock pieces and dissolved mineral carried by running water is called a load. Every stream from the smallest trickle to the biggest river carries a load. For example, near its mouth, the Mississippi River moves a load of about 15 tons each second.

Passage 7

Solids can be divided into two major groups—ionic solids and molecular solids. Ionic solids are formed by a chemical bond called an electrovalent, or ionic, bond. Molecular solids are formed by a chemical bond called a covalent bond. But how does an ionic bond differ from a covalent bond? In an ionic bond, electrons from the outer orbitals of one atom are transferred to the outer orbitals of a second atom. In the formation of a covalent bond, electrons are shared between the outer orbitals of the atoms that form the bond.

Passage 8

Oparin suggested that the atmosphere of primitive earth was mainly made of gases such as ammonia (NH_3), methane (CH_4), hydrogen (H_2), and water vapor (H_2O). Such an atmosphere would have allowed far more of the sun's radiant energy to reach the earth than reaches it now. According to Oparin's hypothesis, energy from lightning, ultraviolet light from the sun, or gamma radiation split some of these gas molecules. Splitting of the gas molecules resulted in the bonding of carbon, hydrogen, oxygen and nitrogen in new ways to form new molecules. The new organic molecules collected in shallow pools forming a sort of "organic soup." A warm rain continually added more molecules. Through millions of years the soup became more concentrated. Simple molecules reacted together to form more complex molecules. Oparin believed that the first cells could have formed in such a soup.

Passage 9

The year's at the spring
And day's at the morn;
Morning's at seven;
The hillside's dew-pearled;
The lark's on the wing;
The snail's on the thorn:
God's in his heaven—
All's right with the world !

A RECIPE, AN EQUATION, AND A POEM

Pecan Pie

Serve this very rich pie in small wedges.

Set the oven at 450°.

Line a 9-inch pie pan with Plain Pastry (p. 407)

Mix and pour into the pie pan

   3 eggs, slightly beaten

   1/2 cup brown or white sugar

   1/4 teaspoon salt

   1 cup light corn syrup

   1/2 teaspoon vanilla

   1 cup pecans, broken in pieces

Bake 10 minutes. Reduce the heat to 350° and

bake 35 minutes longer. Chill. When ready to

serve, spread over the top 1/2 cup heavy cream, whipped

Garnish with pecan halves

   The Fannie Farmer Cookbook

   Eleventh Ed. Boston, Mass.: Little

   Brown and Company, 1965 (p. 418)

Name the sum:

$$\frac{1}{2} + \frac{1}{2} = a$$

$$\frac{1}{4} + \frac{2}{4} + \frac{1}{4} = b$$

$$\frac{1}{8} + \frac{3}{8} + \frac{3}{8} + \frac{1}{8} = c$$

$$\frac{1}{16} + \frac{4}{16} + \frac{6}{16} + \frac{4}{16} + \frac{1}{16} = d$$

Continue the equation pattern for 2 more rows.

How can you name the numerator of the sum for each row?

   Modern School Mathematics (Grade 8) by Mary P.

   Dolciani. Boston, Mass.: Houghton Mifflin Co., 1978.

Much Madness

Much madness is divinest sense

To a discerning eye;

Much sense the starkest madness.

'Tis the majority

In this, as all, prevails.

Assent, and you are sane;

Demur,—you're straightway dangerous,

And handled with a chain.

   Emily Dickinson

LANGUAGE IN YOUR TEXTBOOK

Directions: Select three representative passages in your content area textbook to analyze.

PASSAGES

If organized in paragraphs, what is the mode of development used in each passage: temporal exposition (time), topical exposition, narration, or procedures?

Passage 1.

    2.

    3.

If not in paragraphs, explain the structure:

Explain the *purpose* of each passage:
1.

2.

3.

How and where is the topic of each passage clearly presented?
1.

2.

3.

List the transition words used, if any, in each passage that show logical relationships (*however, therefore, first*, etc.):
1.

2.

3.

What kind of background knowledge is required of the reader in each passage?
1.

2.

3.

SENTENCES

Are sentences varied and appropriate in their complexity for the age level intended?

1.

2.

3.

Is each sentence loaded with several concepts or just one clear idea?

1.

2.

3.

What kinds of transformations are common in each passage (passives, questions, requests, negatives)?

1.

2.

3.

Does every referent (pronouns, etc.) have a clear antecedent especially across sentences? List the referents and their antecedents in each passage.

1.

2.

3.

WORDS

Which words in each passage have multiple connotative meanings?

1.

2.

3.

Which difficult words would be easier for readers with a simple synonym in each passage?

1.

2.

3.

How are new vocabulary words presented in the context of each passage (as appositives, highlighted, italicized, underlined, etc.)?

1.

2.

3.

CONCEPTS (main ideas)

From titles and subheadings, what major points that extend throughout the entire passage can be clearly identified in each passage?

1.

2.

3.

From the topic sentences, what points can be identified that clarify and restrict the main idea?

1.

2.

3.

From the details, examples, or reasons given in each passage, what are the specific points that can be identified?

1.

2.

3.

OVERALL LANGUAGE USE

Comment on the writing in your textbook. What about it makes it easy or difficult to read, in your opinion?

DEVELOPING SENTENCES:
NARRATION—HEIGHTENING THE EFFECT OF THE VERB

Sensory detail

Examples: 1 It was as if Jincey had glimpsed some universal beauty
      2 —of sorrow, perhaps,
      2 or of nobility—
      2 too poignant for her to bear.

Francis Gray Patton, "The Terrible Miss Dove"

  1 Visibly the swiftness and power of the masses of water increased,
      2 swirling into quicker and quicker movements its living black surface,
      2 dispersing its pattern,
      2 carrying away more and more of it
         3 on the hastening current.

Carl Stephenson, "Leiningen Versus the Ants"

Practice: 1 The waves crashed to the shore,
      2 _____
      2 _____

  1 The model posed for the artist
      2 _____
      2 _____

Intangible (emotional) detail

Examples: 2 His mouth dry,
      2 his heart down,
  1 Nick reeled in.

Ernest Hemingway, "Big Two-Hearted River"

  1 But he had already jerked straight around,
      2 stared,
      2 glared again,
      2 and seen but the quiet day.

Henry James, *The Turn of the Screw*

Practice: 1 She ran into the bus station,
      2 _____
      2 _____
      2 _____
      2 _____
  1 Joe stared into space.

Metaphorical Detail

Examples: 2 Shivering a little,
  1 She lay back beneath her coat,
      2 with closed eyes,
      2 her night-dark hair spread out on my pillow,
      2 her hand cold as earth in mine.

Robert Nathan, *A Portrait of Jenny*

Practice: 2 Riding his motorcycle,
      2 in his black leather jacket,
  1 _____

DEVELOPING SENTENCES:
DESCRIPTION—HEIGHTENING THE EFFECT OF THE NOUN

Sensory Detail

Example: 2 With his bustling gray hair, bulky nose, and lucid eyes,

        1 he had the look of an aging and shabby eagle.

                                  Carl Stephenson, "Leiningen Versus the Ants"

        1 The firelight fell on him;

          2 he was hideous;

          2 it was a sinister apparition.

                                      Victor Hugo, *Les Miserables*

Practice: 1 The newborn colt stood up in the barn,

        2 _____

        2 _____

        2 Running his hands over the smooth, shiny chrome,

      1 _____

        2 _____

Intangible (Emotional) Detail

Examples: 1 It was not anger,

          2 nor surprise,

          2 nor disapproval,

          2 nor honor,

          2 nor any of the sentiments

            3 that she had been prepared for.

                                O. Henry, "The Gift of the Magi"

        2 For under the level gaze of Miss Dove

      1 she would begin to feel

          2 —though she wore her handsomest tweeds and perhaps

             a gardenia for courage—

          2 that she was about ten years old and her petticoat was showing.

                        Francis Gray Patton, "The Terrible Miss Dove"

Practice: 1   The ballerina danced magnificently

    2 _____

    2 _____

    2 Feeling guilty,

1 _____

    2 _____

Metaphorical Detail

Examples: 1   He was a big brute of man,
            2   a veritable gorilla,
            2   one of those hard-hitting, rough-housing chaps,
            2   and clever with his fists as well.

                              Jack London, "The Heathen"

    2   However frequently a twelve-year-old boy was washed,
1   he always smelled like a bird's nest.

                     Francis Gray Patton, "The Terrible Miss Dove"

Practice: 2 _____

1   my life is just beginning

    2 _____

1   There must be a reason

    2 _____

    2 _____

Examples: 1   He went home
            2   like a man stung by a whole swarm of bees,
            2   like a man scalded with boiling water.

                       Anton Chekhov, "A Slander"

Practice: 1   The batter hit the ball

    2 _____

    2 _____

1   She slapped him in the face

    2 _____

DEVELOPING SENTENCES: EXPOSITION—USING LOGICAL ORDER

Time-Order

Examples: 2 Following its usual pattern,
             1 the weather, fine in the early morning, worsened
               2 as the day advanced,
             1 and soon they were moving
               2 through gray clouds and squalls of snow.
                        James Ramsey Ullman, "Victory on Everest"

             2 Even then,
             1 there had to be a catastrophe
               2 before he could realize his desire.
                        Haroun Tazieff, "Caves of Adventure"

             1 Most of my books have themes, or underlying ideas,
               2 which you can find
               2 if you explore like this below the surface of the story.
                        Howard Pease, "A Letter to a Fan"

Practice: 2 When I was stationed in Bermuda,

             1 _____

             2 _____

             2 If I try hard enough,

             1 _____

Topic (Examples, Details, Logical Connectors) Development

Examples: 2 On the other hand,
             1 I can remember few of my teachers and little of the subjects
               2 which seemed to me irrelevant to my life.
                        Lincoln Steffens, "Preparing for College"

             1 I can vision only dimly the grace of a Pavlova,
               2 although I know something of the delight of rhythm,
               2 for often I can sense the beat of music
               2 as it vibrates through the floor.
                        Helen Keller, "Three Days to See"

             1 I must find a balance somewhere,
                or an alternating rhythm between these two extremes:
             2 a swinging of the pendulum
                 3 between solitude and communion,
                 3 between retreat and return.
                      Anne Morrow Lindburgh, "Gift from the Sea"

Practice: 1 The child stood sobbing in the rain

             2 _____

             2 Because he was so tall,

              1 _____

             2 _____

PURPOSE IN WRITING

Directions: Following are four possible reasons for writing something to a reader in a school assignment. For each reason given below, write out two or more sentences that will demonstrate the purpose.

Reason for writing—*to express a viewpoint or opinion*
    (*Hint:* write about your religious beliefs.)

Reason for writing—*to use the imagination (creative writing)*
    (*Hint:* describe a haunted house.)

Reason for writing—*to persuade the reader to do something*
    (*Hint:* convince the reader to contribute money to a cause.)

Reason for writing—*to present facts*
    (*Hint:* give some facts about the room you are in.)

PURPOSE FOR WRITING

Directions: Each writer of the following selections had a specific reason for writing. Identify the purpose for each communication.

Selection 1

Maria and Henry Mitchell, two of the ten children in a family, were born and grew up on the island of Nantucket, located off the southern coast of Massachusetts. Their father, William, was interested in navigation and astronomy and encouraged his children to explore the skies with him.

Maria (1818-1889) did excellent work in arithmetic and was able to help her father with astronomical calculations. She went on to study and explore on her own. In 1847 she discovered a new comet, for which she was awarded a gold medal by the King of Denmark. Some years later, Matthew Vassar invited her to be the first professor of astronomy at his new college at Poughkeepsie, New York.

Henry (1830-1902) went into the Coast Survey and studied the tides. He was considered to be the leading hydrographer in America in his day.

[Mary P. Dolciani, William Wooten, and Edwin Beckenbach, *Algebra*, Book 1 (Boston: Houghton Mifflin, 1980), p. 15.]

Selection 2

Dark hills at evening in the west,
Where sunset hovers like a sound
Of golden horns that sang to rest
Old bones of warriors under ground,
Far now from all the bannered ways
Where flash the legions of the sun,
You fade—as if the last of days
Were fading, and all wars were done.

[E. A. Robinson, "The Dark Hills." Reprinted with permission of Macmillan Company from *Collected Poems* by Edwin Arlington Robinson. Copyright 1920 by Edwin Arlington Robinson, renewed 1948 by Ruth Nivison.]

Selection 3

It was in the Year of the Dry Summer that Paul Bunyan's loggers first encountered mosquitoes. That was the season Paul Bunyan invented thunder. Day after day, week after week, month after month, the great hero-leader of the loggers toiled through experiments with all the sounds he could imagine. Just as cows, pigs, dogs, hens, and ducks could be called, so could clouds be called, thought Paul Bunyan. Seventeen thousand various kinds of calls the great logger tried that summer before he hit on the sound of thunder. Then his labors were rewarded. Paul Bunyan had not thundered once before a stray cloud rolled up from the west. He thundered on, and by midnight so many clouds had gathered that the Dry Summer ended in a downpour that was a deluge instead of a rain. Ever since that parched season the weather has used the thunder which Paul Bunyan invented for it.

[James Stevens, *"An American Hercules"*]

Selection 4

The Stevens Party left Council Bluffs on May 18, 1844. Before doing so, they performed what may well have been the act that contributed most to their final success—they elected Elisha Stevens to be their captain.

He was an unusual enough sort of fellow, that Stevens—about forty years old, with a big hawk nose and a peaked head; strange-acting, too. He seemed friendly enough, but he was solitary, having his own wagon but neither chick nor child. Born in South Carolina, raised in Georgia, he had trapped in the Rockies for some years, then spent a while in Louisiana, and now finally he was off for California, though no one knows why.

[George Stewart, "The Smart Ones Got Through" in *Adventures in American Literature*, p. 207.]

Selection 5

Maybe what I am trying to say is that a film must act, a book has time to think and wonder. There is the essential difference which keeps me, for all my love of movie-going and film-writing, still a confirmed novel writer and an enthusiastic novel reader. In the flush of TV spectaculars, wider and wider screeneramas, and all the rest of our frightful, fruitful mechanical advancements, the book is still the essential civilizing influence, able to penetrate the unknowns of human aspiration.

[Budd Schulberg, "Why Write It if You Can't Sell It to Pictures?" in *Adventures in American Literature*, p. 184.]

Selection 6

Take a look at and a test-drive in the new Mazda RX-7GS. It is, quite simply, a superbly balanced, highly responsive machine of incredible capability. And the more sophisticated your own driving abilities, the more you'll find to marvel at as you feel it master the road.

[In *Newsweek* magazine, January 12, 1981.]

RELATIONSHIPS OF WRITER TO AUDIENCE

Directions: Below are four kinds of relationships between a writer and a reader. Each one progresses from personal and informal to impersonal and formal.
    Write three or more sentences to illustrate each one of the kinds of relationships. Notice how your language changes according to your relationship with the reader.

Reflection—writing to yourself, as in a diary

Conversation—writing gossip to a friend and expecting an answer

Correspondence—writing to someone who is at a distance (not necessarily a letter) about a subject known to both writer and reader

Public Narrative—writing formally to a large, unknown audience about an impersonal subject

AUDIENCE/PURPOSE/TONE

Holden Caulfield

If you really want to hear about it, the first thing you'll probably want to know is where I was born, and what my lousy childhood was like, and how my parents were occupied and all before they had me, and all that David Copperfield kind of crap, but I don't feel like going into it, if you want to know the truth. In the first place, that stuff bores me, and in the second place, my parents would have about two hemorrhages apiece if I told anything pretty personal about them. They're quite touchy about anything like that, especially my father. They're nice and all—I'm not saying that—but they're also touchy as hell. Besides, I'm not going to tell you my whole goddam autobiography or anything. I'll just tell you about this madman stuff that happened to me around last Christmas just before I got pretty run-down and had to come out here and take it easy.

David Copperfield

Whether I shall turn out to be the hero of my own life, or whether that station will be held by anybody else, these pages must show. To begin my life with the beginning of my life, I record that I was born (as I have been informed and believe) on a Friday, at twelve o'clock at night. It was remarked that the clock began to strike, and I began to cry simultaneously.

In consideration of the day and hour of my birth, it was declared by the nurse and by some sage women in the neighborhood who had taken a lively interest in me several months before there was any possibility of our becoming personally acquainted, first that I was destined to be unlucky in life; and secondly, that I was privileged to see ghosts and spirits: both these gifts inevitably attaching, as they believed, to all unlucky infants of either gender born towards the small hours on a Friday night.

Source: From Walker Gibson, *Persona: A Style Study for Readers and Writers* (New York: Random House, 1969), p. 53.

AUDIENCE/PURPOSE PREWRITING WORKSHEET

Directions: Answer the following questions regarding your decisions on the audience and the purpose for your writing:

	Yes	No
1. I have clearly identified the audience to whom I am writing.		
2. The audience I am directing this to is: _____		
3. I realize the familiarity of the audience with my subject and will explain it according to their understanding.		
4. The vocabulary used is suitable for the level of audience.		
5. The style I choose is appropriate with an informal style for more familiar audiences, and a more formal style for unknown audiences.		
6. My purpose for writing is made very clear to the reader.		
7. My purpose for writing this is: _____		
8. The form of composition (essay, story, letter, report, etc.) I have chosen is appropriate for the subject and my reason for writing.		
9. The form of composition I choose to write in is: _____		
10. I clearly understand my purpose in writing this and what kind of audience I am writing to.		

THE BUSINESS LETTER

Make sure that your business letter is the best representation of yourself with regard to effective communication and appearance as is possible. The general form to be used for writing an effective business letter is given below.

1. A business letter is usually typewritten on an 8½ X 11 inch sheet of paper.
2. Your return address is typed nine single spaces down from the top. Then type the addressee's address four single spaces down. Leave double spaces between parts of the letter and between paragraphs.
3. Use either the semiblock form, in which paragraphs are indented five spaces, or the block form, in which there is no indentation.
4. Use only one side of the paper. Fold the paper in thirds, folding up from the bottom first.

A model of a good business letter form is included below:

(9 spaces)

> Your Name
> 1815 Overland Avenue
> City, State   Zip Code
> Date

(4 spaces)

Mr. John Smith
445 Street Place
City, State   Zip Code

Dear Mr. Smith:

Thank you so much for the information you sent me regarding the business transaction we discussed recently.

As soon as I have carefully read all the information you sent me, I will be in touch with you again.

In the event you have additional information relative to costs involved, please let me know.

Yours truly,

(4 spaces)

Your Name

Mr. John Smith
445 Street Place
City, State   Zip Code

Your Name
1815 Overland Avenue
City, State   Zip Code

A RESUME

Name: Your Name
         1815 Overland Avenue
         City, State Zip Code
         Telephone Number

Personal Statistics (Optional):
         Age
         Weight, height
         Marital status
         Social security number

Educational Background: (start with most recent)
         College   Dates of attendance
         Address
         Phone number

         High School   Dates of attendance
         Address
         Phone Number

Work Experience: (start with most recent)
         Employment   Position
         Address
         Employer to contact
         Dates of employment
         Phone number

         Employer   Position
         Address
         Employer to contact
         Phone number

Professional, Club, Community and Service Activities
         Clubs at school, positions held, honors awarded
         Community organizations you belong to
         Charitable contributions (participation for charitable purposes)
         Church activities
         Awards won
         Services performed

Career Goals
    My career plans include finishing college with a degree in nursing so that I may be of
service to people. My experience and background appear suitable for the job description
you have advertised, and my interests in nursing would be complemented in such a position.
I am particularly interested in obtaining work in such a capacity.

LETTER OF APPLICATION

The following is a model letter of application. An effective letter of application has several major characteristics:

1. It conforms to all the requirements of a good business letter and is free of all errors. Proofread it carefully.
2. The first paragraph may mention the source of information about the position or award, the second may give information about qualifications for it, the third may list references, and the fourth may suggest further communication.
3. The message should be closely tailored to responding to specifics about the job description or award and presented with sincerity.

LETTER OF APPLICATION—MODEL

Your Name
Address
City, State   Zip Code
Date

Mr. Samuel Zelinko
382 Houseman Street
City, State   Zip Code

Dear Mr. Zelinko:

According to your advertisement in Sunday's newspaper, you wish to employ a reliable boy to help with deliveries and to do errands after school hours and on Saturdays. I would very much like to have you consider me for this work.

I am sixteen years old and am now in the tenth grade. For two summers I have been employed with the Local Pharmacy Company as a delivery boy and general helper. Mr. John Jones is my employer and he can inform you of my qualifications and work experience. His telephone number is 846-2045.

Other references are my minister at church, Rev. Mr. Charles Smith, whose telephone number is 846-3456. Also, the counselor at Washington High School will provide me a reference. Mr. James may be reached at 846-2344.

Thank you for considering my application. I should be very happy to meet with you. My telephone number is 846-7654.

Truly,

Harry Harbor

FACT OR OPINION

Directions: Read the story below. Determine if the numbered items are fact or opinion. Use what you learn here to apply to your statements in news stories, editorials, or other kind of writing.

A businessman had just turned off the lights in the store when a man appeared and demanded money. The owner opened a cash register. The contents of the cash register were scooped up and the man sped away. A member of the police force was notified promptly.

Circle F *if the statement is definitely a* fact. *Circle* O *if the statement is not a fact.*

1. A man appeared after the owner had turned off his store lights.   F   O

2. The robber was a man.   F   O

3. The man did not demand money.   F   O

4. The man who opened a cash register was the owner.   F   O

5. The store owner scooped up the contents of the cash register and ran away.   F   O

6. Someone opened a cash register.   F   O

7. After the man who demanded the money scooped up the contents of the cash register, he ran away.   F   O

8. While the cash register contained money, the story does *not* state *how much.* F   O

9. The robber demanded money of the owner.   F   O

10. The robber opened the cash register.   F   O

11. After the store lights were turned off, a man appeared.   F   O

12. The robber did not take the money with him.   F   O

13. The robber did not demand money of the owner.   F   O

14. The owner opened a cash register.   F   O

15. The age of the store owner was not revealed in the story.   F   O

16. Taking the contents of the cash register with him, the man ran out of the store.   F   O

17. The story concerns a series of events in which only three persons are referred to: the owner of the store, a man who demanded money, and a member of the police force.   F   O

18. The following events were included in the story: someone demanded money, a cash register was opened, its contents were scooped up, and a man dashed out of the store.   F   O

THE NEWS STORY AND THE EDITORIAL COLUMN

JOSEPH KRAFT

The tightening of the Soviet screw

WASHINGTON — The Russians are prepared to pounce, but they want to cut the costs of naked invasion. So creeping intervention is the name of the Soviet game in Poland.

Cracks are beginning to show in the Polish resistance. With President Reagan in the hospital and the secretary of state abroad, the focus in the United States and in allied countries lacks steadiness.

Diplomatic and propaganda pressures have mounted apace with military moves. The visit of Soviet President Leonid Brezhnev to the Czech Party Congress in Prague comes under that heading. So does the statement by the Czech leader, Gustav Husak, that the Warsaw Pact countries are "determined to maintain the status of Poland as a socialist country." The tone of menace in the Soviet press has heightened steadily.

A meeting of the Polish Parliament set for Monday this week was canceled. In announcing the cancellation, Polish authorities cited "indisposition" of the prime minister, Gen. Wojchiech Jaruzelski. Warsaw then said its delegation to the Prague Party Congress would be led by former Foreign Minister Stefan Olszowski, not Party Secretary Stanislaw Kania.

OLSZOWSKI HAS been known, since the independent trade union, Solidarity, struck against the government in August, as a partisan of tough, repressive tactics. The prime minister and party secretary, by contrast, have always opposed using force against Solidarity. What seems to be happening in Poland is a growth in the challenge posed by hard-liners around Olszowski to the more moderate leadership of Jaruzelski and Kania.

The preferred Russian scenario would probably begin with a victory for hard-liners in Warsaw. Next would come use of force by the Polish government against Solidarity and its partisans. Then, if necessary, an appeal for help by the Polish regime to the "socialist fraternity." Thus, instead of invading, the Russians would merely be slouching toward Warsaw in response to the plea of a friendly government.

The United States and its allies will determine in large part the price Russia has to pay for interference in Polish affairs. So the clear interest of the Atlantic allies is to keep the spotlight of attention steadily focused on Poland and Russia.

Two egregious examples of blurred focus, however, have cropped up.

First, there was the remark by Defense Secretary Caspar Weinberger, in London, that a Soviet invasion of Poland might trigger American military aid to China. That comment opens a whole other, extremely complicated subject. It gives the Russians at least the color of a pretext for not showing restraint. Indeed, if the idea is to make the Soviets invade, China is a good subject.

Second, there was the reluctance of the German foreign minister, Hans-Dietrich Genscher, to press the Polish question during a visit to Moscow last week. Herr Genscher talked with Brezhnev and other high Soviet officials about theater nuclear weapons, in Europe. But he didn't force the Polish issue, because the Russians showed sensitivity — which, in fact, is exactly the reason to come across loud and clear on the subject.

THE MOOD in Washington, however, does not exactly favor sharp concentration on Poland. The White House emphasis is on reassuring the country that President Reagan is alive and well and telling more jokes than ever. In keeping with that stance, the secretaries of state and defense were sent abroad last week on previously scheduled visits of no special moment.

Los Angeles Times

Polish Situation Still Is Considered Serious

(Related Stories On Page 3)

WASHINGTON (UPI) — The apparent end of Warsaw Pact maneuvers around Poland means Moscow is giving Polish leaders a little more time to solve their labor crisis, but the situation remains serious, U.S. officials said Tuesday.

The officials said the threat of invasion clearly had eased but the United States remains uncertain of Soviet intentions.

A statement issued by the State Department press office in late afternoon noted that the announced end to the Warsaw Pact exercises applies only to Soyuz 81 "and not to all military exercises in and around Poland."

"As of today we continue to observe an unusual level of military activity in the area. We will, of course, continue to watch the situation closely," the statement said. Officials said Poland's economic and political problems are chronic and the source of future problems for Warsaw as well as Moscow.

Food is scarce, industrial production is down 12 percent from last fall, and Poland has a hard currency debt to the West of more than $21 billion.

The maneuvers in and around Poland began March 17 and were expected to last a week. They were extended indefinitely, prompting concerns in the West an invasion would result.

President Reagan, recovering from an assassination attempt, sent Soviet President Leonid Brezhnev a note warning of the economic and political consequences of a Warsaw Pact invasion.

But Tuesday the Soviet —POLISH

(Continued on Page 32)

news agency Tass, as well as those in East European capitals, said the large maneuvers had ended and the troops were returning "home."

And in Prague, Brezhnev gave a lukewarm endorsement of the Polish communist leadership, telling the Czech Communist Party Congress he believed Warsaw could uphold the Socialist system.

"If he meant to say the Poles should be allowed to solve their own problems without outside interference, we welcome this," State Department spokesman William J. Dyess said. "Its been our consistent position.

"From what we have seen of Mr. Brezhnev's remarks, they do not give a clear picture of Soviet intentions and we believe it is too early to draw any firm conclusions."

Dyess said the United States remained concerned about Soviet military activity in and around Poland "and the threatening public posture taken by the Soviets and other East European countries."

"We were seeking some rational explanation for the Soviet activity, and we are still somewhat uncertain as to what the Soviet intentions are, and why the Soyuz 81 excercise was continued several days beyond the time it was supposed to end, if indeed it has now ended," Dyess said.

HUMAN INTEREST STORY

Directions: Read the human-interest feature below. Using the facts of the story, rewrite it as a first-person narrative.

Face Scarlet, She Asked: Give Me a Break, Rheff

COVENTRY, England (AP) — Moviegoers were reaching for their handkerchiefs as Rhett Butler was walking out on Scarlett O'Hara in the 228th and final minute of "Gone With the Wind." Suddenly, the screen went blank — the projector had broken down.

Enter Alan Taylor and Linda Burke. Taylor, 24, assistant manager at Coventry's ABC Cinema, and Miss Burke, 23, an ice cream saleswoman, acted out the final scene live on stage.

The impromptu actors didn't quite match the performance of Clark Gable and Vivien Leigh, nor their exact lines, but the audience roared its approval, according to accounts of the incident in British tabloids Monday.

The final scene, a la Taylor and Burke:

"Oh, Rheff. What am I going to do if you leave me?"

"The name is Rhett ... Frankly, I don't give a damn."

"Home. I'll go home. I'll find some way of getting you back. After all, tomorrow is another day."

Reprinted by permission of Associated Press.

LEAD PARAGRAPHS

Directions: The narrative lead has been cut out of the story following. Write an opening lead for this story and check the original to compare your lead to it.

A Toothpick Clock--
Wooden You Know?

Zevenbergen just spent 15 months, $15 and 15,000 toothpicks building a 4-foot-tall grandfather clock that keeps perfect time.

One of the top teens nationally recognized by the publishers of Who's Who Among American High School Students, Zevenbergen first got involved in his unusual hobby when he was in the eighth grade. Given a simple art assignment, he built a Liberty Bell, crack and all, constructed with 750 toothpicks divided in half.

"I REALLY WAS FASCINATED by all the things you could do with toothpicks," he explained. His fascination turned into motivation after a replica he made of the Eiffel Tower won him blue ribbon honors at the Osceola (Iowa) County Fair when he was a freshman in high school.

Once his new-found skill was established, he sought something "more challenging," like building a working grandfather clock.

"I copied a grandfather clock from a picture and worked out all my own dimensions to reproduce it with toothpicks," the teen related. He began with 20 boxes of picks and some glue in April 1979.

His first setback came during that summer. The warm weather and accompanying humidity forced him out of his basement workshop when a panel warped and had to be redone.

"I REALLY GOT TIRED of it at that point," Zevenbergen recalls, "and I stopped working on it for three months.

"Then suddenly I wanted to finish it and became determined to prove to myself that it could be done."

"As proud as I was of the clock," Zevenbergen now says, "I was pretty relieved when it was done." He said he isn't ready to begin any new toothpick projects in the immediate future. But his family and friends may think twice about offering him a toothpick after dinner.

CHICAGO (AP) — When David Zevenbergen picks up a toothpick, it's not to spear an hors d'oeuvre. The Sibley, Iowa, teen has more timely ideas for his toothpicks.

Reprinted by permission of Associated Press.

NEWSPAPER OBITUARIES

Directions: Read the following obituaries and decide what kind of information is given about each person. Examine the format in which the information is given. Write your own obituary including the kinds of information and following the format given in the example.

Paul F. Deeb

A memorial mass for Paul Deeb, 34, Scottsdale, Ariz., formerly of the Denver area, was Tuesday at Our Lady of Perpetual Help Roman Catholic Church in Scottsdale.

Deeb died Friday at Scottsdale Memorial Hospital. He was born July 20, 1946, in Detroit, Mich.

The family moved to the Denver area in 1950. Deeb was educated at Cherry Hills Elementary School and Cherry Creek High School. He operated the Deeb Carpet Studio in Scottsdale.

Survivors include his parents, Mr. and Mrs. G.F. Deeb, Scottsdale; and a sister, Elaine Carty, Mesa, Ariz.

Virginia K. Eatherton

Memorial services for Virginia Kathryn Eatherton, 59, Colorado Springs, will be at 1 p.m. Thursday at Divine Science Church, 1400 Williams St.

She was killed in a robbery at her motel in Colorado Springs Saturday.

Mrs. Eatherton was born May 5, 1921, in Woonsocket, S.D. She was married to Norman Allen Eatherton Oct. 15, 1942. They were divorced in 1962.

Mrs. Eatherton is survived by a son, Gordon, Denver; a daughter, Norma Lee Propp, Yuma; a brother, John Tuin, Paonia; a sister, Marge Spink, Costa Rica; and four grandchildren.

Donations may be sent to the Virginia Eatherton Memorial Fund, 450 S. Locust St., Denver 80224. All funds are to be donated to Addiction Research and Treatment Services, 3818 W. Princeton Circle, Denver.

Laura A. Eader

Mass of Christian Burial was said Monday night at Sts. Peter and Paul Roman Catholic Church in Wheat Ridge for Laura A. "Dovie" Eader, 97, of 1590 Yates St., formerly of 439 Lafayette St. Burial was Tuesday in Mount Olivet.

Mrs. Eader died Thursday at Eventide of Lakewood.

She was born Jan. 3, 1884, in Gary, Ohio, was educated in Denver and spent most of her life in Denver. She had been married to William H. Eader, who worked for The Denver Post for 52 years and served as foreman of the photo engraving department. Eader died in 1961.

Mrs. Eader was a longtime member of the Denver Press Council.

Survivors include a sister, Lena M. Dillehay, Denver; two nephews and two nieces.

ADVERTISEMENTS

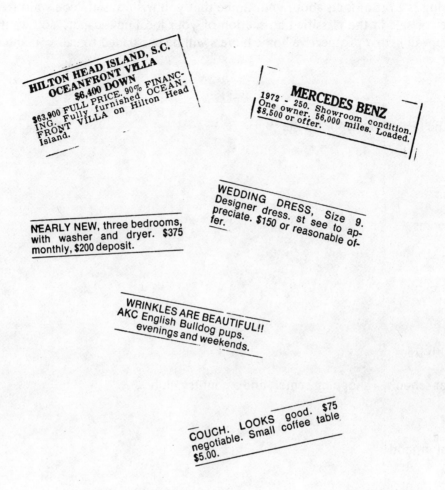

HILTON HEAD ISLAND, S.C. OCEANFRONT VILLA
$6,400 DOWN
$63,900 FULL PRICE. 90% FINANC-ING. Fully furnished OCEAN-FRONT VILLA on Hilton Head Island.

MERCEDES BENZ
1972 - 250. Showroom condition. One owner. 56,000 miles. Loaded. $8,500 or offer.

WEDDING DRESS, Size 9. Designer dress. st see to ap-preciate. $150 or reasonable of-fer.

NEARLY NEW, three bedrooms, with washer and dryer. $375 monthly, $200 deposit.

WRINKLES ARE BEAUTIFUL!! AKC English Bulldog pups. evenings and weekends.

COUCH. LOOKS good. $75 negotiable. Small coffee table $5.00.

ADVERTISING

The following is a list of facts about your home that you wish to sell. You want to advertise your house for sale in the classified ad section of your local newspaper. You want to make the ad so appealing that prospective home buyers will be persuaded to call you and come see your house.

These are the facts about your house:

eight rooms

three bedrooms

two stories

fireplace

garage

large lot with trees

located near schools, a shopping center, and a country club

gas furnace

quiet neighborhood

Include all the facts in your ad, use abbreviations, and limit your ad to seventy-words or less.

THE COMIC STRIP

Directions: Write the end of this comic strip episode using dialogue that reveals the characters' personalities and develops the story. After you have finished, check the original ending on the next page and compare.

INTERVIEWS

Directions: Personifying abstract words helps in learning and remembering them. Use the following questions to interview your new vocabulary word.

Why do you exist?

Where do you come from?

Why do we need you?

Where can we find you today?

Are you of benefit to society?

Are you necessary to life?

Why should I value you?

Are you controversial in any way?

ANALOGIES

Compare known things you can visualize to new information you need to learn in school subjects. For example, in music class, provide colors to understand types of music such as purple for classical, orange for rock, blue for jazz. With analogies you can relate new concepts to ones you are already familiar with in order to understand the new ones better.

Known	New	Example
colors		types of music
mountains		Civil War generals
houses		periods of art
trees		types of literature
rooms in a house		periods in history
bodies of water		human circulatory system
land formations		polygons
animals		
flowers		
foods		
armies		

ANALOGIES

Directions: Analogies test sensitivity to relationships between words and ideas. You are asked to analyze relationships and to recognize relationships that are similar to each other. Each of the groups below consists of two words that have a certain relationship to each other, followed by five lettered pairs of related words. Select the lettered pair of words that relate to each other in the same way *as do the words of the original pair.*

1. PART-WHOLE
   borderland:country::(a)water:land
   (b)rock:soil (c)margin:page (d)danger:
   safety (e)shelf:edge

2. CONCRETE-ABSTRACT
   ointment:burn:: (a)water:fire
   (b)sympathy:sorrow (c)medicine:
   doctor (d)powder:face (e)pain:agony

3. CAUSE-EFFECT
   repetition:monotony:: (a)familiarity:
   recognition (b)interest:boredom
   (c)dissipation:depravity (d)attempt:
   achievement (e)callowness:inexperience

4. INSTRUMENT TO FUNCTION
   Bicycle:locomotion:: (a)canoe:paddle
   (b)hero:worship (c)hay:horse
   (d)spectacles:vision (e)statement:
   contention

5. ACTION TO OBJECT
   trigger:bullet:: (a)handle:drawer
   (b)holster:gun (c)bulb:light
   (d)switch:current (e)pulley:rope

6. MALE AND FEMALE
   boar:sow: (a) parent:scion (b) wizard:
   witch (c) vixen:fox (d) protagonist:
   heroine (e) pheasant:quail

7. CLASSIFICATIONS
   astronomer:stars:: (a)cryptologist:
   insects (b)etymologist:plants
   (c)entomologist:words (d)philatelist:
   coins (e)ornithologist:birds

8. SYMBOLS OF IDEAS
   Old Glory:United States:: (a)lion:
   unicorn (b)elephant:Republican Party
   (c)Red Cross:Clara Barton (d)tradition:
   innovation (e)GOP:Republican Party

9. REWARD TO AN ACT
   profit:selling:: (a)cost:price
   (b)fame:bravery (c)praying:loving
   (d)medal:service (e)money:work

10. PRODUCER TO PRODUCT
    Author:novel:: (a)teacher:student
    (b)reader:interest (c)hero:win
    (d)carpenter:cabinet (e)doctor:cure

11. IMPLEMENT TO USER
    stethoscope:physician::pestle:
    (a)sculptor (b)pharmacist (c)teacher
    (d)author (e)farmer

12. TYPE-CHARACTERISTIC
    wolf:rapacious:: (a)miser:prodigal
    (b)horde:irresistible (c)mantis:
    preying (d)fox:cunning (e)cat:
    mewing

13. SIZE, DEGREE, AMOUNT
    wind:gale:: (a)inundation:flood
    (b) revelry:riot (c)penchant:
    proclivity (d)rubble:structure
    (e)rostrum:stage

14. FORM
    ball:circle:: (a)carton:square
    (b)cube:sphere (c)globe:wheel
    (d)plane:solid (e)round:circular

15. TIME SEQUENCE
    instantaneous:procrastination::
    (a)immediate:delay (b)forthwith:
    lying (c)dilatory:presently
    (d)now:henceforth (e)demure:demur

16. HOMONYM
    veil:vale::feign: (a) emulate
    (b) simulate (c) fain (d) cower
    (e) dissimulate

17. GRAMMATICAL
    walked:walks::risen: (a)raised
    (b)rise (c)rises (d)raises (e)raise

18. ANTONYMS
    Construct:demolish::build: (a)set up
    (b)raze (c)work (d)put together
    (e)take responsibility

19. RHYME
    Linger:finger::miner: (a)coal (b)major
    (c)digit (d)hand (e)signer

20. ATTITUDE TO OBJECT
    sympathy:protagonist:: (a)hate:
    villain (b)cry:misfortune (c)love:
    store (d)here:affection (e)sadness:pity

21. FAMILY
    father:daughter:: (a)son:daughter
    (b)son-in-law:daughter (c)uncle:nephew
    (d)uncle:aunt (e)grandfather:mother

SYNONYMS AND ANTONYMS

Directions: Choose the lettered word that is most nearly similar *or* opposite *in meaning to the word in capital letters, and write its letter in the space supplied. No question has both a synonym and antonym; each question has one or the other.*

____ 1. TACITURN: A. understood   B. unmannerly   C. acceptable   D. voluble
       E. placid

____ 2. VICTUALS: A. viands   B. rites   C. prey   D. successes   E. likenesses

____ 3. TRUSS: A. clothe   B. douse   C. reckon   D. braid   E. unloose

____ 4. PAUPERIZE: A. enslave   B. engulf   C. enmesh   D. enact   E. enrich

____ 5. RECONNAISSANCE: A. rebirth   B. survey   C. knowledge   D. assistance
       E. recognition

____ 6. GARISH: A. mute   B. showy   C. pacific   D. coordinated   E. coarse

____ 7. DRENCH: A. sparkle   B. soil   C. root out   D. wet thoroughly   E. inundate

____ 8. SUPPLEMENT: A. mortify   B. reign   C. deduct   D. curse   E. starve

____ 9. DEFTLY: A. safely   B. honorably   C. hastily   D. stealthily   E. adeptly

____ 10. PARASITE: A. catalyst   B. heaven   C. barnacle   D. emetic   E. host

____ 11. PREDATORY: A. preferring   B. pillaging   C. arranging   D. praising
       E. disciplinary

____ 12. NEOPHYTE: A. wood nymph   B. old man   C. resident   D. veteran   E. fungus

____ 13. SALUTARY: A. colloquial   B. cheerful   C. noxious   D. bloody   E. stunted

____ 14. PROCLIVITY: A. curiosity   B. penchant   C. arrogance   D. amusement
       E. slope

____ 15. JEOPARDIZE: A. manufacture   B. plan   C. protect   D. contradict   E. console

____ 16. INSIPID: A. eaten away   B. incipient   C. enervating   D. tasty   E. stalwart

____ 17. TRIBUNAL: A. court   B. bailiff   C. font   D. three-cornered hat   E. incinerator

____ 18. PRUNE: A. pluck   B. furrow   C. replant   D. trim   E. fertilize

____ 19. EVANESCENT: A. transitory   B. pallid   C. bubbling   D. burgeoning
       E. spacious

____ 20. INVEIGH: A. call on   B. measure   C. declaim   D. weigh anchor   E. articulate

REBUS GAME

play
play _____

<u>joke's</u>
U _____

C C C C C C _____

cycle
cycle _____

think think _____

w
word _____
r
d

person
   ality _____

* W.W. I
  W.W. II _____

<u>mind</u>
matter _____

<u>GROUND</u> _____
  feet
  feet
  feet
  feet
  feet
  feet

side/side _____

Le
  vel _____

<u>O</u>
B.A. _____
M.A.
Ph.D.

CLOZE EXERCISES

Passage 1

He stared at the _____ , shivering reflection of a fire on the _____ wall of his tent until, exhausted and ill from the monotony of his suffering, he fell asleep.

When another night came the columns, changed to _____ streaks, filed across two pontoon bridges. A glaring fire _____ -tinted the waters of the river. Its rays, shining upon the moving masses of troops, brought forth here and there sudden gleams of _____ or _____ . Upon the other shore a dark and mysterious range of hills was curved against the sky. The insect voices of the night sang solemnly.

Passage 2

On the evening of July ____ , _____ , the troops of the _____ _____ Regiment were trying to relax on the sands of _____ Island on the southern side of the _____ harbor. The day-long bombardment had ended, but the evening was uneasily quiet.

In front of the troops, across a narrow neck of windswept land, loomed the sloping walls of _____ _____ . The _____ bombardment had done no visible damage to the fort. It would have to be taken by a desperate frontal assault. The _____ , commanded by Colonel _____ _____ _____ , had been selected to spearhead the attack.

Passage 3

Larger and more complex organisms usually produce reproductive cells of two different types. The cell produced by the male is usually capable of swimming through a liquid. Such a cell is called a _____ cell. The reproductive cell produced by the female, called an _____ cell, is usually much larger than the _____ cell. Seldom is the _____ cell capable of swimming. For fertilization to occur, the _____ cell must swim to the _____ cell. During fertilization it bores its way into the membrane of the _____ cell and becomes a part of it. The single cell that results is called a _____ _____ cell.

Passage 4

1. In a right triangle there is always one _____ angle.
2. The hypotenuse of a right triangle is the side _____ the right angle.
3. If you know the lengths of _____ sides of a _____ triangle, you can use the Law of _____ to find the _____ side.
4. In the formula $a^2 + b^2 = c^2$, c stands for the length of the _____ of a _____ triangle.
5. The Law of Pythagoras is true for _____ right triangles.

STRUCTURAL MEANING

Sentences reveal their structure and convey meaning through four systems of signals:

a. The order in which the words are uttered—word order;

b. The grouping of words into units (adjectival phrases, noun clauses, etc.) that substitute for single words and do the same work;

c. The use of structure words (*the, by, and,* etc.) that serve as pattern signals to relate other words to each other;

d. The forms of individual words—such as *cat* plus *s* to indicate two or more cats and *cat* plus *ty* to suggest attributes associated with cats.

With the above points in mind, study the following stanza from Lewis Carroll's "Jabberwocky":

> 'Twas brillig and the slithy toves
> Did gyre and gimble in the wabe;
> All mimsy were the borogoves,
> And the mome raths outgrabe . . .

1. To what part of speech does each of the "words" in this stanza belong?

2. Which of the words have lexical meaning?

3. Which of the words have only structural meaning?

4. What part does the position of each word in relation to the other words play in classifying the words as parts of speech?

5. Fill in the following dashes so as to make both lexical and structural sense:

> "Twas _____ and the _____ y _____ s
> Did _____ and _____ in the _____ ;
> All _____ y were the _____ s,
> And the _____ _____ s _____ .

What meanings have you carried over from "Jabberwocky"? What meanings have you added?

Write brief definitions of *lexical* and *structural* meaning.

Directions: Read the story and answer the four questions.

Once upon a time there was a green, roly-poly, undulating catermillar that glid his twills amongst the reaves of gless. A statim of anguint came uponst his meanor infesting his pearance.

"Oh, Bretty Bairford," he cried. "There is something very quiant with your fraughtin."

"Something very quiant with my fraughtin?" explauded Bretty Bairford. "What do you mean?"

"Come and see!" whimpested the green, undulating catermillar. "Hancher down into the reaves of gless where your fraughtin is and look."

So the catermillar and Bretty Bairford hanchered down to take a look.

"You glid arie wendest me tofa," said Betty Bairford. "I'll meet you there."

When Bretty wendest at the tofa, the green, undulating catermillar hiefed its roly-poly twill and pointed.

"See? Your fraughtin has a ghorid glitch in it."

"Oh," laughed Bretty Bairford. "I don't mind having to eat stooples every day, but I abstremolutely hate to iron clothes."

Note: All references to persons living or dead are purely unintentional.

Questions:

1. Why was the catermillar in a statin of anguint?

2. What was quiant with Bretty Bairford's fraughtin?

3. Do you think Bretty Bairford thought of a good way to solve her problem?

4. Tell about a time when you solved a problem you had that was like this.

COMPOUND WORDS

Group 1

1. grandmother	16. playground
2. workshop	17. railroad
3. footstep	18. everybody
4. sunshine	19. snowshoe
5. horseback	20. something
6. pancake	21. newspaper
7. firefly	22. butterfly
8. moonlight	23. peanut
9. fishhook	24. bedroom
10. mailbag	25. pocketbook
11. snowball	26. schoolroom
12. sidewalk	27. Thanksgiving
13. streetcar	28. lighthouse
14. sailboat	29. outside
15. Sunday	30. oatmeal

Group 2

1. anywhere	16. forgot
2. bluebird	17. below
3. understand	18. airplane
4. sometimes	19. herself
5. tonight	20. understand
6. himself	21. forgive
7. airport	22. befall
8. forget	23. become
9. because	24. without
10. income	25. forgive
11. nobody	26. anyone
12. everything	27. football
13. baseball	28. anybody
14. maybe	29. doghouse
15. everyone	30. carport

COMPOUND WORDS

Directions: Some compound words are formed by combining two nouns (doghouse), *while others may be formed from a verb and a noun* (playground). *Still others consist of an adjective and a noun* (backpack), *or a verb followed by an adverb* (lockout). *In the following groups, provide the missing part for the types of compound words.*

Two Nouns	Verb and Noun	Adjective and Noun	Verb and Adverb
book–	sail–	–coat	crack–
house–	drive–	–chair	knock–
table–	work–	–man	turn–
pan–	watch–	–body	be–
horse–	throw–	–shoe	cast–

CLUES TO 100,000 WORDS

Prefix	Its Other Spellings	Its Meaning	Master Words	Root	Its Other Spellings	Its Meaning
1. de	—	down, away	detain	tain	ten, tin	to have, to hold
2. inter-	—	between	intermittent	mitt	miss, mis, mit	to send
3. pre-	—	before	precept	cept	cap, capt, ceiv, cip, ceit	to take, to seize
4. ob-	oc-, of-, op-	to, toward, against	offer	fer	lat, lay	to bear, to carry
5. in-	il-, im-, ir-	into	insist	sist	sta	to stand, incure, persist
6. mono-	—	one, alone	monograph	graph	—	to write
7. epi-	—	over, upon, beside	epilogue	log	ology	speech, science
8. ad-	a-, ac-, af-, ag-, al-, an-, ap-, ar-, as-, at-	to, towards	aspect	spect	spec, spi, spy	to look
9. un- com-	— co-, col- con-, cor-	not with, together	uncomplicated	plic	play, plex, ploy, ply	to fold, bend, twist, interweave
10. non- ex-	— e-, ef-	not out, formerly	nonextended	tend	tens, tent	to stretch
11. re- pro-	— —	back, again forward, in favor of	reproduction	duct	duc, duit, duk	to lead, make, shape, fashion
12. in- dis-	il-, im- ir di-, dif-	not apart from	indisposed	pos	pound, pon, post	to put
13. sub-	suc-, suf- sug-, sup- sur-, sus-	under	oversufficient	fic	fac, fact, fash, fest	to make, to do
14. mis- trans-	— tra-, trand	wrong(ly) across, beyond	mistranscribe	scribe	scrip, scriv	to write

COMMON WORD ROOTS

Directions: A well-known magazine in a study of 20,000 common English words found that over 12,000 were based on Greek or Latin. So many English words come from one Greek or Latin root that if you learn one root, you have a clue to an entire family of words. Practice learning these in the following exercises. Choose one word from each list to complete the sentences below.

I. *DENT*—"tooth" (Latin).
  (1) dentist (2) denture (3) dentifrice (4) dental (5) indention (6) indentured
  Grandfather's _____ causes him much discomfort.
  Pretty girls appear in most _____ advertisements.
  The use of _____ floss stimulates the gums.
  One should visit one's _____ twice a year.
  Paragraph _____s have the appearance of irregular teeth.
  An _____ servant held one part of a written contract edged with teethlike
    notches that matched the other part held by his master.

II. *CHRON*—"time" (Greek)
  (1) chronicle (2) synchronize (3) chronic (4) chronologically (5) chronometer
  (6) anachronism
  The poor fellow has had a sinus infection so long that it has become _____.
  Would you call a lady's hoop skirt for street wear an _____ ?
  A _____ is an instrument that keeps time with great accuracy.
  Much of the literature of the American Colonial period consists of sermons and
    _____s.
  The early movie producers could not _____ voice and action.
  One test question in history was to list the wars of our country _____ .

III. *RUPT*—"break" (Latin)
  (1) erupt (2) abrupt (3) corrupt (4) disrupt (5) interrupt (6) rupture
  In what year did Vesuvius _____ and destroy Pompeii?
  The fire drill will _____ all classes at ten o'clock.
  James felt insulted and made an _____ departure.
  The _____ of friendly relations between the countries is serious.
  The question of return of prisoners of war will _____ negotiations.
  Association with the unrighteous will _____ the weak.

IV. *GRESS*—"step" (Latin)
(1) progress (2) digress (3) Congress (4) egress (5) transgress (6) ingress (7) aggression
(8) regression (9) retrogression

The _____ of the United States is in session.

War was caused by _____ of the dictator state.

To _____ that law meant death.

To _____ often spoils your story.

Do not be discouraged if you _____ slowly at first.

Provide other means of _____ in case of fire.

We hoped for progress, but instead there was _____ .

Every place of _____ was crowded at the stadium because of great mobs.

Destruction of their libraries will cause _____ in their culture.

V. *PAN*—"all" (Greek)
(1) pancreas (2) panacea (3) Pantheon (4) panchromatic (5) pandemonium
(6) pantomime (7) Pandora (8) panorama (9) Pan American Airways (10) Pan American Union

The _____ is an organ of the body that is "all flesh."

All countries of America are represented in the _____ .

_____ means "all mimic."

A _____ affords a wide view of the scene.

A _____ film reproduces all colors.

One can fly over all of North and South America on _____ .

There is no _____ for all ills.

The _____ was built to honor all the Roman gods.

_____ was given all the gifts that the gods could bestow.

When you hear a racket that sounds like all the demons, you call it a _____ .

VI. *POTE, POSS*—"power" (Latin)
(1) impotent (2) potential (3) potency (4) potentate (5) potent (6) posse
(7) plenipotentiary (*pleni*—"full") (8) potentiality (9) omnipotent (*omni*—"all")
(10) possible

Soft drinks are not _____ .

Repeated veto by a few made the council _____ .

This wise man was our _____ in Russia during the war.

Every thief is a _____ murderer.

The woman did not realize the _____ of the sleeping pill.

No one can estimate the _____ of television for future education.

A large _____ is now on the trail of the escaped convict.

Several countries are still ruled by a _____ .

Only God is _____ .

It is not _____ to run fast in this deep snow.

MORPHEMES

Numbers

half	semi:	conscious private annual colon	hemi:	sphere tone
one	uni:	lateral form ocular	mono:	tone lith rail logue
two	bi:	ped valve partisan	di:	meter chromatic
three	tri:	angle	tri:	ped dent logy
four	quad:	ruped ruple	tetra:	meter
five	quin:	tuplicate tillion	penta:	gon meter
six	sex:	tet tain tant	hexa:	gon meter
seven	sept:	September	hept, hepta:	chord gon
eight	octo:	October octet	octa:	octad octagon
nine	nov:	November	nona:	gon genarian
ten	dec, deca:	December decade	dec:	achord agon
hundred	cent:	imeter		
many	multi:	millionaire	poly:	gon
all	omni:	ominpotent	pan:	demonium

Source: Adapted from Burmeister, *Reading Strategies for Middle and Secondary School Teachers,* 1978. Addison-Wesley, pp. 365–387. Reprinted with permission.

ROOTS

villa (farmhouse)	*form (shape)*	*fort (strong)*	*civ (citizen)*
villa	uniform	fortify	civic
village	conform	fortification	civil
villain	deform	fortress	civilized

micro (small)	*journ (daily)*	*mob (move)*	*vict (conquer)*
microscope	journal	mobile	victor
microfilm	journey	mobil	victory
microbe	journalism	automobile	victim

mod (manner)	*cap (head)*	*vin (wine)*	*graph (write)*
model	capital	vineyard	autograph
mode	captain	vinegar	phonograph
modern	decapitate	vine	paragraph

PREFIXES

sub	*in*
marine	visible
plot	accurate
normal	complete
vert	capacitated
merge	harmonious
ject	ept
mit	adequate
let	vincible
way	dependent
due	sensible

dis	*anti*
approve	government
like	religious
agree	biotic
believe	American
allow	aircraft
continue	abolitionist
mount	chronical
bar	toxin
respect	body
count	climax

PREFIXES

Directions: The prefix a *or* an *means "not" or "without." It is often not recognized and thus its negative meaning is not understood. (Before a vowel or the letter* h, an *is used instead of* a.*) Notice the use of the prefix in each word below. Use each word in a sentence that illustrates its meaning.*

a	+	nomaly	not the usual
a	+	typical	unlike the type
a	+	gnostic	not knowing
a	+	moral	no concern for morals
an	+	onymous	without the real name
a	+	symmetrical	not proportional
an	+	emia	without enough red blood cells
a	+	gamous	unmarried
a	+	chromatic	without color
a	+	graphia	unable to write

PREFIXES

Directions: The prefix un *means "not" and gives a negative meaning to a word. Fill in the blank space with the correct answer:*

1. The word *unbelievable* means _____ believable.

2. "He was unaware of the danger" means he was _____ aware of the danger.

3. The prefix *un* means _____ .

4. *Uncertain* means _____ certain.

5. A person who is not comfortable is _____ .

6. Things that are not safe are _____ .

7. The umpire's call was not fair. Her call was _____ .

8. A person who is not happy is _____ .

9. A person out of work is _____ employed. The person is _____ .

10. A person you cannot depend on is _____ dependable.
    That person is _____ .

SUFFIXES

Directions: Below there are twelve words. Each word has two syllables. First, divide the words into syllables. See how many words you can make by matching the beginning part of one word with the ending part of another word. For example, foolish *is divided into* fool *and* ish. *Add the last part of* starting *to* fool *and you can make the word* fooling. *Try to get all thirty.*

foolish	stockade	wooden	starting
quickly	rocky	teacher	wicked
ticket	friendless	kindness	helpful

1. _____   16. _____

2. _____   17. _____

3. _____   18. _____

4. _____   19. _____

5. _____   20. _____

6. _____   21. _____

7. _____   22. _____

8. _____   23. _____

9. _____   24. _____

10. _____   25. _____

11. _____   26. _____

12. _____   27. _____

13. _____   28. _____

14. _____   29. _____

15. _____   30. _____

SUFFIXES

Suffix	Meaning	Example	Definition
able, ible	able to be	audible	able to be heard
al, il, ile	pertaining to	medical	pertaining to medicine
ish	belonging to, like	girlish	like a girl
less	without	friendless	without friends
ness	quality of	kindness	being kind
ous	full of	vigorous	full of vigor (life)
tion	act of	education	act of educating
ful	full	wonderful	full of wonder
ly	like	manly	like a man
ism	practice of, theory	Americanism	theory of American ways

1. Add a suffix to each of the following words to create a new word; then use it in a sentence.

child
courage
dark
grace
help
illustrate
imitate
mischief
move
notice
polite
ready
slow
soft
sweet
worth
pay
blame
brother
danger
politic
law

2. Locate and underline the suffix(es) in these words. Define the words literally.

amorous	foolish	motivation	exceptionally
reprehensible	petition	reservation	masterful
capable	meaningless	departmentalism	mischievousness
ductile	dutiful	brotherhoodism	adaptation

SUFFIXES

Directions: Draw a line from the science to its definition.

The Science	Definition (the study of)
geology	human mind
astrology	birds
herpetology	animals
archaeology	insects
etymology	reptiles and amphibians
biology	earth's history and life
entomology	origins of words
meteorology	life
ornithology	humans
anthropology	stars and how they affect humans
psychology	the atmosphere, weather
zoology	material remains of earlier people

SUFFIXES

Directions: A suffix can change the meaning or the function of a word. Read the sentences and fill in the blanks for the correct meaning for the suffix less, *which means "without." Also check appropriate words and phrases in parentheses.*

1. To be penniless means to be without _____ .

2. In the word *careless*, the suffix *less* means _____ .

3. A homeless person is a person (with___, without___) a _____ .

4. A friendless person is a person without _____ .

5. A windowless room is a room _____ windows.

6. A spotless coat is (clean___, dirty___). It (has___, has no___) spots on it.

7. If a person is said to be reckless, people believe the person is _____ caution.

8. The judge said the prisoner was guiltless. The prisoner was (to blame___, not to blame___).

SUFFIXES

The word *accept* can be made into a describing word by adding *able* to the end of it. *Able* means "able to be."

Form the following words into words that describe by affixing *able* to them. Define each word.

consider	allow
reason	peace
use	break
teach	charge

These words can add *able*, but the final *e* must be dropped before it is added. Spell the words.

desire

move

admire

sale

These words can add *able*, but the spelling is different in other ways. Spell the words.

misery

rely

apply

charity

SPELLING

The following common suffixes, when you recognize them in long words, should help you to understand the word and to spell it.

able, ible, ble	—	able to be
al, ial	—	pertaining to
ant, ent	—	being
ance, ence	—	state of being
ate, ize, fy, yze	—	to do or to make
dom	—	power, office, state
ful	—	full
ion, sion, tion	—	act of
ity, ty, ment	—	condition
ness	—	state of being
ous, ious, tious	—	have the quality of

Underline the suffixes you see in each long word below:

preferential

capitalization

covetousness

transcription

deferential

mischievousness

motivationality

princedom

revocationality

peacefulness

enhancement

reasonableness

SPELLING

The following common prefixes, when you recognize them in long words, should help you to understand the word and to spell it.

inter	between
un, in, ir, il	not
ex	formerly
bene	good
com, co, con	with or together
mis	wrong(ly)
trans	across or beyond
a, ac, ad, at	to or toward

Underline the prefixes you find in the long words given below. Define the words.

illiteracy

copilot

miscommunication

beneficent

irreligious

interconnect

transcontinental

inability

inattendance

Write five more words you know using any of the prefixes listed above.

SPELLING

Directions: "Big words" almost always have parts to them that you can recognize as a root, a prefix, or a suffix. Recognizing these word parts can help you to spell the words better. Following are some word roots to which prefixes and suffixes may be added to form longer words. Add prefixes and suffixes to these roots to make longer, meaningful words.

graph   (to write)

ology   (science)

spec   (to look)

duct   (to make or lead)

fer   (to carry)

mit, mis   (to send)

Underline all the word parts you can recognize in the following word that is the longest in the dictionary. What does it mean?

antidisestablishmentarianism

FIVE-SENTENCE PARAGRAPH

The controlling statement

The controlling statement has three parts:

    idea

    viewpoint

    key terms
       (give three)

        because

        because

        because

Put the three key terms into rough sentence form:

Now develop a five-sentence paragraph using the *idea + viewpoint* for the topic sentence. Develop each *key term* into a complete sentence. The fifth sentence will be the conclusion, which sums up and restates the topic.

OUTLINING

Directions: Use the following sentence as the basis for an outline—each because *becomes a Roman numeral:*

> Popsicles are refreshing because they are cool, because they are
> flavorful, and because they are colorful.

    I. Cool

        A. Frozen

        B. Becomes liquid

   II. Flavorful

        A. Cherry

        B. Grape

  III. Colorful

        A. Red

        B. Purple

This exercise helps in discovering main ideas in reading and for writing, and it develops effective study skills. This outline can be used for organizing longer compositions where each Roman numeral is a paragraph by itself.

WRITING ANSWERS TO ESSAY QUESTIONS

Directions: Use the controlling-statement format for writing answers to essay questions on tests. The idea and viewpoint are already given in the questions.

Supply the key terms (the becauses*) to complete the answer. Develop the key terms fully.*
Example of a social studies question:

What were the causes of the American Revolution?

idea:	American Revolution
viewpoint:	causes were

[These can be answered in separate paragraphs or in a single paragraph depending on the depth required.]

Example of a science or health essay question:

What are the major parts of the circulatory system in the body?

What are the functions of each?

idea:	circulatory system
viewpoint:	parts and functions

Some of the major parts of the circulatory system are the heart, the lungs, the veins, and the arteries.
[Each can then be explained in depth, one per paragraph.]

WRITING ANSWERS TO ESSAY QUESTIONS

Controlling Statement: *Idea*   *Viewpoint*   *Key Terms*

1. How do a state legislature and the national Congress compare?

2. What effect does the difference in the shape of an article have in its density?

3. How do you determine the density of an article?

4. Point out the kinds of buttonhole techniques that may be used to finish a jacket.

5. Why did the South secede from the Union?

6. Compare a plant cell to an animal cell.

7. What were the major shortcomings of the czarist governments?

8. Explain the major characteristics of impressionistic art.

9. Identify the kinds of foods that contain carbohydrates.

10. Describe the characteristics of the climate of countries that exist on the equator. Explain what causes the climate to be that way.

UNITY OF SENTENCES

Topic Sentence

Idea:

Viewpoint:

Three Key terms: 1.

2.

3.

Order to be used:

Space (near to far, top to bottom or reverse,
largest to smallest or reverse, etc.)

Time (past to present, present to future, young
to old)

Cause and effect (if-then, because)

Comparison (likes and differences)

Procedure (directions, instructions, steps)

Write a five-sentence paragraph using the topic sentence (idea + viewpoint), three key terms
developed into sentences in a specific order, and a conclusion:

1

2

3

4

5

TYPES OF ESSAY QUESTIONS

Directions: Identify the order *suggested by the topic (space, time, cause and effect, comparison, procedure).*

1. Why were the French peasants poor just prior to the Revolution?

   Order:

2. Why did Americans move westward from the Colonies?

   Order:

3. How do you determine the density of an article?

   Order:

4. What steps are required to hinge a door?

   Order:

5. Compare a plant cell to an animal cell.

   Order:

6. Explain the major characteristics of the Baroque period.

   Order:

REFERENCE TIES IN MEANING

Directions: Write out the referent for the pronouns used in each selection:

A. As the boat bounced from the top of each wave the wind tore through the hair of the hatless men, and as the craft plopped *her* stern down again the spray splashed past *them*. The crest of each of these waves was a hill, from the top of *which* the men surveyed for a moment a broad tumultuous expanse shining and wind-riven. *It* was probably splendid, *it* was probably glorious, this play of the free sea, wild with lights of emerald and white and amber. [Stephen Crane, "The Open Boat"]

Pronoun	*Referent*
1. her	1.
2. them	2.
3. which	3.
4. it	4.
5. it	5.

B.   Richard Cory

1 Whenever Richard Cory went downtown,
2   We people on the pavement looked at him:
3 He was a gentleman from sole to crown,
4   Clean-favored, and imperially slim.

5 And he was always quietly arrayed,
6   And he was always human when he talked;
7 But still he fluttered pulses when he said,
8   "Good morning," and he glittered when he walked.

9 And he was rich—yes, richer than a king—
10   And admirably schooled in every grace:
11 In fine, we thought that he was everything
12   To make us wish that we were in his place.

13 So on we worked, and waited for the light,
14   And went without the meat, and cursed the bread;
15 And Richard Cory, one calm summer night,
16   Went home and put a bullet through his head.
         Edwin Arlington Robinson, "Richard Cory," in *The Children of the Night*. Copyright under
         the Berne Convention. Reprinted with the permission of Charles Scribner's Sons.

Pronoun	*Referent*
1. We (line 2)	1.
2. him (line 2)	2.
3. He (line 3)	3.
4. we (line 11)	4.
5. us (line 12)	5.
6. we (line 13)	6.
7. his (line 16)	7.

COHESION IN REFERENCE

Directions: Match the pronoun to the word it refers to according to number (singular or plural) and gender (male or female). Then underline the word the pronoun refers to.

1. Every boy on the team had _____ eligibility checked before the season began. (their, his)

2. Each of us tried _____ best, but only fifteen could make the team. (our, their, his or her)

3. Either Susan or Mary will have _____ uniform ready for the game. (their, her).

4. Of all sports, I prefer tennis because it keeps _____ in good condition. (you, me).

5. The boys' team sat on the bench. _____ did not play until the girls had finished. (It, They)

6. The referees called a foul on a player on the girls' team. _____ was fouled out and had to sit on the bench. (They, She, It)

7. The game was played on indoor courts. _____ were surfaced with indoor carpeting. (It, They)

8. George and Sam were battling it out for first place in the tournament. _____ was a regional competition. (He, They, It)

TIES FOR MEANING

Directions: First, determine the type of tie you need. Next, select from that group the word most appropriate to the meaning of your sentence.

Type of tie	Conjunctives
addition	in addition, furthermore, moreover, also, besides, by the way, similarly, equally important
example	for example, for instance, in fact, like, thus, as an illustration, in other words
suggestion	so, therefore, in that case, for this purpose, under the circumstances, to this end, with this object
summary	in summary, in conclusion, therefore, finally, as a result, on the whole, consequently, in brief, accordingly, thus
logical order	*Space:* above, under, nearby, opposite to, adjacent to, near, across, beyond, to the right/left, in the background/foreground *Time:* then, after, one day, subsequently, first, second, meanwhile, immediately, soon, when, yesterday, tomorrow, once, afterward, next, in the meantime *Value:* initially, first, second, secondly, finally, next, last
emphasis	indeed, truly, again, to repeat, in fact
granting a point	granted that, though, even though, in spite of, while it may be true, although
likeness, contradiction, cause	*Similarity:* likewise, in this manner, similarly *Contrast:* in contrast to, however, still, yet, on the other hand, at the same time, rather, conversely, nevertheless, but, while this may be true *Cause and effect:* due to, thus, hence, because, since, therefore, consequently, accordingly, as a result

TIES FOR MEANING

Directions: Some of the meaning ties need to be used more than once. Think carefully about the type of tie the conjunctive represents and how it fits into the context. Choose the tie from the list that follows.

at the same time	late
though	meanwhile
after	that
and	but

California also seized the President's attention _____ that of the whole country. _____ in 1844 a confidential report reached Washington _____. Mexico was willing to sell it to the United States. This excited the interest of Polk, and _____ he became President he tooks steps to send a diplomatic representative to negotiate with Mexico.

_____ , _____ , a new government had taken over in Mexico, _____ it refused to receive the United States negotiator. Many Americans thought _____ this was shabby treatment _____ that Mexico ought to be severely punished.

_____ , a group of Spanish-speaking Californians, with the help of a number of Americans, were trying to stir up a rebellion against Mexican rule of the territory. The American army officer John C. Fremont, supposedly on an exploring expedition, attempted to help push their plans along. _____ he made so many Californians angry with his meddling _____ the plans were dropped.

TIES FOR MEANING

Directions: In the following recipe, provide meaning ties (such as first, secondly, then, and, meanwhile, *etc.) that would make the procedure clearer and easier to understand. Consider the functions of the ties to link text together and to make meaning clearer.*

Bavarian Cream

Mix in a saucepan

> 1 envelope gelatine (1 tablespoon)
> Few grains salt
> 1/4 cup sugar

Beat together until well blended

> 2 egg yolks
> 1 1/4 cups milk

Add to the gelatine. Cook and stir over low heat until the gelatine dissolves (about 5 minutes). Add

> 1/2 teaspoon vanilla

Chill until the mixture begins to stiffen.
Beat until in soft peaks

> 2 egg whites

Beat in, a little at a time

> 1/4 cup sugar

Fold into the gelatine mixture. Fold in

> 1/2 pint heavy cream, beaten stiff

Mold in individual molds or one large mold. Unmold and garnish or flavor as suggested for Spanish Cream. Serves 6.

[*The Fannie Farmer Cookbook*, 11th Edition. (Boston: Little Brown & Company, 1965), p. 379.]

TIES FOR MEANING

Directions: Each of the sentences in the following paragraph begins with one or more words that indicate something in particular is going to happen and that tie meaning in the sentences together. What are the words? What are their roles in each sentence? Think about them and write down your answers.

> Hereafter, whenever we speak of two lines, or two planes, we shall always mean that the lines or planes are different. That is, when we speak of two things, we shall always mean that there are indeed two separate items. But if we say merely that P and Q are points, we mean to allow the possibility that $P = Q$.

[E. Moise and Downs, *Geometry*, (Reading, Mass.: Addison-Wesley Publishing Company, Inc., 1975)]

COHESION IN REPETITION

Directions: Identify the repeated words *and the* synonyms *for each noun given in the two passages below.*

Californians:

1. East is east and West is San Francisco, according to Californians. Californians are a race of people; they are not merely inhabitants of a State. They are the Southerners of the West. Now, Chicagoans are no less loyal to their city; but when you ask them why, they stammer and speak of lake fish and the new Odd Fellows building. But Californians go into detail. [O. Henry, "A Municipal Report"]

Synonyms and Repetitions

_____

_____

_____

_____

2.   Chicago

Hog Butcher for the World
Toolmaker, Stacker of Wheat
Player with Railroads and the Nation's
          Freight Handler;
Stormy, husky, brawling,
City of the Big Shoulders . . .
          [Carl Sandburg, "Chicago," from *Chicago Poems* by
          Carl Sandburg, copyright 1916 by Holt, Rinehart
          and Winston, Inc., copyright 1944 by Carl Sandburg.
          Reprinted by permission of Harcourt Brace
          Jovanovich, Inc.]

Synonyms and Repetitions

_____

_____

_____

_____

_____

_____

SYNONYM TIES FOR MEANING

Parody

Directions: In the following poems, provide a synonym or close synonym for each of the underlined words. Choose words of the same syllable length so that the poetic rhythm remains.

Fog

The fog comes

on little cat feet.

It sits looking

over harbor and city

on silent haunches

and then moves on.

> Carl Sandburg, "Fog," from *Chicago Poems* by Carl Sandburg, copyright 1916 Holt, Rinehart and Winston, Inc., copyright 1944 by Carl Sandburg. Reprinted by permission of Harcourt Brace Jovanovich, Inc.

Comment on Cows

Cows
Do nothing but browse
And drowse
And now and then moo.
That's all they do.
Yet even while grazing
They aren't lazing.
Even while snacking
They aren't slacking.
If not illustrious,
They are inner industrious,
Making milk with all their might
With every bite.
Cream too,
With every chew.
I'd like it fine
Could I combine
In such measure
Business with pleasure.

> "Comment on Cows" by Richard Armour, in *Nights with Amour* (McGraw-Hill Book Co.)

COHESION IN UNSTATED INFORMATION

Directions: For the following recipe, fill in all *the unstated steps that a person would have to go through in order to bake the pie. Start from the very beginning and write out in detail the process and procedure indicated for every direction. Notice how so much information is left out that the reader-baker has to infer and to fill in through experience and prior knowledge. What the reader fills in gives the text its meaning.*

Pecan Pie

Serve this very rich pie in small wedges.

Set the oven at 450°.
Line a 9-inch pie pan with Plain Pastry (p. 407)
Mix and pour into the pie pan
  3 eggs, slightly beaten
  1/2 cup brown or white sugar
  1/4 teaspoon salt
  1 cup light corn syrup
  1/2 teaspoon vanilla
  1 cup pecans, broken in pieces
Bake 10 minutes. Reduce the heat to 350° and
bake 35 minutes longer. Chill. When ready to
serve, spread over the top 1/2 cup heavy cream, whipped
Garnish with pecan halves
    The Fannie Farmer Cookbook
    Eleventh Ed. Boston, Mass.: Little
    Brown and Company, 1965 (p. 418)

COHESION IN ELLIPSIS

Directions: For the following equation problem, write out every detail that a person must understand in order to complete the pattern. What understanding and background are assumed that the reader has? Write out just what it is that the reader-solver must know already in order to solve the problem. For example, the reader would have to understand the + sign as meaning to add. What else would have to be known by the reader? Reader understanding provides meaning for the text.

Name the sum.

$$1/2 + 1/2 = a$$

$$1/4 + 2/4 + 1/4 = b$$

$$1/8 + 3/8 + 3/8 + 1/8 = c$$

$$1/16 + 4/16 + 6/16 + 4/16 + 1/16 = d$$

Continue the equation pattern for 2 more rows.

How can you name the numerator of the sum for each row?

[*Modern School Mathematics* (Grade 8) by Mary P. Dolciani
Boston, Mass.: Houghton Mifflin Co., 1978.]

USING REPETITION TO COMBINE SENTENCES

Directions: Combine each of the following groups of sentences according to the signal given in the parentheses.

Example: We are looking for a new car.
The new car has white sidewalls and chrome trim. (that)

        We are looking for a new car that has white sidewalls and chrome trim.

1. A skier is liable to get upset.
A skier finds rocks instead of snow. (who)

_____

Add another sentence on the subject:

_____

2. The outlaw ran from the sheriff.
The sheriff organized a posse. (who)

_____

3. Although it is usually quiet during the week, the skating rink is very busy on weekends.
The skating rink is the only one in town. (which)

_____

Add another sentence on the subject:

_____

4. The heavy waves changed what had been a calm sea.
The heavy waves crashed against our boat. (that)

_____

Add two more sentences on the subject:

_____

_____

5. I know a talented actress.
The actress starred recently in our school play. (who)

Add three more sentences on the subject:

_____

_____

_____

COMBINING SENTENCES WITH PHRASES

Directions: Combine the following sets of sentences using the signals provided.

Example: He was a big black dog.
             He had a mean snarling growl. (with)

             He was a big black dog with a mean snarling growl.

1. It was a dark stormy night.
   The rain was soaking through my sweater. (with)
   The rain chilled me through and through. (ing)

   _____

   _____

2. Joe was quick.
   Joe was agile.
   Joe was strong.
   Joe played a winning game of tennis.
   His serve was dynamic.
   His forehand was powerfully driven.

   _____

   _____

   _____

   _____

3. The scavengers are searching for treasure.
   The scavengers are diving off the reef.
   The treasure was buried deep in the ocean floor centuries ago.

   _____

   _____

   _____

   Add four or five more sentences to the subject to compose a paragraph.

   _____

   _____

   _____

   _____

   _____

SENTENCE COMBINING WITHOUT SIGNALS

Directions: Combine the following clustered sentences so that they make sense. For example, combine the first cluster, sentences 1 to 4, then 5 to 6, etc.

Rock Concert

1. The singer was young.
2. The singer was swarthy.
3. He stepped into the spotlight.
4. The spotlight was red.

5. His shirt was unbuttoned.
6. The unbuttoning bared his chest.

7. Sounds ballooned around him.
8. The sounds were of guitars.
9. The sounds were of drums.
10. The sounds were of girls.
11. The girls were screaming.

12. He nodded.
13. He winked.
14. The wink was to his guitarist.
15. The drummer responded with the beat.

16. The singer became animated.
17. His legs were like rubber.
18. His body jerked.
19. His head was thrown back.
20. He wailed a shout.
21. The shout was into the microphone.
22. The microphone was at his lips.

23. His movements were twisting.
24. His movements were strobed.
25. The strobing was with floodlights.

26. His voice was a garble.
27. The garble was loud.
28. The auditorium swirled.
29. The swirling was rock.
30. The rock was "heavy."

[From *Sentence Combining* by William Strong, p. 40. Copyright © 1973 by Random House, Inc. Reprinted by permission of the publisher.]

PICTURE ARRANGEMENTS APPLICABLE TO THE CONTENT AREA MODES

Content Area	Picture Arrangements	Writing Mode
Math Science Home economics Industrial arts Foreign languages	Events in a sequence or steps in a process: contests, sports events, beginning to ending of an activity	Procedural—a direction or step-by-step relating of a process using words of transition
Social studies English Science	On a central theme or idea that has numerous examples; characters involved in persuasion, advertisements	Topic exposition—argument or clear topic. Statement with supporting details and logical connections
Social studies Home economics Industrial arts Physical education English	Events leading up to a solution, before-and-after effects of an event	Time-order—problem solution, cause and effect
Social studies English Home economics Science Foreign languages	Descriptive scene with characters performing an action in a particular setting; pictures showing likenesses and differences in characters, scenes, events	Narration/description—tell a story using description, characters, a plot; compare and contrast using coordinating conjunctions such as *but, or, yet*

ATOMISTIC EVALUATION

	CONTENT	STYLE		MECHANICS
		Organization	Sentence Structure	
Superior (A–B)	central idea defined clearly idea supported with concrete, relevant details	planning evident paragraphs unified and developed introduction original consistent development word choice appropriate to audience and purpose transitions effective	varied sentences complete sentences effective sentences	usage standard correct punctuation spelling accurate verb tenses consistent clear and matching subject-verb agreements
Average (C)	central idea too general or trite detail not developed detail irrelevant detail not consistently supportive of idea	planning evident but not carried through transitions clear but monotonous paragraphs usually developed and unified	well-constructed sentences but lacking freshness, power, or effectiveness	occasional deviations from standard usage, punctuation, spelling
Needs Improvement (D–F)	no clear central idea confused detail unsupportive detail detail not relevant	no plan or purpose evident paragraphs under-developed, not unified transitions unclear	sentences confused, incomplete, childish, not unified	frequent errors in usage, punctuation, spelling

CONSTRUCTING A MATRIX

Directions: *Write in what you think is expected from a writing assignment given in class. What is expected for a superior 1, for a lesser 2, etc.? Collaborate with your teacher and others in your class so that all of you understand clearly what is expected in your performance at each level. Name the specific criterion or item that the writing assignment is based on. For example, a persuasive writing assignment might have the criterion of appeal and a descriptive assignment have the criterion of effective adjectives or describers.*

CRITERION

Superior
1

2

EXPECTATIONS

3

4

Weakest
5

Copyright © 1984 by Allyn and Bacon, Inc. Reproduction of this material is restricted to use with *A Guidebook for Teaching Writing in Content Areas* by Sherry Hill Howie.

COMPOSITION RATING SCALE

Assignment	Student	Date
	Purpose	

A. Content – 50 percent

Convincing						Unconvincing
persuasive, sincere, enthusiastic, certain						
Organized						Jumbled
logical, planned, orderly, systematic						
Thoughtful						Superficial
reflective, perceptive, probing, inquiring						
Broad						Limited
comprehensive, complete, extensive range of data, inclusive						
Specific						Vague
concrete, definite, detailed, exact						

B. Style – 30 percent

Fluent						Restricted
expressive, colorful, descriptive, smooth						
Cultivated						Awkward
varied, mature, appropriate						
Strong						Weak
effective, striking, forceful, fresh, stimulating						

C. Mechanics – 20 percent

Organization						Incorrect form
paragraphing, heading, punctuation, spelling						
Language standard						Substandard
sentence structure, agreement, references, etc.						

Source: Used in Cleveland Heights–University Heights City School District, Cleveland Heights, Ohio. Adapted and used with permission.

APPENDIX D

Feedback Form

Your comments about this book will be very helpful to us in planning other books in the *Guidebook for Teaching* Series and in making revisions in *A Guidebook for Teaching Writing in Content Areas*. Please tear out the form that appears on the following page and use it to let us know your reactions to *A Guidebook for Teaching Writing in Content Areas*. The author promises a personal reply. Mail the form to:

Dr. Sherry Hill Howie
c/o Longwood Division
Allyn and Bacon, Inc.
7 Wells Avenue
Newton, Massachusetts 02159

Your school: _____

Address: _____

City and state: _____

Date: _____

Dr. Sherry Hill Howie
c/o Longwood Division
Allyn and Bacon, Inc.
7 Wells Avenue
Newton, Massachusetts 02159

Dear Sherry:

My name is _____ and I want to tell you what
I think of your book *A Guidebook for Teaching Writing in Content Areas.* I like certain
things about the book, including:

I do, however, think that the book could be improved in the following ways:

There are some other things that I wish the book had included, such as:

Here is something that happened in my class when I used an idea from your book:

Sincerely yours,

_____